Riding the Millennial Storm

Riding the Millennial Storm

MARC FABER'S PATH TO PROFIT IN THE NEW FINANCIAL MARKETS

Nury Vittachi

John Wiley & Sons (Asia) Pte Ltd

Singapore • New York • Chichester • Brisbane • Toronto • Weinheim

Other Wiley Editorial Offices
John Wiley & Sons, Inc.
605 Third Avenue, New York, NY 10158-0012, USA
John Wiley & Sons Ltd
Baffins Lane, Chichester, West Sussex PO19 1UD, England
John Wiley & Sons (Canada) Ltd
22 Worchester Road, Rexdale, Ontario M9W 1L1, Canada
Jacaranda Wiley Ltd
33 Park Road, (PO Box 1226) Milton, Queensland 4064, Australia
Wiley-VCH
Pappelallee 3, 69469 Weinheim, Germany

Library of Congress Cataloging-in-Publication Data:
Vittachi, Nury, 1958–
    Riding the millennial storm: Marc Faber's path to profit in the new financial markets/Nury Vittachi; with Marc Faber — 2nd ed.
    p. cm.
  ISBN 0-471-83205-7 (alk. paper)
  1. Financial crises. I. Faber, Marc. II. Title
  HB3722 . V57 1998
  332.6 — ddc21
                                                                98-42023
                                                                CIP

ISBN 0-471-83205-7

Typeset in 12/14 point, Adobe Garamond by Linographic Services Pte Ltd
Printed in Singapore by Kyodo Printing Co (S'pore) Pte Ltd
10 9 8 7 6 5 4 3 2 1

CONTENTS

—··—··—··—··—··—··—··—··—··—··—··—··—

Contents

Contents

PROLOGUE

— · — · — · — · — · — · — · — · — · — · — · — · — · — ·

Conference appearances by Marc Faber are often followed by animated discussions between confused reporters. They know that the Hong Kong-based investment advisor has become an economic icon. They all have press clippings in which he is called 'The Prince of Pessimism' or 'The Godfather of Gloom.'

But that doesn't really gel with what they have just seen — an investment analyst with a somewhat chequered career whose enthusiastic words conjure up a bright future for some of the world's poorer countries, and who is confident that his advice can steer people away from financial losses and towards potentially huge capital gains.

Whence does this contradiction arise? Perhaps the fundamental train of thought behind Faber's investment philosophy is best summed up by his favorite anecdote.

It's a bitterly cold day. You have lost all feeling in your nose. Your ears are hurting. You hunch your shoulders together to bury your head under the raised lapels of your greatcoat.

You turn a corner and you see a frozen pond. Can you risk taking a short cut across? Or would it be safer to walk to the bridge half a mile down the road?

You notice a man on the other side of the pond. He gingerly steps on to it. It holds the weight of one foot. He carefully places the other foot on the ice.

A young woman behind follows his lead. As you watch, some children arrive with skates, and more adults follow them. Soon, the whole village is having a party on the ice. Each person has given the next person the confidence to join the party. The more people clamber on to the ice, the safer it feels. It's logical, isn't it? Or is it?

Something makes you stop. You turn around. You walk away. Behind you, you hear the crack and the first scream.

That is Marc Faber's vision. Yes, you could say it's a dark vision; but really, it does the opposite of what most sunglasses do — instead of increasing obscurity, it enhances clarity. As an increasing number of heavy bodies add themselves to the ice, human nature makes them feel that the safety factor is increasing. But the clear-thinking observer realizes that their added weight means the opposite is true. Each fresh body on the ice makes it more — not less — likely that the ice will crack.

The global investment business today is a business in exactly the same way that the street market in Camden Town or Bangkok is. It is manned by salespeople, and they all have products they want you to buy. They make sure that what they sell is attractive. They tell you uplifting stories of how buyers of their services have generated wealth for themselves. They attract you to the ice. There are lots of people on it, so it must be safe.

Faber provides an interesting service by pointing out that periods of wealth destruction are just as inevitable as periods of wealth generation. It's a truism with which the investment services industry naturally feels uncomfortable.

While much of his thinking comes across as original, Faber fully admits that his research, like that of the economic historians he so admires, is built on the works of others — the frozen pond metaphor was first circulated by the economist F. Lavington in the early 1920s.

'If Faber's not really a pessimist, what is he, then?' a television reporter asked me after a press conference in the spring of 1998. To properly answer that question, I realized, would take a whole book. And this is it.

THE BEGINNING OF
THE END

The Richest Place on Earth

Two men and a woman are sitting around a desk in the office of a real estate agent in Tokyo, their brows knotted. There is an unusual problem with Mr Takashi's proposed home loan.

The female property dealer, a helmet-headed Office Lady from Osaka, takes the time to explain the situation to him carefully. 'Even if you work all your life until retirement, you will not have earned enough to pay this mortgage. So we have inserted a clause which means that the debt will be passed on to your son, when he is born. Understand?'

Mr Takashi nods, happy to commit his unborn child to pay a multibillion-yen bill. After all, he is sure that Number One Child, who will probably be a boy, will be only too proud to shoulder the burden for his family. Perhaps he will wait until the child is a toddler, three or four years old, before he tells him about the debt he is carrying. Besides, it won't be a burden, as such. It's an *investment*. At some stage, he or the boy will surely be able to sell it for a huge profit and so ensure the family's financial security.

'Understand,' Mr Takashi says quietly.

The world's media greets this innovation far more noisily, trumpeting it as the ultimate example of financial extremism sweeping through the newly crowned richest country in the world.

The late 1980s was a crazy time in Japan. Every day brought a fresh record in the Nikkei Index. The market capitalization of Tokyo blue-chip NTT, at its height, exceeded the entire market capitalization of the German stock market. Every financial journal, domestic and foreign, featured examples of the extravagances of the new rich. Japan became known as the world capital of useless inventions. There were the shoes with no soles 'for the man who likes to feel grass with his toes'; there was the outdoor lamp which was solar-powered and thus worked only when not needed; there was the talking toilet-roll holder which would congratulate its owner on a successful bowel movement. There were literally books full of similar products, known in Japanese as *Chindogu*.

The frivolous, wasteful products seemed like froth. There was so much money sloshing around the small Asia-Pacific country that there were bucks galore for any kind of offbeat invention, however marginal its value. Were these signs of a bubble? No; the inventions were widely interpreted as a surface manifestation of the genuine underlying power of the Japanese economy: an economic strength that had never been seen before in history.

The financial miracle was real enough: you could feel it. You just had to walk along the Ginza in Tokyo on any shopping day in the late 1980s. Count the Louis Vuitton handbags swinging on the shoulders of the women; look at the men balancing dozens of bags of shopping, the children playing with their electronic toys, the pedigree dogs wearing Burberry-style pooch jackets.

Salaries in Japan had rocketed, and almost everyone had one. Unemployment had tumbled, and averaged less than 3 percent throughout the decade. It was a miracle with muscle: growth had been strong, with the country's economy expanding at an annual average of 4 percent throughout the 1980s. Inflation, which had been an uncomfortable 8 percent at the start of the decade, had dropped to near zero. Society was peaceful, successful, free, democratic, and rich. Japan had made it. The American Dream had been realized — but on the opposite side of the Pacific.

How did they do it? That's what economists around the world were asking. Clearly, there was a range of reasons. Good industrial planning, most analysts agreed, was a key factor. Japan's Ministry of International Trade and Industry had kept the cost of capital low, enabling businesses to borrow heavily and beef up their production capacity. To some extent, the whole island nation was one massive manufacturing and production machine. Resources had wisely been directed to particularly strong sectors, such as consumer electronics (every consumer in the world appeared to want a Sony Walkman) and cars (the Toyota Corolla had become the world's best-selling car).

Critics complained that the Japanese government had sneakily structured international trade so that it was a one-way valve. Japanese goods could go out and bring foreign money in, much more easily than foreign goods could enter Japan. This was not entirely true, as Japan had long been a major importer of goods. But certain sectors, such as cars, were protected. Other nations, such as the United States and the countries of Europe, were complaining, but they could do little about it. They were too busy trying to escape from their own problems of high unemployment and chronic inflation, a pair of economic diseases that together produce a condition known as stagflation.

Had Japan become Utopia? Not quite. There were many shortcomings. Salarymen worked too hard, and the rat race to success at the office was often a march of death. Pressure was high for many people, and this was most distressingly manifested in the high rate of suicide among schoolchildren. One oft-discussed shortcoming was the lack of innovation in Japan; everything seemed to be copied. But some commentators suggested that this was proving to be a boon, rather than a problem. The West went to all the trouble of inventing things; Japan re-made them, but smaller, better, and cheaper.

While the Western nations, most famously the United Kingdom at the end of the 1970s, were plagued with strikes, labor relations in Japan were as smooth as silk. Lifetime employment was the norm, salarymen slaved year-round without taking disruptive holidays, and the *Keiretsu* — cartel-like structures which controlled links between manufacturers and retailers — kept the links in the production chain in their proper places.

It all seemed too good to be true. Even the government's sternest critics dared not suggest that this was an imaginary boom planted in the unadventurous Japanese press by the ruling Liberal Democratic Party. Journals all over the world agreed this was a genuine economic miracle. You only had to look at the macroeconomic figures on the financial pages: Japan racked up US$400 billion in trade surpluses with the rest of the world during the 1980s. That sort of cash infusion into an economy had to make a huge difference.

It *had* done. For a while. But time was up.

It's All Downhill from Here

Dr Doom glances at his watch. He is flying down a mountain at high speed. His motorbike is huge. It's bigger than the van he has just overtaken. It's bigger than a Tokyo apartment. It's bigger than the ego of the man in the black Mercedes-Benz he has just cut up — and that must be saying something, considering the vehicle's personalized number plate and tinted windows.

The 1000cc monster bike (European, of course) skims lightly over the tarmac of the steep, winding streets of Hong Kong's craggy Mid-Levels suburbs early one morning in January 1990. They say that Hong Kong, like New York, is a city that never sleeps. It's a lie. Other than the elderly, who wake at first light in all cities, the people of the glittering super-city on the coast of southern China are generally late risers. At 7.30 am, the newspaper vendors are only beginning to set up on the pavements, and the roads are quiet. Only Garden Road, the main artery from the mountain-top suburbs to the commercial flatlands, has a significant amount of traffic on it. And that traffic is making way for a two-wheeled blur, driven by a man who seems to be enjoying the steepness of the slope a little too much.

It is an unusually cold morning, with the barometer dropping to 60 degrees Fahrenheit, and a sharp north-easterly zephyr coming off the South China Sea. But Dr Doom, a colorful financial forecaster who sometimes appears in public in his everyday guise of mild-mannered investment advisor Marc Faber, is impervious to the weather. His mind is occupied, crunching numbers like a computer. The figures are the recent closing scores of the Nikkei Index, the stock counter which is the main gauge of health for the richest place on earth.

Faber had spent the last few weeks watching the main Japanese stock counter, and there had been a host of signs which revealed that the end of the Japanese boom really had begun. Stock prices had topped out and fallen a little. Investors thought they had experienced a correction. Ha! They were going to plummet, much further, much faster, and much harder than had ever been seen before in that country.

The Nikkei had started to lose its footing a few weeks earlier, and was falling, stumbling, step by step. This was no blip. This was no 'correction,' a lovely euphemism that suggests that crashes are a good thing. This was the end of Japan's late 20th century stock-market boom.

And yet people were still refusing to see it. In his motorcycle pannier was the January 4 issue of the *Far Eastern Economic Review*, which featured a cheery forecast about the Nikkei Index's prospects for 1990: 'With so little to worry about, the Tokyo Stock Exchange should perform excellently again.' As he replayed the line in his mind, Dr Doom couldn't help but laugh.

Even the ghosts in the machine agreed with him that the end had come. The Nikkei's record high, achieved on December 28, 1989, had been interpreted by a Japanese numerologist as conveying a message: 'Descent into a pit from which there is no recovery.' Japanese stockbrokers had cheerfully joked about the 'message' —

and then forgotten it. Faber, like them, didn't take ghosts seriously, but he didn't forget it.

Two weeks later, even the Westerners in the investment community felt the ghost in the machine was sending them a message. On January 16, the Nikkei Index had dropped precisely 666 points — the Number of the Beast, whose arrival prefigured the end of time. Investors, of course, laughed off another ridiculous portent and kept on pumping the money in — and why shouldn't they? The indicators, in the long run, were all positive. The good times, they believed, were only beginning. Look at all the evidence.

It had been as recently as the end of 1987 that Japan's Economic Planning Agency (EPA) had valued the national stock of real estate at 1686 trillion yen, a figure which probably understated its market value. The total value of U.S. real estate at the end of 1987 was a comparatively paltry US$3.361 trillion. In December 1988, the EPA had announced that Japan had accumulated 5338 trillion yen (US$43.75 trillion) worth of 'national assets' by the end of the previous year, making it easily the world's richest country.

Japanese consumers were bewitched by these and other examples of their nation's financial supremacy, which were continually replayed by the media. The people of Japan, the press said, could sell their island, put their money in suitcases, fly across the Pacific Ocean, and buy the United States — four times over. This amazing feat would be financially possible, despite the fact that Japan is less than one-twentieth the size of the United States.

Faber knew that this fanciful but popular analogy left out one inconvenient fact. To sell Japan, the people of that country would need a buyer — but there was no one else in the world who would or could buy at those prices. Japan's property sector had embarked on a game it could play only by itself; a game that was thus sure to end in disaster in a world where economies were being increasingly globalized.

The Zurich-born financier was a voracious reader, and he had seen a mounting number of fulsome, detailed, enthusiastic justifications of the high price of Japanese property — in his mind, a clear warning sign. Between 1986 and 1988 alone, the value of property in Japan had doubled. But investors failed to see this as a dangerous spike, since the climb in land values had a long history. The value of Japanese real estate had increased 462 times between 1955 and 1987. Amateur and professional economists put the growth down to a supply and demand equation. People wanted apartments and offices in Tokyo or other major cities, and there was simply no more land available. Japan is a mountainous country, and no significant new supply of land had been added for decades. Prices therefore had to be squeezed upward. The supply showed no signs of increasing, so why should demand slow?

Faber had watched in horror as the bubble grew huge — and then spread across the world. Since 1986, Japanese landowners, cheered by the huge perceived value of their holdings, had been using their property as collateral for bank loans which enabled them to invest vast amounts of money, first in the Tokyo stock market and then in overseas assets such as U.S. stocks and bonds. They eventually diversified into a range of assets, from Florida golf courses to European paintings. In 1989, Japanese buyers accounted for more than 40 percent of the purchases by value at the major autumn sales of art in London and New York. Also in Faber's bag was a recent copy of an international newspaper which carried an article about a Japanese tycoon who had done more than invest in art — Yasumichi Morishita had spent US$53 million on buying a large chunk of Christie's, the second-largest art auction house in the world. Features on the business pages kept up the same theme: Japan's enormous capital accumulation had made it the world's largest aid donor. The superlatives flowed on and on.

Earlier that week, Faber had clipped an item about Japanese stocks from a Hong Kong business publication; they had dipped slightly after hitting a high at the end of the previous month. 'The market could pluck up courage for a rebound. Japan is still awash with cash, and private investors, who cannot put their money into the real estate market because of scarce supply and absurdly high price levels, need something to invest in,' wrote a breathless stock-watcher.

There would be something almost biblical about the suddenness of the financial disaster that was about to befall Japan and reverberate around the world, Faber mused. He saw the steel towers of Hong Kong's Central financial district below him, several of which were owned or part-owned by Japanese companies. He gunned the BMW RS 100 bike up to 60 miles an hour and leaned to the left, moving across three lanes into Queen's Road Central. It was like the man in the parable: eat (hand-massaged Kobe beef), drink ($500 bottles of imported cognac), and make merry (by selling apartments to your unborn children), for tomorrow your portfolios die. He switched into third gear and sped through a red traffic light in front of the HongkongBank headquarters.

Faber, who ran the Hong Kong operation of Drexel Burnham Lambert, the huge Wall Street junk bond operation, knew that he wasn't the only voice in the emerging markets field who had been warning that the end had come for the boom on the Tokyo Stock Exchange. Indeed, by early 1990, it was becoming the common view among economists that Japanese asset growth would have to tail off in the first few years of the 1990s.

But the Swiss investment advisor was predicting something far stronger: a total implosion which would see stock prices cut in half — at the very least. A share-market catastrophe that would cause the Japanese banking system to fall to its knees for a decade or more. A crash that would be repeated over the next few years in many of the 'bubble' economies of East Asia, creating a quite different picture of the global economy in 2000 than was expected.

He had expressed these unpopular theories repeatedly, usually earning himself sneers and general unpopularity. Politicians, always trying to foster general bullishness, particularly disliked him. In 1988, Faber had written: 'The world is accepting a ridiculous overvaluation in the Japanese market on the grounds that there is so much liquidity in Japan, while conveniently overlooking the fact that a great deal of the liquidity is borrowed money.'

His views had earned him the nickname 'Dr Doom', a title he happily accepted. He was so convinced of the correctness of his predictions, that he had stuck his money, and that of his investors, where his mouth was. He instructed his clients to 'short' the Nikkei

Index — that is, structure their investments to climb upward when (there was no 'if' about it) the Tokyo share market crashed. Each $4.05 'put' — expiry date 1992 — stood to rise dramatically if he was right.

Among the other prophecies of doom was a notable book called *1990 dai Nihonjin e no Keikoku* [A warning to Japan for the 1990s], published in 1989, in which Johsen Takahashi, chief economist of the Mitsubishi Research Institute, said Japan was possibly now at the peak of its wealth in asset terms, with the amount due to fall rapidly in absolute terms during the 1990s as savings levels contracted. Takahashi argued that the country had only a limited time in which to find ways of diverting its wealth into useful channels before the bubble burst.

But Faber's prediction had been far harsher than this. He said that Tokyo would not see a return to its stock-market highs for a period of years. 'They may not be repeated for another 15–20 years, if then,' he had told his clients.

Yet he was not surprised that other people in the financial world were unable to see that Japan had achieved its wealth largely through asset inflation, without a corresponding increase in tangible wealth. For investment bankers, the temptation to look on the positive side was almost irresistible. *Forbes* magazine had recently reported that Japan had 30 US-dollar billionaires — more than any other country after the United States. Add to that another 400,000 or so individuals whose land holdings alone were worth US$2 million, and you have a community which leaves bankers drooling on to their Gieves and Hawkes pinstripes. Someone's got to look after all that money — and collect commissions on it.

Faber arrived at the New World Tower in Queen's Road Central. He parked his motorbike in the car park built into the lower floors and carried his helmet up to his cluttered office.

On his Reuters telex, he saw news reports about Japan's continuing financial problems. The Nikkei, which had started to retreat from its high at the end of December, was expected to continue to fall. Other analysts were suddenly turning seriously bearish. There was a rising feeling of panic in the Tokyo financial district. People were beginning to realize that this was more than just a hiccup in the endless ascension of the stock market of the Rising Sun. The end had begun.

Faber's phone rang. He snatched it up.

'Yes?'

'It's Dick. It's gonna blow, Marc. The whole damn thing is coming down fast. This is it. Ka-boom! The end. Armageddon.'

'Yes. The Nikkei, I think, is in free fall — total collapse.'

'No, not the Nikkei, you dummy — Drexel Burnham Lambert. Your job.'

Marc Faber sat down.

Doom is on the Way

An all-sugar diet quickly becomes cloying. Hundreds of thousands of financial research reports and business journals circulate in the world's major cities every week, and the bulk of them carry sweet-tasting news about companies and economies. This is particularly true of the business pages' profiles of chief executive officers and the thick books of analysis issued by finance houses. Executives don't like letting strangers into their offices, so how can a reporter or analyst get a turn with the CEO unless they let it be known that a positive write-up is likely? This is particularly true of Asia, the world capital of lapdog journalism, where packets of money regularly swap hands at press conferences.

Among professional brokers' reports worldwide, 'buy' recommendations are a dime a dozen. If an analyst finds a real stinker in his tray, he doesn't need to use that unpleasant word 'sell.' There are lots of mild euphemisms he can use: it is a 'hold,' or 'one for the risk-takers,' or better still, 'a long-term investment.' That last phrase sounds completely positive; yet too often it means that the stock's possible (or probable) worthlessness will only become apparent to the buyer a few years down the line, when the tipster has moved onward and upward.

'Broker research is useful — assuming you have a pet dog in need of house-training,' said William Kaye, managing partner of Asian

Hedge Fund, quoted in the *Far Eastern Economic Review* of April 18, 1996.

Financial reporters looking for authoritative analysis for newspapers or broadcast use find it easy to get someone to make positive noises about company X or Y. But who will go on the record, in front of whirring tape-recorders and cameras, to bad-mouth the most powerful people in the community?

In this large bowl of sugary soup, the casual observer finds one large, unapologetic lump of salt. The name of unashamed pessimist Marc Faber became a household word in his home town of Hong Kong during the 1980s, and his fame had spread throughout Asia by the end of that decade. As the turbulent 1990s started, he gained a reputation around the world for his criticism of the darlings of other investment gurus. Japan? Dead and buried. United States' technology stocks? Sell 'em short. The Asian tigers? Get out while you can.

This was no knee-jerk, blanket condemnation of all rivals' recommendations. Faber wasn't negative about everything. He frequently selected and highlighted investments the value of which he prophesied would travel upward — but again, these tended not to be the favorites of other tipsters. The disastrous London Docklands? A worthwhile investment for those with patience. Strife-torn Russia? Get in there quick. Pakistan, Mexico, Sri Lanka? Well worth a punt.

It was in the pages of Hong Kong's *South China Morning Post* that the casual observer first became familiar with him; the financial advisor appeared in its pages through the 1980s more often than many politicians of the time. Although the nickname 'Dr Doom' was first coined for him by the broking community, Hong Kong newspapers' financial gossip columns soon started using it as a straight label for him, without quotation marks. 'Doctor Doom had a good day yesterday ...' began a 1990 article about Faber's joy at winning a bet in which he correctly forecast trouble for a major construction development.

In the past ten years, readers of virtually all the major global publications in the business field have read his name. It appears regularly in the international mainstream press as well, popping up in the reports of Reuters, the Associated Press, and the other wire services that feed the press worldwide. During the boom years of the early 1990s, he was simply stereotyped as the incarnation of pessimism. The *South China Morning Post* frequently tacked the word 'Superbear' in front of his name. Other terms used by the media in general included 'prophet of doom' and 'doomsayer.' (The name 'Dr Doom' has no connection to the Marvel Comics character of that name, but stems from Jeremiah, the biblical prophet of doom. Although Faber, who has a doctorate, does not insist on the use of the title, he is listed as 'Doctor' on the masthead of his regular newsletter, *The Gloom, Boom & Doom Report*.)

Since the mid-1980s, Faber has appeared in screeds of articles under the title of 'The Bear,' almost invariably with a smiling optimist on the other side of the page bearing the caption 'The Bull.' A typical example of such a news feature was published in *Barron's*, the financial weekly, on April 3, 1995, carrying the semantically confused headline: 'Biggs vs. Faber: Are They Emerging — Or Submerging — Markets?' This report claimed to feature

> ... two celebrated and knowledgeable old hands, Barton Biggs, chairman of Morgan Stanley Asset Management, and Marc Faber, who runs Hong Kong-based Marc Faber Ltd, which specializes in investments in developing economies. Barton and Marc share extraordinarily keen intelligence and long and profound experience investing in emerging countries. What they conspicuously don't share is a common outlook on the prospects for emerging markets. Barton is a raging bull; Marc is an unapologetic bear.

The same stereotypes were replayed on stage at large numbers of financial conferences. A typical example was one organized by Credit Lyonnais in Hong Kong in June 1997, with Faber as The Bear, Gary Coull, managing director of Credit Lyonnais Hong Kong, as The Bull, and a financial reporter as The Critic.

The press loves to simplify, and Faber, with his easy accessibility and willingness to put his neck on the block, was the perfect 'rent-a-quote' for reporters needing a negative voice to balance their stories.

If there's only one pot of salt in a crowded kitchen, every cook will want to use it. The *Wall Street Journal* put it straightforwardly: Faber is 'the region's [Asia's] most notorious bear.' Other reporters used phrases that rather sourly suggested he was an automatic naysayer: *The Economist* introduced him as that 'congenital bear Marc Faber.'

This cartoon character, largely an invention of the press, quickly established a special niche in the consciousness of the financial world. Even the most sober reports hinted at the investment advisor's larger-than-life status. The *Financial Times* of London, with classic British understatement, described him as 'not your average fund manager,' before going on to say that he is 'something of an icon.'

In recent years, the references in the international press have become more favorable, as an increasing number of Faber's predictions appear to have been fulfilled. *Fortune*, in its May 26, 1997, issue, talked of 'Marc Faber, congenital contrarian and shrewd Swiss investment advisor in Hong Kong.'

Following the turmoil in Asian markets in the latter half of 1997, many of the references became unashamedly laudatory. *Barron's* printed this in its issue of December 15, 1997: 'We spoke with Marc last Friday morning and, first off, congratulated him on his prophecies come true; almost alone among world market watchers, he had foreseen the Asian crackup. Legions of filthy rich have been turning into deserving poor.' That joyful last sentence neatly encapsulates the cheery *schadenfraude* that was detectable in the Western media's reports on the tumble of the smug tiger economies of East Asia, and gives one reason why they have become so happy with Faber.

Forbes, the glossy business bi-weekly published out of New York, was equally congratulatory, listing his successes in the issue dated January 26, 1998:

> When we last checked in with Marc Faber, the Swiss-born doomsayer and money manager was skeptical about Asia's emerging markets. He warned that the Malaysian and Thai stockmarkets were over-valued, that Hong Kong's best days were behind it, and that Chinese shares were of dubious quality (October 24, 1994). Good call, Marc.

Asia-based publications also patted him on the back. *Hong Kong Week*, a supplement of the *Asian Wall Street Journal*, said on December 28, 1997: 'Confirmed contrarian Marc Faber, director of Marc Faber Ltd, was among the earliest to predict the bear market.'

By this time, the Asian vernacular press was also taking an interest in him. The editors of *Apple Daily* (slogan: 'An *Apple* a day keeps the lies away'), a lively Hong Kong newspaper, decided it was worthwhile to translate Faber's essays into Chinese characters for the edification of its readers.

An exception was Faber's original main supporter, the *South China Morning Post*, which appeared to have grown tired of him by 1998. When, in February of that year, he was reported to have business links with a company that provided strike-breakers for a dispute-hit dockyard firm in Australia, the paper's reporters suggested that unionists may wish to picket his office in Central. In the event, no such thing happened. Attacks on the strength of unions are seen as good things in capitalism-mad Hong Kong. When Faber showed an obvious reluctance to engage in public battle on the issue by giving them quotes and photographs, *Post* reporters made snide comments, painting him as a 'publicity-hungry' investment advisor who had suddenly become shy. Faber accepted a call from one *South China Morning Post* reporter, only to be asked: 'Are you a fascist?'

But political issues apart, it was clear that by the end of the 1990s, Faber was clearly established in that ephemeral thing referred to as 'the media consciousness' as a major voice prophesying economic doom. He was portrayed as having a penchant for emphasizing the dark side, a talent for delivering provocative forecasts for the new millennium, and a cheery fearlessness about pooh-poohing the pronouncements of more mainstream forecasters. Unfortunately for him and other prophets in the field, the financial world entered an extraordinarily unpredictable phase in the late 1990s.

Fins de Siècle

A century comes to an end, and the world is dominated by a single superpower. The colonial era is waning fast, and the citizens of planet Earth are entering an age of technological wonders. This refers to the year 2000, the dominance of the United States, and the dawn of the era of the microchip, right?

It could, but people living 100 years ago would have said it applied to the year 1900, at which time the single global superpower was the British Empire, and the new technological wonders included such revolutionary developments as the car, the telephone, the radio, and the light bulb.

When musing on *fins de siècle*, one is struck as much by the similarities as by the differences. In 1900, the major medium for transmitting large amounts of information was the book. In the year 2000, the same holds true — at least for some of us. But these and other parallels aside, the two *fins de siècle* could not be more different. Advances in transport and electronics have transformed our lives in ways that could never have been foreseen. The changes in our individual lives are obvious, from the moment your digital alarm clock wakes you up, to the last late-night news bulletin that puts you to sleep.

Less obvious but equally momentous are the macroeconomic changes, particularly the way in which finance has become a huge, flowing, global river. (It is not by chance that the word 'liquidity' is the most used metaphor in finance.) Today, foreign exchange markets turn over some US$1.2 trillion every day. Hot money surges around the world, transforming the lives of individuals and countries, for better or worse. Sometimes it pools in certain places, such as the United States in the 1950s. Sometimes it withdraws suddenly, leaving a drought, as in Indonesia in late 1997.

Today's financial prophets have an unimaginably difficult job to accurately forecast what will change and, importantly, what will stay the same, even in the next six months. It appears impossible to say with any confidence what will happen in the next few decades or half-century. Any economic futurist who wrote about the year 2000 as recently as 1997 would have to make major revisions following the global financial adjustments that took place, starting in Asia, from the second half of that year onwards.

And it wasn't all bad news. The overriding global economics story of the 1980s had been the United States' trade deficit. By the middle of the 1990s, everything had changed. The Dow Jones Industrial Average was rocketing once more into record territory, as economists released an unceasing torrent of good news. In 1997, unemployment in the United States fell to between 4 and 5 percent, not far from Japan's 1980s' figure of 3 percent. The economic growth of the United States averaged 2 percent through the 1990s — nothing like the 8 percent growth enjoyed by Indonesia and Malaysia in 1996, but then, look what happened to them. Growth in the United States had been slow but it was steady, and, matched with low inflation and low unemployment, turned out to be a textbook example of a plodding tortoise doing better, in the long run, than the breathless hare.

Inflation? In early 1998, the United States' tortoise had achieved the Holy Grail of all government economists: a combination of positive growth and negligible inflation. At the same time, fast-growing Asia was stalling. Economists were predicting 50–60 percent inflation for that year for Indonesia's hare, and stagflation for Malaysia's. Some economists were forecasting zero growth for 1998 even for the rich Singaporean hare, which had enjoyed 7.6 percent growth in 1997.

By 1997, which country had the smallest debt compared to its size? Stand up the United States. The final figure for the U.S. trade deficit in 1997 was expected to be US$70 billion, less than 1.4 percent of gross domestic product. This is the lowest of any of the industrialized countries.

The causes of the transformation in the United States range from the pleasantly predictable to the genuinely surprising. The supporters of helmsman Alan Greenspan, chairman of the Federal Reserve, were certainly not surprised that he managed to keep his feet flipping between the accelerator and the brake deftly enough to hold inflation down without slowing growth. His efforts were helped by unexpected political factors, international and domestic.

The end of the Cold War, and the resultant slashing of military budgets, was well-timed. The long-awaited peace dividend predicted in the late 1980s really did seem to come about, although it took its time. On the domestic front, President Bill Clinton was constantly hit by scandals — but all centered on his personal ethics, or lack of, and the economy over which he presided stayed firmly on track.

Again, the temptation is to simplify: in the late 1990s, East done bad, West done good. The truth, as ever, is more complex. There was a great deal of financial progress in the East. The East Asian miracle was not nullified, but merely derailed, perhaps temporarily, in some quarters. The average citizen of China, Hong Kong, or Singapore was no poorer at the end of tumultuous 1997 than at the beginning.

And by the middle of 1998, economists were picking through the rubble of the Asian miracle and finding an education. The Asia-Pacific crash forced governments to learn tough but necessary lessons about global and domestic economics, and some were implementing important reforms. For example, broking industry reforms are to be implemented in Japan in 1998–2002, under the name 'the Big Bang' (the nickname for a technique of wholesale financial deregulation that occurred in Britain 12 years ago and Wall Street 23 years ago). The steps to be taken in this period include: a lifting of foreign exchange controls, so that any corporation or individual can trade in international currencies; a change of rules, so that banks will be allowed to enter the equities business; the lifting of restrictions on derivatives trading; and the decontrolling of commissions on smaller broking transactions.

The result, if all goes well, will be a slicker, more efficient financial machine. And it's not just fine-tuning for the sake of it. The pickings are potentially important on a world scale. Japan sits on an estimated US$10 trillion in underperforming household savings. That's enough to make a difference in a lot of lives.

Japan (along with Hong Kong and Singapore) may be leading the way in financial reform for other big economies in Asia, but it is only during a crash that the virtues or otherwise of playing with a new set of rules become apparent. It has become clear that a vital financial aim for all governments is to create financial structures so strong that it is almost impossible for major banks to crash, and if one does, for the system to allow it to do so without harming its depositors. Can such a system exist? When Drexel Burnham Lambert crashed in 1990, its officers, including one Marc Faber in an office in Hong Kong, had the unpleasant job of finding out.

The Longest Night

'Damn. This hasn't come at a very convenient time,' Faber groaned. His secretary, Pauline Leung, nodded sympathetically. Having his company collapse in February 1990, at the same time as his predictions for the Japanese share market were dramatically fulfilled, was a definite inconvenience. Instead of breaking out the champagne and whiling away the hours counting the profits made on shorting the Nikkei, Faber spent a painful day on the telephone, talking to client after client, realizing the value of the personal touch during a crisis. Television news reports were filled with pictures of junked computers piled on the pavements outside the Wall Street headquarters of Drexel Burnham Lambert, and interviews with shell-shocked former employees. Some of Faber's clients, who had millions of dollars in Drexel accounts, were in tears.

Faber, at first, was in relatively relaxed form. If anything, the crisis seemed to make him less tense, as it released him from a business relationship which had been less than unalloyed bliss. He reckoned that in its own way, the collapse of the junk bond kings who employed him had been as inevitable as the bursting of the Japanese bubble. You gamble a few times, and you may win or lose. You gamble a great many times, and you definitely lose.

Drexel's New York head office had constantly urged him to get more intimately involved with the firm by buying share options in it. Faber had resisted, and over the years had gathered only a token $50,000 worth of equity in the company, despite having been titular head of Drexel Burnham Lambert (HK) Ltd since 1978.

And even on that gloomy day in 1990, his news for his clients wasn't as bad as it seemed. He knew full well that the U.S. finance industry was insured to the hilt, with strict procedures in place that protected public money in the event of almost any form of bank collapse, including the fall of a junk bond dealer. Faber was able to reassure his clients that their shareholdings were safe; they would simply be transferred, under Securities and Exchange Commission (SEC) rules, to another brokerage. The Securities Investors Protection Corporation would look after them, he told his clients. Then, Drexel itself had an additional US$10 million insurance on each account.

Yet it was still a complicated mess to sort out. The Hong Kong office of the company had offered an unusually large range of products, so a typical account would have included various amounts of cash in U.S. equities, Eurodollar bonds, yen bonds, deutschemark bonds, cash deposits, commodities, S&P futures, Nikkei futures, gold, and so on. With cash accounts, transfers were easy. With margin accounts in various foreign currencies, it was trickier. But his clients' accounts, as he promised, were almost immediately transferred to Kidder Peabody, Schroders Wertheim, Shearson Lehman, and other U.S. finance houses.

But Faber discovered he had made one small, but serious, miscalculation. Not everything was guaranteed. The exceptions were the commodity accounts, which were held through a subsidiary called Drexel Burnham Lambert Commodities Ltd. This had been capitalized at a tiny US$500,000. When it became clear that this firm may have gone bankrupt with his clients' money in its belly, Faber became worried. He remained in a cold sweat on the phone the rest of that day and all night, trying to sort out the problem. It proved to be as complete a nightmare as he could have imagined. He spoke repeatedly to the affected clients, while his staff dialled and redialled phones, trying to get through to the chaotic Drexel Burnham Lambert back office in New York.

One client, a British aristocrat, was in tears at the thought that he might lose part of his investment, although the man was extremely wealthy and had only US$30,000 in the commodities account. Faber, who sometimes lost more than that in minutes on a single ill-judged stock transaction, had trouble being patient with him — especially since the man kept calling back, and wept through the night.

Some clients demanded all their money back instantly in order to transfer to another company. 'Some were obnoxious,' he recalls. Others were extremely calm, with the long-term ones happy to assure Faber that he continued to have their full support.

Faber eventually managed to get through to the Drexel back office in New York. He got the clerk to go through his commodities accounts in the main computer and transfer them to securities accounts, where they would be safer.

He finally lowered the telephone handset at 6 am the following morning, as dawn once again broke over The Peak. Crisis over. Rubbing his eyes, he decided he needed some cheering up. He switched his screen over to the Nikkei Index, where reports on the disaster were still in full flow.

A reporter phoned him at about 10 am, when he was having breakfast. 'Morning, Dr Doom. Too bad about Drexel,' the caller said. 'But it must be satisfying that you seem to have been proved right about Tokyo. You must be making a mint.'

Faber sighed. 'Yes, it is good to be right about that. But unfortunately, my accounts are rather frozen here because of the Drexel problem. But I still have some shorts on the Nikkei, so I can enjoy the carnage a bit.'

Beginning, Muddle, End

Four months later, in June 1990, the landlord of the New World Tower in Queen's Road Central, Hong Kong, had a new deal with his tenant on the 27th floor. Several rooms had been released, and walls moved. The tenant had a much smaller office. Gone was the door sign which said 'Drexel Burnham Lambert (HK) Ltd.' In its place was 'Marc Faber Ltd.' The 45 employees had been pared down to 12. The operation had been relaunched.

Before the end of that year, the Nikkei Index had fallen, as Faber had predicted, to less than half of its high. His $4.05 'puts' had risen to an amazing $130 each — the investment had multiplied itself by a factor of 33. On its way down, the index had pulled down virtually all of the other Asian markets. The August 2 invasion of Kuwait by Iraq dealt another blow to world stock markets. The spotlight shifted away from Asia, landing squarely on Baghdad and Washington.

In Japan, the people in the financial sector who still had jobs were on a roller coaster. Nineteen-ninety was not a good year for them. Equity prices had fallen heavily in February. From a high of 38,915.87 on December 29, 1989, it stopped falling at 29,843.24 in February. A summer rebound took it back up to 33,100 in July, and many investors piled in. Faber forbid his clients to do so. The mid-year rebound was the first of many false turning points that would entrap thousands of investors over the following years, the most notable being Singapore trader Nick Leeson, whose gamble on an upturn in the Nikkei Index caused the collapse of Barings Bank. Like Leeson five years later, those who jumped in to buy at 'bargain prices' in the summer of 1990 were caught short by fresh tumbles in the fall, triggered by global problems (the Gulf crisis) as well as domestic ones. (One bank revealed that its huge property-related debts were many times larger than its shareholdings.) There was a further 11 percent decline in the Nikkei Index between August 20 and 24, when it fell to 23,737.63, and on October 1, it fell below the 20,000 point barrier. 'Down into the wilderness, never to return,' exactly as the ghost had said.

Although land prices outside Tokyo continued to rise for a while, prices of speculative projects throughout Japan fell and orders for condominiums dropped in 1990. Nothing more was heard from estate agents attempting to sign up unborn babies for large mortgages.

The damage wasn't confined to Japan. The fall in the country's export of capital and its outbound direct investment in manufacturing hurt other South Asian markets, notably Thailand. But there was one victim of the 1990 Asian stock-market blues which lost even more than Japan, and that was Taiwan. Again,

February and August of 1990 turned out to be key months. From a record high in February, Taiwan's weighted index fell spectacularly, losing almost 80 percent of its value by August of that year. Wiped out was some NT$5900 billion in paper assets — this was equal to one-and-a-half times Taiwan's total gross national product in 1989. By November, the index had climbed dramatically, in what observers saw as a desperate attempt by small investors (the country had an estimated five million individual punters) to play the game again and recoup their losses. The Taiwan share market had revealed itself to be the worst sort of casino, with prices of counters having no relation to fundamentals.

It was a tough year, and it was only in December, when the markets had started to discount the problems in the Gulf, that brokers began to relax.

Faber is on the phone to one of his clients, a Malaysian billionaire.

'So, the stock markets have finally settled. The crisis is over now, right?'

'No,' says Faber. 'This is part of the great restructuring of the end of the century. This isn't the end. This is the beginning.'

2

Prepare to Meet Thy Doom

_._._._._._._._._._._._._._._._._

Cutting Remarks

'**H**ave you heard about Dr Doom? He's made this bet. He has to cut off his favorite dangly bit. It's seven inches long. It's going to be sliced off, inch by inch, a little bit each day. The whole operation is going to be incredibly painful.'

The listener, a florid bond-trader nursing a vodka, looks up sharply. 'Faber's going to cut *it* off?'

'I mean his ponytail. To a guy like him, that's much more painful.' Traders at Brown's Wine Bar laugh, and pass around the newspaper write-up of the wager.

Similar conversations flow around another crowded bar a mile away, the Foreign Correspondents' Club of Hong Kong. But there, the gossipers keep their voices down. The butt of the jokes is standing just a few yards away.

It's seven on a Tuesday evening and Marc

Faber is leaning on the bar, holding a glass of Grolsch. He is six foot tall, and towers over David, the wizened Chinese barman at the club. The Swiss financial man has a surprisingly lean physique for a businessman with a penchant for European beer and plutonium-hot Thai curries. But the wispiness and transparency of his hair give away his age, which was 50. The little remaining hair is pulled back into a short ponytail, retained apparently for reasons of nostalgia, and kept in place by an unfussy band from his daughter's dressing table. Instead of a dark suit, he is wearing a yellow sweater over a colored shirt.

It's not difficult to see why Faber attracts undue attention in a world over-supplied with visionaries who claim to be able to spot the emerging market that will make you — yes, *you* — an instant fortune. For a start, he *looks* different. With his ponytail, casual clothes, and motorbike, he would fit better into a rock group or an advertising agency than a finance house. Then there is his bizarre habit of starting speeches on economic matters with esoteric bits of history — the habits of the Phoenician sailors one millennium BC, for example.

'One more?' asks the barman.

'Yes, please, David.' Faber is perfectly fluent in English, but speaks with a distinctive lilting Swiss accent, and uses the Germanic *'Ja'* instead of 'Yes' when he gets enthusiastic — and he gets fired up a lot, littering his sentences with intensifiers. His favorite word is 'unbelievably,' which he uses constantly: *'Ja,* Sri Lankan hotels are *unbelievably* cheap right now.'

By Wall Street standards, he dresses atrociously. Feeling no affinity for the standard moneyman's dark-blue suit, he appears in public, at conferences, and in television interviews in whatever he feels comfortable in — casual clothes, a pale suit, a sports jacket, or, at his most formal, a dark suit livened with a comic tie.

'I think maybe I will be going for a little hair cut tomorrow,' he says, smiling in my direction. I nod. You see, Faber and this reporter have a history. The investment guru has been the target of many of the present writer's most sarcastic quips in the financial gossip pages. We are old sparring partners — I play The Critic when he plays The

Bear at conferences — and most people think I was the first to dub him 'Dr Doom,' although I wasn't. I was just one of a pack of newshounds who would phone him at work or at home, at any hour of the day, and offer him 'free publicity' — although he knew as well as we did that we were just using him. This was the game, with someone like Faber who was good enough not to mind being ill-treated. He was praised and then vilified, pedestalled and then toppled, garlanded and then mocked, celebrated and then insulted, up one day and down the next.

The latest game had a touch of spice to it. He was predicting a crash on the Hong Kong share market. Faber would cut off one centimeter of hair for every 50 points the market rose. If it fell 50 points, he had nothing to gain but his honor. The bullish investment community, hoping he would lose, would get double or nothing. If the market rose, they would see their share values go up, and have the joy of seeing Faber's ponytail disappear. If the market fell, the drop in the value of their shares was the less significant of their losses — his grinning, told-you-so visage in the newspaper would be the main punishment.

Since Faber's ponytail was only 16 centimeters long, he stood to lose it all if there was an 800-point rise in the market. Given the volatility of the Hang Seng Index, this could happen in the space of two days without arousing undue comment.

November 5, 1992, had been a bright, cool day. The sun was shining, the Hang Seng Index was moving steadily upward, and turnover was running at a heady HK$1 billion an hour. Members of the financial community — commission-based stockbrokers, in particular — went gaily about their tasks, a skip in their step, a song in their hearts, and enzymes dripping from their mouths.

All except one. Marc Faber was sitting in Faces restaurant in Central with the table covered in charts, tables, and research documents. 'It's a trap,' he told his dining companions. 'The Hang Seng is going to plummet. People think it's a rising market, but it has actually topped out. I am quite sure of it.' We had all heard him deliver this line before — and he had been disastrously wrong the previous time, we reminded him.

Faber said he was so sure about it this time that he would bet anything — even his precious ponytail. He would cut off one centimeter for every 50 points the market rose, he announced. 'Starting today.'

And so the bet had started. Since at least one analyst had predicted that the index would rise from its present level of about 6350 to 7200 within six months, this was judged to be a brave enough wager. Faber stood to lose his entire ponytail.

'What if you've cut the whole thing off and it goes up further?' I asked.

'Then I'll have to cut something else off. Perhaps your readers can nominate something?' he replied.

Details of the wager duly appeared in the following day's press. Readers were quick to phone in with suggestions about what else Faber could cut off. The only printable suggestion came from an accountant at Ernst & Young, who said Faber should be punished by being forced to cut off all contact with stock markets for a week — and not be allowed to read any financial news.

At 10 am the following day, the market opened for business and the Hang Seng Index went steadily upward. Faber's spirits went steadily downward. By mid-morning, it had risen more than 50 points from the previous night's close, standing at 6401.

A photographer from the *South China Morning Post* was booked to travel to Faber's office in Central and photograph him having his ponytail shortened by a suitably large and theatrical pair of shears. But the market suddenly turned around, and the photographer was told to stand by and wait for further instructions. The market fell for the rest of the day, closing 32 points down.

Faber did a great deal of gloating for the rest of the week. He had correctly predicted a turn — albeit a minor one — and the market sagged a little more each day.

Then, on the Thursday of the following week, there was a muscular rally and the afternoon session closed with the counter standing at 6447 — some 96 points more than where it had stood at the time of the bet.

Faber made an appointment with his hairdresser the following morning. But as his tresses fell, so did the index — by 80 points. Had he been a little slower in keeping his promise, he would have saved both the hair on his head and the HK$300 he paid society hairdresser André Norman for the unwanted trim. 'It was the most expensive centimeter I've ever had cut,' Faber said later that day.

The index returned to falling mode that day and for the next few days. Faber was out of Hong Kong, delivering a speech at the Templeton Global Conference in Palm Beach, Florida. But he kept a close eye on the Hang Seng Index every time he passed a financial monitor. 'I slept very well,' he said on the phone from the conference. 'Some very important chart points have been decisively broken. A close below 6000 will almost certainly seal the fate of the market.' Within a minute, the index dipped below 6000. 'It looks like my ponytail is going to remain intact,' he said. 'I am greatly relieved.'

The market continued to fall, and Faber called my office at the *South China Morning Post* from a *Business Week* conference at the Regent hotel in Hong Kong. 'I've taken some of those Chinese 101 pills to make my hair grow back,' he said. Faber explained that the market had 'reached what technical analysts call a "broadening top," which is a very negative sign.' I pointed out that if he had been wrong, the large bald patch on his head would have become his very own broadening top.

The ponytail wager was just one of several highly public bets Marc Faber has taken with the financial community. Objecting to the wild bullishness of the leasing agents for the Bank of China headquarters in 1990, Faber had promised to parachute off the top of it if the agents managed to lease out all the offices. Since it was 70 stories high, there was a lot of space to fill. But it was also a long way down.

Faber had sneaked into the building when the deadline for the wager arrived and discovered large numbers of empty offices. 'You could hire the place out as tennis courts,' he had quipped to the embarrassed property agents. The investment advisor's willingness to take risks in public has marked him out as an eccentric in the strait-laced and conservative Hong Kong business community.

Then there is his office. His rooms often cause first-time visitors to lose their power of speech. The office is laden with historical memorabilia — not just the odd trinket in a glass box, but statues of Chairman Mao, full-size flags, paintings, Buddha figurines, busts, and so on. The walls are lined with books — not financial analyses or annual reports, but real, solid hardback books, with history and Asian culture among the main themes. On the shelves we find Confucius, Aristotle, the Bible, Plato, Socrates, Nicolaus Copernicus, Galileo Galilei, Mahatma Gandhi, Isaac Newton, Karl Marx, Lenin, Mao Tse-tung, Simon Bolivar, Christopher Columbus, Vasco da Gama, Jean Jacques Rousseau, Charles Louis de Secondat Montesquieu, and Charles Darwin.

But eccentricity alone is not enough to make him a draw to investors. On the contrary, the conservative Asian investors on his doorstep would be repelled by it. There are other reasons for their loyalty. Importantly, Faber's method of analysis is different. He thinks it is wrong that most finance house economists spend their time in expensive offices in Wall Street or the Tokyo business district setting up complex computer models. Faber is more likely to be found on a lake in Argentina, or on a mountain in Tajikistan, or in a castle in Romania. Every few weeks he returns to his office in Hong Kong with a suitcase full of data from a newly explored society, and will spend days analyzing it and seeing how it changes his world picture.

His contacts are different. No bi-weekly shuffle along the brokers' wine bars in New York's Battery Park for him. He is more likely to be seen in a Cambodian nightclub chatting to some secretive Asian tycoon, or sharing dim sum with an old Chinese family in a members-only club in Kowloon. In fact, the entire range of sources on which he bases his predictions are different. This is a key to the enthusiasm with which clients greet his monthly newsletter.

While you might expect your investment advisor to appear with charts predicting the likely movement of stock or commodity prices, Faber is more likely to turn up to a meeting with a picture showing the number of rings in a recently felled oak: Nature's own long-term record of weather conditions that could yield useful information on crop futures. His predictions are less likely to be underpinned by 40-

day moving averages or this quarter's leading indicators, than by examination of the fortunes of pre-industrial cities in the 15th or 16th century. His understanding of how organizations grow and acquire their competitors is more likely to be illustrated with the record of a recent military skirmish than a textbook flow-chart of acquisition procedures.

There is also the fact that he is often demonstrably wrong. This may look like a black mark, but in financial circles, this is the sign of a man who makes precise, measurable predictions, and is a quality that gains a financial prophet respect in professional circles. He has suffered for his mistakes, too, by going 'short' (wagering cash that a market or commodity will fall) on investments which have soared. And he admits it. 'As far as the first half of 1987 was concerned, I was totally wrong,' he wrote disarmingly about the Dow Jones Industrial Average in 1988. Furthermore, his besetting sin — the taking of profits too early — is one that doesn't damage his clients' wealth. It's a simple axiom of investment that occurs to too few people: no one loses money by taking profits. And Faber maintains, with some justification, that he tends to be right when it really counts.

But the most important factor of all is: his advice provides clients with opportunities for stunning capital gains. He inspires passionate loyalty among his followers, who have seen his offbeat predictions regularly fulfilled. And his rivals and critics also subscribe to and read his newsletter. 'Whatever you think about Marc, you cannot fault the quality of his analysis, which is always excellent,' says Peter Everington, managing director of Regent Pacific, one of the fastest growing investment companies in Asia. It's actually the first part of that sentence that sticks in the mind: 'Whatever you think about Marc, ...' It implies a negativity. It must be admitted that many people in the investment community don't like Faber, thinking that his fame is undeserved and his reasoning false.

He doesn't dress right ... he gets an unfair share of publicity ... he gets it wrong all the time ... 'He's predicted 20 out of the last ten crashes,' a rival economist from a British finance house in Hong Kong complained.

Yet, as Everington indicates, even those who totally disagree with

Faber's conclusions will still read what he has to say. Innovative thinking in finance is rare, and the few sources need to be mined carefully. Faber's theories cannot be boiled down to a simple formula in the 'pop economics' fashion that is so common today, although wags in Hong Kong sometimes talk of 'Doom Thought' — a pun on the Chinese communists' canon of dull Deng Xiaoping speeches known as 'Deng Thought.' Yet there are consistent underlying attributes in Faber's writings and speeches: a focus on large-scale historical trends, a hyper-contrarian attitude, a gift for lateral thinking, a cynicism about fast profits, a talent for finding useful links between apparently unconnected trends, an emphasis on fresh research, a staggeringly wide range of interests, a refreshing disrespect for convention, an ability to find patterns in seemingly random screeds of data, a joy in spending as well as saving money, a driving, almost Blackbeard-like hunger to dig up new and undiscovered sources of treasure, and a preference for profiting from a downward slope rather than a rising one. Despite his heavy focus on research, he has a contradictory habit of occasionally acting purely on impulse.

A Hotel on a Mountain

Acting on impulse killed Arnold von Winkelried. It also made him live forever. This was quite a feat in the early Middle Ages, from which relatively few names have emerged. The scene of Arnold's impetuous action was the battle of Sempach in what is now Switzerland, in 1386. The Swiss and Austrian armies seemed well matched as they hurled jeers, threats, and spears at each other. The battle was stalled. Neither side seemed able to make any significant headway against the other.

Then, Arnold von Winkelried, a citizen of Unterwalden, rushed forward from the Swiss side. He wasn't covered, and seemed to be heading for certain death — à la Kevin Costner in *Dances With Wolves*. Whether Winkelried had a brilliant sense of timing or whether he was fired by a suicidal impulse is not known. What is clear is that he raced to make a one-man assault on the Austrian lines at what turned out to be a critical moment in the battle.

Seemingly impervious to the arrows and other missiles which pierced his flesh, he ran along the Austrian front line, terrifying his opponents and snatching their spears from them. His collection of enemy weapons clutched to his chest, he eventually fell dead of his wounds.

His countrymen surged through the opening he had created and eventually gained a victory which assured Switzerland of its independence. His fellow soldiers declared, over his heavily punctured body, that Winkelried would never be forgotten.

That's the legend, anyway. Historians in Switzerland today are not agreed on the precise details of the incident, but most are convinced that Winkelried existed and that he was a military star; he is still fondly remembered today as a national hero. One thing that is little known is that his daughter married a man named Odermatt. But let us return to this gentleman's offspring later.

First, we should clear up some misconceptions about this mountainous country which many people first glimpse on the lids of chocolate boxes. Switzerland is that place in Europe which remains neutral and never fights wars, and it is rich because of all the cuckoo clocks and Swiss banks, right?

Up to a point, Lord Copper. Until late in the 19th century, most of the Swiss region was very poor, and it has a history of small-scale wars with its neighbors. Despite its reputation as a neutral place, Marc Faber believes the origin of Switzerland's wealth can most honestly be traced to warfare. Its rural areas were located mainly in mountain valleys and were unsuited for agriculture, so a large number of young Swiss left their farms throughout the Middle Ages and became mercenaries.

For several hundred years, these hired fighters were Switzerland's largest export item, and the country benefited as they remitted their loot to their families. But it wasn't just hard cash they eventually returned with. Many who had served in foreign armies became fluent in foreign languages and familiar with new techniques, products, and ideas. Upon retirement they frequently set up small trading or manufacturing businesses, taking advantage of the very low wages paid in the impoverished Swiss mountain regions.

This led to the rise of the Swiss textile industry, especially in Glarus and around Zurich and St Gallen, which, by the early part of the 19th century, employed one-quarter of the country's population. This industry gave birth to a textile machinery and machine tool industry. Today, machines and machine tools are Switzerland's largest export earner, followed by the chemical industry and tourism. Cuckoo clocks appear nowhere in the equation. (They actually originated in Germany.)

This cosmopolitan streak and an apparent in-bred talent for business innovation emerged in several individuals who became pioneers in various fields. Some, whose names include Geigy, Nestlé, Sulzer, and Suchard, built global businesses from Switzerland. Others went to the United States in the 19th century and became 'names' there, including Studebaker, Chevrolet, Bandalier, and General Sutter.

The second half of the 19th century saw a new specialization blossom in Switzerland, in the shape of the rise of the Swiss hotelier. Cesar Ritz was a Swiss national who moved to London to try out his hostelry skills there. He famously turned around the fortunes of the ailing Hotel Savoy in London and then proceeded to open several hotels in Europe. The Ritz in Paris became legendary, and the Grand Hotel in Rome was the world's first hotel with private bathrooms, then considered an astonishing luxury.

Now let us return to Winkelried, or more precisely, to his offspring. Some 600 years after the warrior's dramatic death, his descendant, Adelbert Odermatt, son of the owner of a horse-carriage conveyance business, showed that he had the same talent (or good fortune) with timing. As a young man, he worked in the transportation company based on the family stables. They rented out horses and carriages the same way that Hertz Rent-a-Car today provides hatchbacks to people on the move.

But soon after the turn of the century, Adelbert and his father Melchior recognized the tourist potential of the Swiss mountains, and gathered together enough cash to start a hotel called the

Bellevue Terminus in a village called Engelberg on a snowy crag. Initially, Adelbert's timing seemed bad. He had just completed the 300-room hotel when the First World War broke out, and business slumped. But the downturn proved to be temporary, and the tourists flocked back after 1918. Adelbert Odermatt's business thrived. The hotel went through the boom years of the 1920s with the rooms packed during the holiday seasons. Engelberg was the place to be, and where better to stay than at the Bellevue?

Odermatt's wife, Helen, worked day and night supervising the kitchens and the restaurants, while the man of the house made the bar his kingdom, and passed many hours entertaining the guests with stories of Swiss life and references to his famous ancestor. His wife turned out to have a remarkable talent with languages, which proved useful as the tourists arrived from further and further afield. Although she was from a tiny village on a mountain and had never been out of the country, Helen soon spoke and wrote fluent English, French, German, and Italian.

Odermatt, flushed with the success of the venture, financed the first funicular transport system (a cross between a cable-car and a railway carriage) up the mountain. This became an additional tourist attraction.

The average turn-of-the-century tourist was a hiker, but in the 1920s, an increasing number of visitors were interested in the new winter sports that were taking the hill countries of continental Europe by storm. Skiing was not native to Switzerland. It was actually introduced by the British, although they have no real ski-able mountains in their country. The British army had been posted to Norway for training in winter conditions, and had picked up the Norwegian technique of strapping wooden planks on their feet for sliding games. A single hand stick was used, swung from side to side, rather like a solo canoeist uses his oar.

Other sports such as bob-sleighing were also growing in popularity, and Odermatt sometimes spent more time entertaining himself in the snow than his guests did. He became extremely skilled and eventually became a national bob-sleigh champion. Twice he was on the Swiss bob-sleigh team at the Olympic Games. Helen, on her occasional breaks from running the kitchens and restaurants, became one of the first women who skied in Switzerland. She skied extremely well (and fast). Doing a schuss gave her great pleasure, and did so even when she took to the slopes at the age of 70.

The hardworking hoteliers found time to have four daughters, one of whom died of illness at the age of 14. The oldest, Gabriela, a dark-haired beauty, started a dalliance with one of the hotel guests — Paul Faber, the son of a hydraulic engineer working for Brown Bouveri. He appeared to be a suitably well-bred suitor for a Winkelried descendant. He came from a family that traced its roots back to the Huguenots, a clan which had been expelled from France in the 17th century and moved to Switzerland, where it started the watchmaking industry.

Business at the Bellevue Terminus went through many dramatic ups and downs — the Depression in the 1930s caused a slump which lasted until 1935, when the visitors flocked back and the hotel had to be expanded. Then came the Second World War, which brought tremendous hardship to Swiss mountain resorts (too close to Hitler's stamping grounds, you see).

At last, in the 1950s, skiing became a popular international sport and the Swiss ski resorts took their place among the top attractions in Europe. Even then, the hotel family could not relax. By that stage, many new mountain resorts, such as St Moritz and Zermatt, began to compete with Engelberg, which was slowly displaced as the mecca of the jet set. Engelberg's proximity to Zurich, once an asset, became something of a liability — for hoteliers, anyway. Skiers could comfortably drive up to the slopes in the morning and return home in the evening without actually staying in one of the slowly deteriorating large hotels, most of which eventually went bankrupt.

Gabriela had married Paul in 1940, and the couple set up home in Zurich. But they made frequent visits to the family hotel on the mountain. They took their two children with them. The first was Alexander, born in 1944, and the second Markus, born on February 28, 1946. They wanted to call the younger child 'Marc' but were constrained by Swiss laws, which did not allow short forms of names to be registered.

As a child, Marc spent a lot of time at the Bellevue and heard much about the cyclical and seasonal nature of the tourism industry. The hotel was only open for the short winter and summer seasons, and had to make its money fast, so that it could survive the bleak off-season periods. He was also fascinated by the different strands of business at the hotel — the restaurants, the guest rooms, the winter sports facilities — and how they interrelated.

The family gatherings in the hotel were a noisy affair. As well as Gabriela's family, the other two sisters, Felicitas and Margot, would also bring their families. A long table would be set up in a private room between the guests' main dining room and the restaurant 'office' — really a food station which received dishes from the basement kitchens and assigned them to the correct tables. The children were given a strict rule: they could not open their mouths to speak unless someone asked them a question. Nevertheless, the parties were noisy and the conversation would rise to a deafening pitch, at which time Odermatt would thump the table with his fist and roar, *'Potz Chaib Ruhe!'* ('Damn well shut up,' in the Innerschweizer dialect) to demand peace.

Marc's father had trained as a doctor, and his medical practice flourished. He quickly became the best-known knee surgeon in Switzerland. The country's best footballers and skiers would come to him to have their leg injuries dealt with. The surgeon took a business-like attitude to his job, and ran his operating theater on a strict timetable. He worked hard, and it was said that he did as many operations as all the other knee specialists put together. Whenever the young Faber boys would mention their surname, they would be asked: 'Are you related to Doctor Faber, the knee surgeon?'

But Faber senior was truly only married to his scalpel; the surgeon's other marriage did not thrive. When Markus was five, his parents divorced. He, his brother, and mother moved from Zurich to Geneva, and lived on a small allowance from their father. The surgeon remarried, and eventually produced two more children, providing Alexander and Markus with two half-sisters.

Meanwhile, their mother, Gabriela, worked as a tourist guide. When Markus was ten, Gabriela decided she wanted to move back to Zurich. The children remained in touch with their father, although he was more of a visiting uncle than a parent. At the age of 11, Markus asked for a bicycle. His father turned him down, saying it was too dangerous. The young boy believed that the father was just being mean, and determined to buy it by his own means. He got a job as a delivery boy for a Zurich pharmacist. He was paid 50 Swiss centimes (about 10 U.S. cents) an hour, so he calculated that he had to work for some 350 hours to raise the 175 Swiss francs needed to realize his dreams. He recalls the incident as his first encounter with practical economics.

Shortly afterwards, Gabriela set herself up in the real estate business in Zurich, and conditions for the family improved. Soon, enough money was coming in for the family to be considered upper middle-class, and to have holidays abroad — they went to Italy, Yugoslavia; Spain, and Britain. Marc went to a good private school in Switzerland and was sent to stay with friends in London at the age of 13 to learn English.

Although he recalls that they were never counted as wealthy, the family was comfortable enough. But they, like many Swiss, were fascinated with the countries outside their small nation — one in particular. In the late 1950s and the 1960s, only one place was considered Utopia. 'I remember as a child how we always talked about America,' Faber says. 'America was the first country to commercialize television, it built big and prestigious cars, it invented computers, and it ran factories more efficiently than anyone else. At a time when most Swiss families still washed their laundry by hand, we found it hard to believe that practically every house in America had a washing machine. Whatever America produced was better and bigger; its many new inventions and gadgets made us feel very provincial. America was a dream country and we children were always fascinated to hear stories from people who had visited the United States.'

Adelbert Odermatt died in 1954 with no will written and his paperwork in disarray. As a result, there was much acrimony in the fight to claim rights to the hotel. Land inheritance laws were biased in favor of men, and Helen, despite the work she had put into the hotel all her life, was pushed out. She owned a building in Engleberg, and ran it as a small penzione-type hotel until her death in 1980, aged 90.

The youngest male Faber was not a good student at school. He was not academic by nature, and it was clear he would rather be out doing something active than sitting at a desk looking at books. The classes in his schools were large and the atmosphere was strict. If you failed, you were kicked out to repeat the year. Of the 36 students who started in his class, only 19 remained when it was time for the exams. Five or six of Faber's best friends were ejected from the class, further diminishing his interest in staying in it. The schedule was gruelling. In summer, school would start at 7 am and continue until noon. At 2 pm it would start again, sometimes going on until 6 in the evening. There was always at least two hours of homework to be done. Marc did the minimum he felt was necessary to avoid punishment.

The only subject he really liked was history — here were stories of real people doing real things, stories you could learn from and which could provide models for your own life.

Marc's older brother, Alexander, proved to have a talent for languages, while Marc's better subjects were left-brain topics — maths, physics, and geometry. He scraped through his exams and found himself with a chance to go to university.

In the 1960s, the Beatles were singing 'Can't Buy Me Love,' yet Marc decided to study economics. He chose the subject for rather negative reasons: Alexander had chosen to study law, and he wanted to be different. It proved to be a good choice. He had a professor called Niehans who brought the subject to life, and Marc Faber suddenly found himself with an interest which was to last through his life.

At this stage, he discovered that he had inherited something from his grandfather — a love of winter sports. He had a natural talent for skiing, and was soon invited on to the university's ski team. It quickly became apparent that he had enough skill to be a national-class skier, and could possibly have a future as a world-class ski racer.

It wasn't long after starting his studies at the University of Zurich that Marc found himself facing a tough decision. He could head out into the snowdrifts and practice the slalom with his friends. Or he could start work on that pile of economics books which lay on his desk.

It was no contest. He grabbed his skis and headed out into the blinding glare of the white slopes.

A Present from Father Christmas

Marc Faber, like many investment advisors, writes a regular newsletter. His eight- or 12-page monthly publication, like those of his peers, is filled with discussions of present trends, a smattering of graphs and charts, and pointers toward stocks worth buying (or, more often, shorting). It started life in the 1980s as a typewritten, photocopied letter sent to all clients of Drexel Burnham Lambert (HK) Ltd, under such exciting titles as 'US Market Bi-Weekly Technical Comment' and 'Monthly Comment on Asian Stock Markets.'

After Drexel's (and Japan's) collapse in early 1990, Faber's reputation as Asia's premier prophet of doom was firmly established. The number of reporters who phoned him for regular comments was growing fast, with his secretary sometimes fielding a dozen calls in a morning. The newsletter was relaunched with superior design and printing, carrying the tongue-in-cheek title of *The Gloom, Boom & Doom Report*, much better to reflect Faber's idiosyncratic personality.

But his letter has never been the sort of hot-off-the-press tipsheet that the great mass of investors will queue to snatch off the countertop. From the point of view of the average reader, it is undeniably rather hit or miss. Each month it focuses on one topic, often arbitrarily chosen, in enormous depth — and if that subject doesn't interest you — well, tough. You just have to wait until next month and see if that presses any buttons.

Some issues feature scholarly quote-filled studies of arcane financial subjects which would mainly interest trained economists. An issue entitled 'Is Deflation a Possibility?' featured a graph showing the average prices of anthracite and bessemer pig-iron between 1870 and 1900 — not a topic widely discussed in the bars of Tokyo or New York. Others focus on a specific country, industry sector, or trend. Then there are the slightly off-the-wall topics chosen for no discernible reason at all, other than the fact that they interest Faber.

One can only guess what his baffled clients thought when they received an issue in July 1996, entitled 'The Land of Michael the Brave.' Who? Where? Only at the end of a lengthy first paragraph does he reveal that the country about which he is writing this month is Romania.

Despite this uncompromising format, Faber's newsletters are widely circulated and discussed. A thousand copies are printed each month; they go to clients in 30 countries and are frequently quoted in the media. Their erudition and adherence to issues of serious economics have their own special appeal. Then there is the growing feeling, as you read them, that these are views that you simply will not find anywhere else.

Faber has a long record of good advice delivered.

In 1982, Faber purchased zero coupon bonds in Wall Street shortly before bond prices soared. In March 1985, he published a newsletter entitled 'The Philippines — A Contrarian's Delight.' The Manila stock market almost immediately started to climb, rising by a multiple of 30 times from 1985 until the emerging markets crash of 1994.

In July 1986, Faber published a newsletter entitled 'Thailand Now Attractive,' announcing that 'stocks are dirt cheap.' Although the Thailand SET Index had been perfectly flat for more than five years, within weeks of Faber's prediction, it started to move upward, climbing tenfold by 1991 and 17 times by 1994.

In September 1987, Faber identified Latin America as a place to watch and told his readers: 'We feel the Chilean stock market ... is significantly undervalued.' So did other buyers. In the next three years, the Chilean stock market became one of the world's best-performing markets.

In December 1988, in a newsletter entitled 'Argentina — A Treasure Among Depressed Markets,' Faber wrote: 'The economic pendulum has swung towards extreme undervaluation. We suggest that investors accumulate properties and equities on any sign of weakness.' The market rose in 1989, fell back, and then started a major climb, reaching 16 times its 1988 price by 1992.

Faber's October 1987 newsletter, although not predicting a worldwide crash, did warn that 'free falls in peripheral markets will occur ... Asian markets are vulnerable to a sharp sell-off.'

In January 1989, he wrote that oil servicing stocks 'have the potential to double in two years.' They actually doubled in less than one year.

In June 1989, he wrote a newsletter entitled 'After Tiananmen.' He told readers to 'buy Hong Kong blue chips at the now depressed prices.' The Hang Seng Index stood at 2765 at the time. The index rose steadily for the following nine years, peaking at 16,640 in 1997.

Although Asia is Faber's major focus, he also had some good calls in the Western world. In December 1991, he told investors to 'buy Bund Call Warrants at DM3.20.' They doubled within a year.

In February 1994, he told investors about one of his more unusual strategies — to accumulate stocks during times of hyper-inflation. In this particular case, the focus was on Russia. 'Hyper-inflation periods provide the most unusual buying opportunity. Russian financial assets are extremely depressed and the only risk in buying Russian shares is time.' By 1997, the shares he had tipped had risen by 20 times.

The most talked-about issue of each year is the December one, which always contains an extra pull-out entitled 'A Present From Father Christmas.' This is a selection of hot tips designed to bring investors a January windfall. The hits have been much appreciated. The misses have been honestly admitted. In 1996, Faber wrote: 'For several years in a row we were very successful at finding rewarding investment opportunities, both long and short. However, I am embarrassed to admit that last year's idea to short U.S. semi-conductor stocks, including Micron Technology, was a disaster — at least until the month of July. My apologies.'

Faber, unusually among so-called financial gurus, is blessed with a streak of disarming honesty. In January 1997, he wrote: 'I have to admit that the strength of the recent bull market in the U.S. has taught me to use the word "impossible" more carefully.'

He used part of one 1996 newsletter to discuss the difficulties of writing such a publication.

> In order to have a successful newsletter (large readership), I am impelled to write about popular, 'in vogue' themes. Yet, popular themes cannot be particularly rewarding from an investment point of view; hence, I should write about out-of-the-ordinary and extremely unpopular themes. After all, the strongest bull markets emerge from sectors in which the fewest investors are positioned.
>
> However, if I wrote, month after month, about direct investment in Kazakhstan, Far East Russia, Uganda and Iran, and advised on Kabul property, as well as 'how to make a fortune with Christmas cards', I doubt that many of my readers would renew their subscriptions.

(That line about making money out of Christmas cards wasn't a joke. Faber, noting that internet bulls reckon Christmas cards will become obsolete, believes they might be worthwhile collectibles. He told his clients: 'The great thing about them is that while you presently receive them free of charge (no downside risk except storage charges), your grandchildren are likely to consider them a rarity — a precious collector's item worth much more than telephone cards.')

Often the newsletter will show strong evidence of Faber's historical bent. There are not many financial tipsheets which will start with a sentence such as the following: 'In AD 794, the Japanese emperor Kwammu moved the capital of Japan from Nagoaka to an area which he renamed Heian-kyo (capital of peace and tranquility).'

Other newsletters give practical tips about visiting the places examined: 'Kyoto is perfectly safe at night. There is no mugging, and honest and reliable taxi drivers will deliver even unconscious drunks safely to their homes without robbing them.' (The reader cannot help but wonder whether this note is autobiographical.)

But rather than attempt to describe some of the more unusual newsletters, I hereby quote from a couple. This one gives a mixture of practical tips and economic advice in anecdotal form:

> A visitor entering the old town [of Marrakesh] through the main gate and proceeding to Place Djeema Al Fna will find it difficult to fend off the incredibly persistent and irritating hordes of tourist guides whose principal objective is to lead their clients to shops in the souk and rip them off as much as possible.
>
> My brother and I managed to avoid the Moroccan guide plague by entering the medina equipped with a map and a compass — Marrakesh is like a labyrinth — through a gate in the north of the city's ramparts, from where the guide mafia does not expect any visitors.
>
> Even so, we could not avoid being taken for a small ride. In one of the shops of the souk, I decided to buy a 'magic' box. The storekeeper asked US$25 for it. I intended to make a counter-offer of $10, but my brother was quicker and bid $2. At first I thought the shopkeeper would throw us out — although I remember such spreads from Mike Milken's junk bond department. But to my great surprise, a heated bargaining session followed, until my brother finally settled for $4. I felt so sorry for the poor shopkeeper that I gave him an extra dollar.
>
> Two days later, I saw an identical magic box in the souvenir shop of the luxurious Sheraton hotel in Casablanca, where it was selling for $3. Two doctorate-holders, an economist and a lawyer, had thus been taken for a ride by a simple, uneducated Moroccan shopkeeper. This was another reason for my turning quite bullish about Morocco.

Following the publication of this report, the Morocco market rose fourfold.

In another newsletter, he combines his specialisms of history and economics to draw some illuminating parallels:

> Let us forget about markets for a moment and consider the following: prior to our age of market economies and capitalism, some other form of 'capitalism' existed.

However this capitalism was not based on creating wealth through progress in all spheres of society and the production and distribution of goods and services, but through conquest (the acquisition of territories and wealth by force — so-called unfriendly takeovers).

From our schooldays we all remember the incredible military achievements of conquerors such as Cyrus the Great (559–530 BC), Alexander the Great (356–323 BC), Julius Caesar (100–44 BC), Charlemagne (AD 742–814), Umar ibn al-Khattab (586–644), Genghis Khan (1167–1225), and, much later, Napoleon Bonaparte (1769–1821).

Their empires were in steep bull trends for a while ... but eventually (frequently after the conqueror's death) toppled like a house of cards ... the great conquerors of antiquity were the first 'businessmen' to make extensive use of leverage. Their armies never grew much in terms of size, but the territories they controlled expanded almost exponentially. As a result, the acquired empire grew disproportionately per unit of soldier ...

But one victory after another led to euphoria, carelessness, and total misjudgment of risks. While most great military leaders were careful not to waste their armies at the beginning of their careers, they later fell victim to their own success and began to neglect the risks associated with the conquest of larger and larger territories (the acquisition of additional assets).

Take, for instance, Napoleon. The Russian campaign of 1812 was, from a risk–reward point of view, a complete absurdity (it was an incredibly leveraged, high-risk low-reward transaction, typical of the terminal or climactic phase of an empire's uptrend) ...

Markets are no different from empires. They expand, rise in value, become ever-extended, and eventually collapse. In a modern market economy, conquerors are business leaders, successful speculators, adventurous fund managers and leverage buyout artists.

The generals are their immediate subordinates (ambitious junior partners among hedge funds, derivative traders, research prima donnas, etc) who are all sharing in the profits of their 'conquerors'.

The solders are the individual investors — usually uninformed, greedy, and displaying strong crowd behaviour [psychology] and rapid changes of sentiment.

In a dreamier mood, in his newsletter of December 1997, he talked about a gift he had been given:

> Not long ago my daughter Nantamada gave me the novel *The Alchemist* by the Brazilian writer Paulo Coelho. It is one of the most wonderful books I have ever read. If you don't know what to give your friends and relatives for Christmas, here is a present that will please both young and old, liberals and conservatives. It is the story of Santiago, a young Andalusian (southern Spain) shepherd boy who dreamed that he would find a hidden treasure at the Egyptian pyramids.

Faber then retold the entire story of the book before concluding:

> *The Alchemist* is not just a well-written novel (I find the French translation better than the English one); it contains much wisdom for investors. The road to the hidden treasure is paved with hardship, and the shepherd boy loses all of his belongings three times before finding it.

Faber admits that the average investor won't learn what the NASDAQ is going to do by reading such a story, 'but what he learns will do his soul a lot more good than the acquisition of a few more dollars'.

On Forecasting

It's 90 degrees in the shade. Faber is in Phuket, Thailand, at a telecommunications conference organized by Chase Manhattan Bank. Physically, it's paradise, and culturally, it's fascinating — particularly the night-life. (He jotted down a note he later put in his newsletter: 'It's a beautiful place — if you are rich and accompanied, stay at the Amanpuri Resort. But if you are interested in an in-depth study of "ladymen", stay in the midst of their natural habitat along Patong Beach.')

There were a number of representatives from Asian telephone companies present, and executives from hardware suppliers such as

Motorola, Nokia, and Ericsson. Needless to say, everyone was rabidly bullish about everything connected with the telecommunications industry.

Faber made a presentation that would definitely have failed to win him any 'Mr Popularity' award. He had already started speaking on stage when he realized that he had forgotten to take the telecommunications industry out of his list of forthcoming big-time losers. He pressed on with his hard-hitting speech, undaunted.

'Wow! You should have seen the audience,' he told friends later. 'Especially a young lady who worked for one of the banks. You could smell, fifty yards against the wind, that she had recently completed an MBA — you know, at one of those "prestigious" business schools where arrogance is the first subject on the timetable.'

This young woman's presentation followed Faber's, and she bitterly disagreed with all his remarks. Fortunately for him, that night, Nokia's shares tumbled by 35 percent in New York on poor results.

That was a neat coincidence, and it allowed him to have the last laugh. But he knew that it didn't really prove anything. It is important to realize this, Faber admits. Any smooth-talking forecaster can prove he is always right. And his equally smooth-talking rivals can prove that he is always wrong. This is one of the problems of making predictions. You can prove whatever you like, given enough data to select from.

Some of Faber's investors bought gold in 1985. Three years later, a selection of them met up in a bar in London and were talking about it. The Japanese investor commented that he was depressed about how far the yellow metal had dropped — a painful 30 percent over three years. But an American banker begged to differ. 'Fallen? What are you talking about? Gold has risen, like, 75 percent since 1985.' A peripatetic investor disagreed with both the opinions offered, suggesting that it had changed little in price. Of course, they were all correct, in terms of their own currency. It all depends on perspective. To a Japanese (or a Swiss), gold fell during that period, while to someone from the United States, it climbed steadily.

After years of watching people make predictions, Marc Faber can swiftly demonstrate how a wily analyst can make a completely wrong-headed forecast seem like it was right on the button.

The U.S. market crashed famously in 1929, and the Hong Kong market in 1973. Both markets fell 90 percent from their highs, and many companies collapsed. But a smart prophet can successfully draw positive examples even from these crashes. If you bought shares at their highs (381 for the Dow Jones in 1929, and 1700 for the Hang Seng Index in early 1973), these markets would have amply rewarded long-term investors. Thus it can be argued that the markets at the time of their crashes didn't show excessive speculation, at least not from a genuinely long-term perspective.

Equally, real estate purchased in 1836 in Chicago, in 1886 in California, and in 1926 in Florida — right at the peak of their respective booms — hit the short-term investor very hard, since prices collapsed. But the ultra long-term investor (or the grandchildren of the patient initial investor) would be quite content with the rise in value of the land by the present day.

So, choosing your parameters is a serious matter for serious forecasters. Another is timing. Was the Japanese stock market already dangerously speculative in 1988? Yes, there is no doubt that it was. But investors who bought into it then enjoyed the benefits of stocks rising a further 30 percent in the 12 months preceding the peak in December 1989.

The silver market of the late 1970s serves as a fascinating example of the same forecasting danger. In December 1979, silver had risen to $18 an ounce, having more than doubled during the preceding 12 months. The precious metal markets were already extremely speculative, and thus should have been a bad buy at US$18, according to the bears (and all common sense). But silver soared to more than $40 in a dramatic four-week rise, so the bulls claimed they were right. Silver then collapsed to $11 in May 1980, and stood at less than $4 in 1992, so the bears then said they were right. Two lots of forecasters were making totally opposing predictions. Who was right? They both were. It was one's timing which defined whether one made a lot of money fast or got badly burned.

But the professional forecaster's worst problem is history. That's history in the sense of wars and revolutions and earth-moving discoveries. These don't fit easily into financial models, however fancy your computer is. This factor you can file under 'the sheer cussedness of life' and put into a box with the words of John Mayward Keynes on the front: 'The inevitable never happens. It is the unexpected always.'

To illustrate this, Faber asks his clients to visualize themselves as a powerful person wishing to invest in Asia in the year 1800. Your most logical choices would have been Calcutta, which was the administrative center of the British Empire, or Batavia, the capital of the Dutch East Indies. Today, Calcutta has lost all its luster; and Batavia, now called Jakarta, is one of the region's poorer performers.

Imagine if you were making the same decision a century or so later, say in 1920. The most important city in Asia was Shanghai, a lively, bustling place known as 'the Paris of the East.' Other places which looked set to boom were Canton (now Guangzhou), Macau, Saigon (Ho Chi Minh City), Rangoon, and Manila (which was under United States' rule) — none of which thrived.

At that time, both Singapore and Hong Kong were already relatively important trading centers and bases for British garrisons. But they had no industries of their own, so they didn't seem to be worthwhile conduits for investment. Seoul and Taipei? You probably wouldn't even have heard of them. If you had, you wouldn't have paid them much notice, as both were controlled by Japan. Even after the Second World War, there were few signs that the fastest growing economies in the world would be Japan, Hong Kong, Singapore, South Korea, and Taiwan.

The vagaries and sheer unpredictability of history make forecasting a difficult business. And the prophet who doubles as a fund manager cannot wriggle away from complaints so easily. His performance, or lack of it, is there in plain sight on the balance sheet. One of Faber's more tragic mistakes was to have been bearish on the United States' market during the mid-to-late 1990s, when his cunningly constructed bearish portfolios slumped in value while the mom-and-pop investors of middle America made a fortune.

Unlike some of his more weasily counterparts, Marc Faber has an endearing habit of publicly flagellating himself for his mistakes, sometimes to an almost Japanese extent. In 1996, Faber sent his clients a checklist of warning signs that the Dow's rise had run out of steam. But he added a note: 'I leave it up to you, my dear readers, to draw your own conclusions (my own having been so far wrong).'

It's a tough job, and getting it wrong a certain proportion of the time is par for the course. What makes it difficult is the lack of support, Faber says. Part of the challenge any hyper-contrarian faces is the loneliness of his or her view. 'It means that at major turning points I can be wrong for quite some time, as I am betting alone against everyone else,' he says.

One of Faber's most depressing periods was 1986 and the period before the fall (seasonal and financial) of 1987. Recalling that period, he explains: 'I was not making much money, having sold out my positions too soon. Furthermore, I had started to short the market. However, the market did not fall as I expected, but continued to rise. Wherever I went, I heard housewives, nightclub hostesses and other amateur investors talking about how much money they had made, while I, the "great expert," was missing out on the bull run. Although I never doubted that the stock-market mania would end very badly and wipe out the speculators, I nevertheless began to feel rather like an idiot. I questioned what purpose it served to analyse the various factors relating to stock prices if totally ignorant investors could make so much more money than I did.'

The Black Monday crash, when it finally came, vindicated Faber and made him a bit of a star — but not before he had started joking about giving up the business and going to run a taxi company in Thailand.

This anti-populist approach is that much harder if you are doing it with someone else's money. 'The problem with the contrarian investment approach is that it requires a lot of courage and inner strength, because the typical client is not a contrarian and will not appreciate this strategy. The typical client will prefer for you to fail conventionally than to succeed unconventionally.'

For Faber, the middle and latter part of the 1990s was another long, painful period, although his self-confidence was no longer as fragile as it had been a decade earlier. The Dow rose steadily, against the odds. He wrote to his clients in June 1996:

> It is almost impossible to know how much longer the investment mania will last and how much higher prices can move before the bubble is punctured. In fact, today, I feel very much like Isaac Newton who in early 1720 remarked: 'I can calculate the motions of heavenly bodies, but not the madness of people.'

Newton, Faber adds with a laugh, was a very wise man but not necessarily a good investor. He sold his shares in the South Sea Company and made a profit of 100 percent, collecting £7000, a huge sum at the time. He then re-entered the market right at its peak and subsequently lost £20,000.

Travels with an Iconoclast

Callers to Marc Faber's Hong Kong office aren't deflected with 'He's in a meeting.' It's more likely that they'll be told, 'We think he's trekking through some unspellable country in Central Asia.'

'Among emerging-market investors, Mr Faber is famous for touting investments in pariah states and in countries where visitors are advised to wear flak jackets,' a reporter with the *Wall Street Journal* commented on November 26, 1993.

Dr Doom searches out unusual corners of the world, and — even more scary for his investors — he buys odd things when he gets there. One of his more unusual investment purchases was a bunch of North Korean loans. The ultimate immobile investment? No. They have been trading at prices which have varied from two cents in the dollar to about 15, depending on how stable the hermit kingdom was perceived to be at the time. In 1993, Faber put more than US$1.5 million into North Korean debt. If you are going to gamble, you have to gamble reasonably big.

Does such a venture count as foolhardy? Not at all, says Faber, who insists that North Korea could surprisingly easily fit into the modern Asian economic system. The country's 22 million population would doubtless be thrilled to provide paid labor for the relatively rich employers in nearby Japan and South Korea, and they would be excellent value from the point of view of those countries. They would also eventually provide a hungry consumer market for goods from those same nations.

But is a war not likely, eventually? Is it not a terrifyingly unstable place? A war could be good news, suggests Faber in his terrifyingly blasé way. 'Aggression would actually accelerate North Korea's economic integration because it would ensure the immediate demise of current dictator Kim Il-Sung's system,' he argued in September 1993. 'North Korea's arsenal would be destroyed by South Korean, Japanese, and American forces overnight.'

Faber's visits to destinations such as Central Asia, Indochina, Eastern Europe, Africa, and Latin America have given his readers insights into places that most business journals and finance house newsletters never mention. But not all his tours have led to him discovering gold mines, or even individual gems.

While he was cautiously positive about Romania, which he visited in the spring of 1996, a tour of neighboring Ukraine left him horrified. The place was a mess, and systems were set up to make things as difficult as possible for foreign investors. At the country's airport, Faber was told that citizens of different nationalities pay different visa fees. He was asked for a stunning US$180 as a Swiss national. Faber displayed his membership card for a Hong Kong nightclub, and the fee was halved.

The hotels were as inadequate and inhospitable as the ones he had encountered on a visit to Moscow in the 1970s. 'Checking in was almost as tedious a process as filing a U.S. tax return,' he later commented. 'Each floor was guarded 24 hours a day by a fierce female dragon.'

Faber returned to Hong Kong with little that was good to say about the sprawling country. 'Its economy is in a shambles, its foreign investment and tax laws are still murky, and in the absence of a rich neighbor, it only attracts very modest foreign direct investment ... its agricultural sector is unproductive, its nuclear reactors are hazardous, the once-efficient steel mills are technologically outdated, and its resources (principally coal and iron ore) are of no great value,' he wrote.

The only good thing that could be said is that it could hardly get any worse: 'By investing in Ukraine now, one would be getting in at the very bottom of its economic cycle.' But he warned that such a prospect was only for someone well-connected, since there was no business transparency at all, so the average investor would have no idea what they were buying. 'The advantage of this situation is that it has so far kept the herd of foreign investors at bay, and, therefore, the valuation of assets is low. The disadvantage is that unless you have the time to really familiarize yourself with Ukrainian economic conditions, and with individual companies, the right investment choice (or stock selection) is difficult.'

That trip wasn't a great success. Others, fortunately, have produced better results. In the 1980s and early 1990s, Faber had put money for speculative investors into the loans of Vietnam, Cuba, Zambia, Angola, Cameroon, and Nigeria. In the spring of 1994, Faber was buying taigas, a new type of Russian government bond. 'Assets in Russia are grossly undervalued. In particular, the financial assets are very cheap,' he enthused.

Reporters, in general, love Marc Faber. They know that he won't give them the predictable material about technology firms on the NASDAQ Index and how technical analysis shows that Wall Street will continue to climb. In interviews, Faber likes to list off-beat investments. A typical one was printed in the *South China Morning Post* in March 1997, when reporter Deborah Orr asked what was on his shopping list.

'Cocoa,' he replied. 'And now we are going to the Ivory Coast. I think some African countries might be interesting. And we are kind of interested to invest in Central Asia — Kazakhstan and Uzbekistan.'

'What is the attraction there?'

'These are countries at the very early stage of economic development, but potentially a country like Kazakhstan could be another Australia — small population, extremely resource-rich.'

Later, back at the newspaper office, the sub-editors had to get out large atlases to locate and check the spelling of Kazakhstan and Uzbekistan.

This perception that the whole world is his economic hunting ground has sometimes got Faber into trouble. In June 1989, as Chinese troops were scrubbing clean the streets around Tiananmen Square, Faber bought Hong Kong-listed shares of companies with operations in China. Not a politically correct thing to do at the time. Fortunately for his reputation, it was generally decided later that constructive engagement with China was the best way ahead for all concerned.

And this leads to an important point. Faber, like many financiers, has been attacked for his ethics. The criticisms appear valid, considering that he generally side-steps political issues. The only question he really asks about China, Myanmar (Burma), North Korea, and other countries run by oppressive regimes, is: are they good targets for investment? A telling incident in 1997, though, suggests that this can be blamed more on naivety and general insensitivity than anything else.

Australian businessman Chris Corrigan, chairman of Patrick Stevedores, contacted the Swiss economist to help arrange financing for a new dock project in Melbourne. Faber made the requisite calls and soon found investors willing to pledge money for the cause.

Shortly afterward, Faber was astonished to find himself labeled as the organizer of a strike-breaking consortium in an industrial dispute. He told an Australian reporter who asked whether he supported the use of non-union labor: 'God, I wouldn't know. I have no idea what is right or wrong; that is not my concern. I acted as an investment banker.'

There was widespread controversy in Australia for some weeks as to whether the restructuring plan for the dockyard was a genuine investment in the business or an underhand attempt to break the power of the unions which controlled it.

Faber realized he was treading a thin line, and worded his answers to the press as carefully as he could: 'The goal of any business is to make money, and I suppose that if you operate a stevedore operation without unions it would have been more efficient, less costly. I don't think the idea was to smash the unions, but to run the business profitably.'

Faber did once get entangled in politics by accident. In the spring of 1993, during the wager in which he bet his ponytail that Hong Kong's Hang Seng Index wouldn't rise (see Chapter 2), brokers noticed that every upward movement of the index would be halted by a new outburst in the row between Britain and China over Hong Kong's political future. 'The time has come to recognise the existence of the Faber Threshold,' said an unnamed financier in the *South China Morning Post* on March 17. It seemed as if the gods didn't want Faber to lose the bet. I caught Faber, intact-ponytail swinging, just before he jumped on a plane to Brazil. 'Okay, okay, I admit it, it's all me,' he said, when asked whether it was coincidental that his fortunes were mirroring the political troubles of Hong Kong. 'When the market reached 6400 I went to Wong Tai Sin Temple and gave a donation. I then told my good friend [Hong Kong Governor] Chris Patten to gazette the reform bill, and I sent a fax to [Chinese Premier] Li Peng, telling him what to say in his speech at the National People's Congress.'

Travelling through uncharted territories to do first-hand research can be dangerous. On September 3, 1997, doom almost came to Dr Doom. Faber and a friend were booked on a Vietnam Airlines flight from Ho Chi Minh City to Phnom Penh. At the last minute, Faber got a call from his friend Alan Khor, son of Cambodian businessman Teng Bunma, saying he couldn't make their planned rendezvous. Faber switched to a different flight — and the one on which he had been booked crashed, killing almost everyone on board.

Incidentally, Teng Bunma's name was flashed around the world earlier that same year when he reportedly lost his temper at the airport in Phnom Penh, took out a gun and shot a jet, damaging its wheels. The story appeared in the news media around the world as an example of an Asian tycoon expressing his impatience in an eccentric and rather primitive way. Faber phoned Khor for the 'inside story,' and was told that Teng started shooting to attract official attention to himself because there were 'dangerous enemies' approaching him. There are still many places in the world where guns are seen as necessary business negotiation tools.

People frequently tell Faber that he was lucky, being in the emerging markets business well before they started emerging. There's truth in that, but Faber opposes the next logical argument in that line of thinking: that money can no longer be made in emerging markets.

'The opportunities are always there, but they shift from one region, city, commodity, or industry to another. The world is constantly undergoing political, social, and economic changes, and when these changes occur there are always some sectors and regions that lose out while others emerge as the new leaders,' he says. 'In fact, the only difference I can see between the availability of investment opportunities 2000, 100, or even ten years ago, and today, is that the speed of change has accelerated.' Your reward or your punishment will be yours sooner.

Faber is amazed that more people don't do any real exploration. Yes, smart real estate investors bought land in Asia's commercial centers, such as Tokyo, Seoul, Taipei, Hong Kong, Singapore, Bangkok, Jakarta, or Manila, but they did so 15 years ago. The same is true for people who invest in tourism projects, who bought land in Pattaya, Bali, and Phuket in the 1980s. By the mid-1990s it was no longer wise to do so.

The Swiss investment advisor has been advising people today who want opportunities in Asia to instead look at Kaohsiung, Taichung, Shanghai, Dalian, Tianjin, Pusan, Inchon, Khabarovsk, Vladivostok, Chiang Mai, Chiang Rai, Cebu, Iloilo, Zamboanga, Surabaya, Ho Chi Minh City, or Rangoon. For tourist locations, forget Bali and try Hainan, Manado, or Da Nang, he says.

Occasionally Faber finds a product in one location which he reckons would be a hit in another. He became known in Hong Kong in the early 1990s as the importer of Grolsch beer (a concession he later passed on to a trading company).

He later switched to another product, which has in some ways had the opposite effect to alcohol. The product, called Muse, was an insertable drug-based device which fixed erectile dysfunction — a precursor to Viagra, which appeared a year or so later.

Faber admitted that he had never tried Muse — 'So far, there has been no need,' he said modestly — but was convinced it worked. 'I think I may apply to be the company's sole agent for Hong Kong and China.' He rubbed his hands with glee. 'Just think of the vast potential for this drug from the Asian markets, where so many men go out to nightclubs, get drunk, and then have difficulties afterward.'

Between November 1996 and February 1997, when Faber started marketing Muse in Asia, the price of its U.S.-listed maker, Vivus, shot upward from US$27 to US$67. But Faber decided not to recommend the stock to clients. 'Eventually, Vivus stock will collapse because competitors will come in,' he said. 'Or some idiot will take a triple dose and have a permanent reaction, upon which he will sue the company.'

This cheeky sense of humor has made Faber a favorite at international financial conferences, where organizers inevitably ask him to be entertaining as well as informative. For example, there was a moment of drama when Faber stomped on to the stage at a conference held to tie in with the Hong Kong handover to China in 1997. He brandished a copy of *New Era Business*, a supplement published by the *South China Morning Post* on June 27. It recorded the views of many senior business people in Hong Kong, all of whom were uniformly bullish. 'Go and buy ten copies of this,' he said. 'Store it for your grandchildren, so that in ten years they can see how people fall into self-delusion.'

Faber made the following rather pointed predictions: (1) The Hong Kong stock market will eventually be closed because of 'insufficient volume.' (2) *Apple Daily*, the cheeky pro-democracy newspaper of Beijing, will be published from Shanghai and will be China's best-selling newspaper. (3) Exchange Square, the home of the Hong Kong Stock Exchange, will be empty and will be turned into an asylum.

No one believed a word of it, of course. But the fact that anyone had dared to be so outrageous at a time when the business community was paralyzed with fear led to his receiving the biggest round of applause of the conference.

3

WHY ROCK-SOLID, CAST-IRON, SURE-FIRE WINNERS ARE OFTEN LOSERS

The Joy of Falling off Mountains

F aber crouched low, whispered an incantation to give himself luck, and threw himself off the mountain. He flew downward at high speed, literally burning a path through the dazzling, powdery snow.

He slowed down slightly to wind through a demanding passage of slalom poles, twisting so steeply from side to side that his elbows almost touched the ground. Faber was at a championship tournament at St Moritz. He had won the first and second rounds, and was on his third race.

Having completed the slalom track, he accelerated toward the finish line. The race was over. He spun the skis to bring himself to a halt.

That was when he hit a rock. Thrown off balance at high speed, he was carried through the air by centrifugal force and slammed into a stone wall. The last thing he heard before losing consciousness was the sound of his bones snapping.

Life as a ski racer had been glorious. In his late teens and early twenties, the Swiss economics student had refined his talents on the slopes to such a degree that he had been invited to join the university ski team. Faber won the Coupe Mercure twice at a well-known competition in Chamonix.

He had participated in many Swiss championships and World Cup races, but he had never taken it as seriously as the professionals: it was the student races and the camaraderie at the lower levels that he enjoyed most. On one occasion, his team had been defeated by a group from Marseille who performed a striptease in the main square of Chamonix when it had been packed with tourists. Faber and his team-mates, wanting to join in the fun, grabbed bottles of bubble bath from a nearby display (the event had been sponsored by a cosmetics company) and emptied them on to the dance floor where the prize-giving was to be held. The room turned into a giant bubble bath and his team was blackballed from future races.

It was a social time, too. He enjoyed the company of his brother, Alexander, on the slopes, as well as friends from university: particularly one Robi Kappeli, whose father was a prominent Swiss businessman. The elder Kappeli built Ciba-Geigy into one of the world's largest pharmaceutical companies.

Faber and Kappeli spent five years driving around in the latter's Porsche from race to race. They skied during the day, studied when their consciences forced them to, partied at night, and had a ball. When he needed money, Faber worked as a ski instructor. He learned how to make friends with the rich, and how they thought about money. He also learned about self-discipline.

Ski-racing needs courage, stamina, skill, and determination. It also needs luck. The snow in St Moritz had been thin, but just deep enough to cover an ill-placed rock that put Faber on his back. He lost a lot of blood and was flown to Zurich for expert help. At the age of 23, a broken femur in his right leg forced him to give up racing for a six-week stay in hospital and turn his attention back to his economics books. Shortly afterwards, he moved to London to pursue postgraduate studies, arriving in Dover with a crutch and a stick.

Contrarianism for Beginners

Being a contrarian investor is easy, right? You just do the opposite of what everyone else does. Jesus was the first contrarian: 'And I say unto you, those who are first shall be last and those who are last shall be first.'

Would that it were so easy. Faber's had some good calls, but the role of contrarian has not been easy, particularly in the mid-1990s. If contrarianism were as simple as the public thinks it is, then it should be as easy as this: pick this year's duds, its worst-performing, least-favored, most written-off stocks, and the following year those are the stocks that are likely to rise, right? Wrong. Don't try this at home.

One of the analysts Faber most respects, James O'Shaughnessy of Greenwich, Connecticut, sat down with all the stock prices of the Dow Jones Industrial Average from 1954 to 1996 and worked out what would happen if you did just that. He picked each year's losers, and calculated how much he would have gained if he had invested in them as his favored picks for the following year.

Result: disaster. This mega-contrarian system of buying stocks with the worst one-year performance turned out to be the worst of two dozen investment strategies he tested. O'Shaughnessy was glad he didn't try this in a real market with real money. If you followed this simplified contrarianist theory and put $10,000 in the U.S. market in 1951, your account balance would be just $29,351 at the end of 1994, a compound annual return of only 2.54 percent — less than if you had left the cash in your grandmother's bank account (although possibly not her savings and loan account).

There are only a few times when this system works. The worst-performing stocks of any particular year tend to do well only after a bear market has bottomed out and the stock market enters the first phase of a bull market (such as in 1975, 1988, and 1991), or in highly speculative markets (such as 1967). The trouble is, you can't predict when these times will occur.

One alternative is to follow the animal husbandry theory of economists. Think of yourself as a farmer keeping bulls and bears. You count the bulls, and, when they get to a certain density, you declare yourself a bear. When the bears predominate, you take a bullish attitude. Does it work? Contrarian economists certainly keep an eye on what their opposite numbers are saying, and some have even tried doing trend-line charts measuring the changing levels of bullishness of the worldwide community of investment newsletter writers.

Nice in theory, but hard in practice. There's no closed-end list of investment newsletter writers, it's tough to decide who is worth including and who isn't, and these days many of them are so cagey with their predictions (watch out for the phrase 'But on the other hand...') that you can read the whole thing and not know whether they are bulls or bears.

No, being a contrarian is much harder than you think. The first thing you have to do is drink Grolsch and stay up late.

The Ten Commandments

It's 2 am on a Friday in Hong Kong and the U.S. market is having a good day. It's May 1996 and the Dow Jones is floating upward like a helium balloon. FM Select 104 is churning out 'Don't Worry, Be Happy.' Faber is in his office, absently humming 'Everything is Beautiful.' He is sitting at his word processor, waiting for some inspiration for his newsletter.

Earlier that evening (or his first break period, considering Faber's 24-hour schedule) he had been chatting with this reporter about the creed of the mom-and-pop investor. Their Ten Commandments go something like this:

1. Everything comes to the patient investor.
2. The best way to make money is to buy blue chips and then forget about them for a long time.

3. In the long run, stock prices always go up faster than other investments.
4. You can never lose money in real estate, as long as you are willing to wait long enough.
5. Buy a commodity and sit on it.
6. Buy real estate and sit on it.
7. Buy a Ming vase and sit on it (but only metaphorically).
8. If you wait long enough, an untraded position on the S&P will do better than the most vigorously traded mixed portfolio.
9. The best retirement fund is a nice chunk of real estate.
10. Patience is a virtue, so wait at least a week between buying and selling.

Such have been the mantras of the Little Guy for at least a couple of decades, and these views have been encouraged by generation after generation of well-meaning financial advisors. The advice is inspiring, comforting — and often completely wrong.

Faber is completely convinced he is right about this. But how to prove it? He is sitting in his office, surrounded by books and computer printouts. His reading and cross-referencing of literally thousands of charts has led him to believe that prices for both equities and commodities regularly top out and fall, never to recover their highs in real terms, or, in some cases, in any other terms. In other cases, the investment does eventually climb to a new level, but too late for the investor concerned, as he or she will have died of old age. The principle holds true for both physical commodities and equities.

But can commodity and stock prices be lumped together in an economic model? The former is a physical product which produces no income stream, while the latter is quite different, being a paper representation of the right of ownership to a capitalist enterprise that (theoretically) produces a flow of profit. Faber reckons that in purely economic terms, everything can be regarded as a commodity: income-producing considerations such as land, human labor, and capital; and items which don't produce income, such as wheat, cotton, gold, art, semiconductors, paper, soft drinks, cigarettes, and so on. In key ways, and at key times, stocks and commodities behave alike. (In this regard, Faber was interested to see an article in *Barron's* entitled 'When Stocks Trade Like Commodities — History Says There's Big Trouble Ahead.' The article was published early in 1987, the year of the Black Monday crash of October 19.)

As always, Faber delved first into the past. Publicly traded equities hardly existed at all until the second half of the 19th century. The only prices that could be traced back over many centuries were those for commodities and real estate. What could be a more fundamental commodity than man's daily bread?

Looking at these, he noticed a number of points. In real terms, wheat prices are today only a fraction of what they had been in the 1870s. He found it remarkable that the sharp decline in value of this major commodity occurred during the second half of the 19th century and in the 20th century, precisely at a time when the global population was exploding (see Figure 3.1). There were literally hundreds of millions of new mouths each year needing to be filled with basic foodstuffs such as wheat. The amount of bread needed grew by a huge multiple. The price should have skyrocketed. Instead, it plummeted.

What went wrong for wheat investors? Wheat supplies were unexpectedly and dramatically enlarged after 1850 for various reasons. There was the opening of the Americas and Australia, the invention of new agricultural machinery, and the applications of fertilizers. The wheat investors hadn't considered these possibilities, and how could they?

Faber turned his attention from wheat to cotton. The history books showed that in the first half of the 19th century, the southern United States built its wealth on the cotton industry as the fabric became popular and replaced, to a large extent, the woollen cloth which had hitherto been used worldwide. Cotton was considered far more versatile than wool, and everyone wanted cotton goods. A sure-fire winner as an investment? It should have been, but again it wasn't. After peaking during the Civil War, cotton prices collapsed and they still today have not exceeded those highs, even in nominal terms (see Figure 3.2).

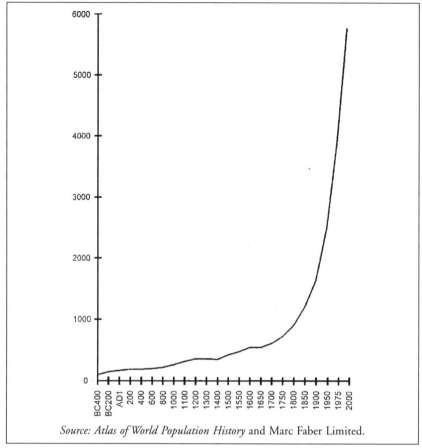

Source: *Atlas of World Population History* and Marc Faber Limited.

Figure 3.1 Total World Population (in millions)

From these and further studies, Faber worked out that analysts and economists, including major figures such as Malthus, had a specific tendency to focus too much on demand while dangerously underestimating the effect of a natural increase in the supply of a popular item. This increase would be the result of the tendency of production capacity to rise, for various reasons. The error would be fatal to their predictions.

Faber studied the long-term economic history of rubber and found an even more telling illustration. Rubber consumption had begun its rapid rise in the second half of the 19th century after

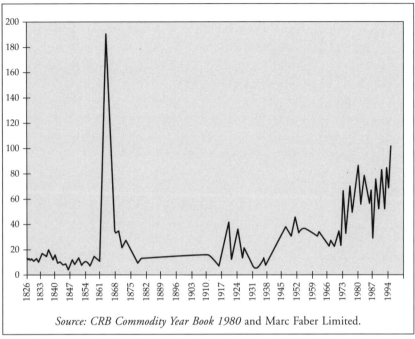

Source: CRB Commodity Year Book 1980 and Marc Faber Limited.

Figure 3.2 Cotton Prices from 1826 to 1995

Charles Goodyear's discovery in 1839 of the vulcanization process, which made sticky latex from trees into a remarkably soft yet tough and durable product with a million uses.

Demand for rubber was fueled by industrialization. A major part of this was the rapid expansion of the U.S. (and later global) automobile industry in the first quarter of the 20th century. The real boom in car production started in 1907. With the market starting to expand at a prodigious rate, rubber should, by all accounts, have been a fabulous investment at that time. Clearly, in the first half of this century, rubber was to the automobile business what semiconductors are to the modern PC industry.

Rubber investors' belief in the growth of the automobile industry wasn't misplaced. Between 1907 and the late 1920s, the automobile industry was the main U.S. growth industry, displacing railways. The number of passenger cars registered in the U.S. rose from less than 100,000 in 1907 to more than 20 million in 1922. By that stage there were more than four million cars being sold a year. In 1923, Henry Ford sold a record 2.1 million of a single car, the classic Model T Ford. His firm alone held a stunning 55 percent share of the U.S. car market.

Every car needed at least four rubber tyres. And after a few years, they needed another set of four rubber tyres. By all logic, rubber should have been one of the surest investments of the century.

What happened? Demand for rubber was soaring in the early decades of the 20th century, yet continuously rising supplies from new production areas actually depressed prices. An increasing number of rubber trees were grown outside Brazil, particularly in South-east Asia. This led to a long-lasting and severe decline in the economic fortunes of the Brazilian city of Manaus, the rubber mecca of the late 19th century. In hindsight, one sees that rubber prices, instead of starting a new uptrend in 1908, actually peaked that year. Those who invested in rubber then, paid the highest prices. What seemed like the key time to invest was actually the worst.

Almost 100 years have passed. The world's industrialization has progressed at rapid speed. Global rubber consumption grew from 33 tons in 1827 to 30,000 tons in 1900 and to more than 5.2 million tons in 1990. We have cars and trucks coming out the wazoo, and they still all have rubber tyres, sometimes 16 on a single vehicle. Faber flipped to the *Wall Street Journal* to check the rubber price today: 94 cents. The investor who bought rubber in 1908 is still waiting for his profit.

(Incidentally, investing in cars themselves during the 1920s' heyday of Henry Ford may also have been an unexpectedly bad investment, particularly in the medium term and to some extent in the relatively long term. During the Great Depression, U.S. car sales plummeted from 5.6 million in 1929 to 1.4 million in 1932, and Ford's sales didn't exceed their 1923 highs until 1955, more than three decades later.)

As Faber worked through the histories of various commodities over an extended period, one point became clear. The popular belief that inflation will always be with us, and prices will always float upward, was quite wrong. Not only was it factually incorrect for general commodities, but it was even wrong for highly attractive commodities which were undergoing a huge increase in demand. The rock-solid, cast-iron, sure-fire winners were losers.

His research showed that real and even nominal prices for some important commodities have been in secular downtrends for more than 100 years. It is all very well to tell the investor to hold on and be patient, but there are limits.

This would be uncomfortable news for commodities investors, but they are a minority. What about real estate? The tendency to put long-term trust in bricks and mortar is almost universal. People buy property or land to use as retirement plans. A good idea?

Faber says not. In hindsight, property has proved just as untrustworthy an investment as other commodities. When did it all start? History reveals that until about 1850, few people in the industrialized world owned equities or bonds, which were still a new form of investment. The merchant class held trade bills, precious metals, and storehouses of commodities which fluctuated greatly in price and through which large fortunes were made and lost. But the landed gentry held its wealth in land and buildings, and believed it was stable for the extremely long term — that is, throughout eternity.

It is important to remember that countries, at that time, consisted of little more than rural land holdings. There were few urban conurbations that a modern citizen would even recognize as a city. In 1800, there were only 12 cities in the entire United States with a population greater than 2500. Even if you lived in a comparatively large 'city,' the chances were that you would know everyone else in town.

Farmland was a good investment in the 17th century, when agricultural prices were rising, and a so-so investment in the 18th century when prices were flat in real terms. But it became a poor investment after the Napoleonic Wars. This was true of both Europe and the United States. In *The Economic History of Modern Britain* by Clapham, Faber read the details of an unexpected downturn for some poor landlord. In the English county of Essex, eight large estates showed a net reduction in rentals of 52.6 percent between

1871 and 1884, while in Suffolk, six similar properties showed a fall of 55 percent. This would have shocked the squires of the manor. The fall in rural property in the U.K. has not been reversed. Real farmland prices in Britain are today much lower than they were at the beginning of the 19th century.

All this was clear evidence to Faber that the advent of industrialization saw a sea change in wealth creation, which shifted out of agriculture into industries, trade, and urban real estate. It would have been extremely difficult to forecast this at the time.

Faber chuckled to himself and scribbled a note to add to his newsletter on safe investments. 'I presume that if investment banks and pension fund consultants had existed in 1800, they would have been able to show that, as an asset class, farmland had provided superior returns over a 200-year period, just as we are told today that equities outperform other types of investment.'

Other examples of real estate investments stuck in long-term downtrends were easy to find. It was clear that properties in the port-town of Bruges or tourist-pulling Venice sell today, in real terms, for a fraction of their 15th or 16th century highs. Property in downtown Detroit is now worth much less than at the height of the auto industry in the 1920s.

With regard to real estate, there was another factor: the prices of many such assets become worthless as a result of decay. The house may fall down. Or the city in which the house is located may slump. Think of the many now-abandoned American gold-mining boomtowns of the 19th century. Or the property assets held prior to the coming of communism and socialism in Shanghai, Rangoon, Saigon, Cairo, and Havana. It is ironic that the English use the phrase 'as safe as houses' for anything that is quite beyond risk. In financial terms, houses are not 'as safe as houses.' Faber believes real estate is relatively dangerous. It is visible, taxable, and confiscatable.

'Asset and commodity prices peak out — there's no doubt about it — and then they enter totally unexpected and prolonged downtrends, which last longer and carry prices to much lower levels than anyone expects. And this happens even when there is growth all around them,' Faber wrote.

The Swiss investment advisor was reminded of the time he stayed in the Philippines with a wealthy sugar-growing family in 1974. Sugar prices had risen to more than 70 cents a pound that year. 'Sugar prices will rise forever,' the sugar king told the pessimistic financier. 'Look at the rising food consumption. Look at the population growth.' It sounded like it made sense. Just over ten years later, in 1985, sugar prices had fallen to 2.5 cents a pound. For the sugar king, life had unexpectedly turned bitter.

So much for commodities, large and small. Faber turned his attention to equities. Again, his first port of call was history.

Investing in shares only became popular in the second half of the 19th century. But active stock markets had developed much earlier, in the 17th and 18th centuries, in Holland, England, and France. Arguably the most successful 17th century company was the Dutch East India Company, run by a famous team of pioneering merchant sailors. Every business person knew its name. Its shares were widely held. When it was launched in 1602, the company had a share capital of 6.5 million florins, divided into shares of 3000 florins each. The initial capital of the Dutch East India Company corresponded to 64 tons of gold — worth almost $1 billion at today's prices.

The investors believed they would get a good return from this well-backed firm of ship-borne trader–explorers, and they were right. Between 1602 and 1720, the company was a true growth stock, and dividends averaged between 20 percent and 40 percent of the original paid-up capital. At its peak in 1720, the shares were worth 35,000 florins each. One hundred and 18 years of good returns, it must be said, is a pretty impressive long-term record. Now here was a safe bet.

But was it? The English made inroads into the long-distance Asia-to-Europe trade in the 1700s, and the Dutch lost their monopoly. By 1780, the company had become insolvent and it was taken over by the government of Holland. So, even a share with an exceptionally long and worthy record can become worthless.

Another revealing example is the story of U.S. railroad stocks during the 19th century. The U.S. was going through a remarkable period of growth, both in economic and in population terms. The biggest industry of the time was the railroad. This was truly the age of the railway. Lines were being laid between all the major cities. Between 1852 and 1900, the number of miles of track in operation grew by a multiple of 14. From the second half of the 19th century to the early 1920s, railways were the largest single industry in the country. By 1925, in terms of capital, the railroad industry was still larger than the U.S. public utility companies such as electricity and gas suppliers, streetcar firms, telephone companies, and so on. The railroad industry was more than twice the size of the iron and steel industry and almost ten times larger than the auto industry.

If any industry deserved to be the ultimate growth stock, it was the railway. It certainly started as a good investment, with a boom in related equities from 1849 onward, peaking in 1852. But the problems came early. The Crimean War caused a drop in investments from Europe, and the stock bottomed out in 1857. There was a U.S. stock-market boom which peaked in 1864, but most railroad stocks failed to regain their 1852 highs. From then on, the trend in railroad equities was downward for the rest of the century, despite the huge growth in the amount of railway activity going on.

There could be no better example of a growth industry in a rapidly growing business in an economically growing country. 'Yet its stock prices performed poorly for half a century and badly underperformed industrial issues in the early part of the next,' wrote Faber.

What was the problem? First, the increase in the number of individual railway firms meant that there was cut-throat competition, and freight rates had to be slashed. Second, railroad construction needed a lot of capital, so a huge supply of new securities had to be issued. But these had to compete with other railroad issues, not just in the United States, but from all over the world. The values of the issues were thus depressed. Third, U.S. railways had large bond issues outstanding. In the deflationary times of the latter part of the 19th century, these proved painful. Fourth, the Interstate Commerce Commission was established in 1887, and began to regulate and over-regulate. Faber identified two particular laws — the Hepburn Acts of

1906 and the *Mann-Elkins Act* of 1910 — as giving the Commission significant power over the rates railways could charge. 'This had a devastating effect on their earnings between 1910 and 1921. Inflation accelerated while rate increases were continually denied,' said Faber. Profits collapsed and railway equities failed to participate in the 1918–1920 rally of industrial shares. Railroads remained a bad investment right up until 1932.

What this means is that even the most spectacular growth of an industry does not in itself indicate that its equities will grow in a similar way, or even grow at all.

Faber's study of railroads has scared him away from recommending investments today in emerging markets' infrastructure projects. 'One can be sure that any number of state or provincial commissions will keep rates down,' he says. 'Their employees, having been educated at American universities, will have studied with great amusement the history of the growing power of the Interstate Commerce Commission. Being eager to apply what Western capitalism has taught them, they will happily cap the rate of return which utilities in their emerging economies will be permitted to earn. They will do this in order to keep inflation from getting out of hand — especially if the infrastructure projects are financed by foreigners.'

Railroads aren't the only example from that time. Faber notes that the majority of common stock-holders in the U.S. didn't do well in the latter half of the 19th century and the early years of the 20th century, despite the tremendous economic growth of that period. Of course, there was good news just around the corner. Stock-buyers enjoyed boom prices in the 1920s — just in time to be wiped out by the crash of 1929 and the Great Depression which followed.

Things picked up after 1932, but along came a war, from 1939 to 1945. Stocks in the United States as a whole were generally depressed in the late 1940s, when a post-war depression was feared. At its low of 161 points in 1949, the Dow Jones had a dividend yield of 8 percent, while bonds were yielding only 2.5 percent. Yet from 1949 to the late 1960s, stocks rose rapidly, and once again became a fashion. What happened to people who got into the stock market in the 1960s? The market slowed down in the late 1960s and early 1970s, and a bear market followed in 1973 and 1974. The 1970s were an unhappy decade for equity-holders, with cash providing a higher return than equities.

Faber was amused to see a report in *Barron's* of May 23, 1994, in which John Liscio calculated that someone who invested in Dow stocks in 1966 would have had to wait until 1986 to catch up with someone who had simply placed their money in U.S. Government Treasury Bills.

Here we have another strand in Doom Thought: stocks perform best following a period during which growth expectations are low; conversely, they perform poorly during a time of great optimism regarding future growth.

Why have people in recent times had such strong faith in the myth that stocks always go up? Faber believes that one of the reasons is the unusually low volatility of the Dow Jones Industrial Averages and the S&P 500 since 1992. In 1992, the S&P fluctuated by only 11.8 percent, while in 1993 and 1994, the figure fell to only 9.8 percent. 'Never before this century has the annual volatility been so low, and this for three years running,' he remarks. Thereafter, volatility increased, but all on the upside. The period 1982–1998 was the best-performing 16-year spell in U.S. financial history. For the sake of comparison, the volatility of the S&P in the 1930s is shown in Table 3.1.

There have also been high-volatility years more recently. In 1970, the Dow moved in a range of 35 percent; in 1974, the figure was 60 percent; and in 1987, it was 50 percent. It is no coincidence that these were also years which featured crashes.

Most of the 1990s have been a relatively calming time for Wall Street investors. From the lows of 1990, the Dow sailed through much of the decade without dipping more than 10 percent, which is unique for the post-Second World War period. In fact, from 1982 to the end of the century, the Dow has barely finished any year lower than it started. It was down 3.7 percent in 1984 and down 4 percent in 1990. Otherwise, the news was all good.

'All this contributes to an equity cult,' says Faber.

Table 3.1 Stock Market Annual Volatility, 1929–1940

	DJIA (%)	S&P 500 (%)
1929	91.8	80.7
1930	86.7	79.5
1931	163.4	122.4
1932	115.5	111.5
1933	116.5	120.6
1934	29.5	41.4
1935	53.5	67.0
1936	29.2	32.0
1937	71.1	83.7
1938	60.0	62.2
1939	28.3	30.0
1940	36.7	42.0

Source: Robert Prechter Elliot Wave Int'l.

Getting it Wrong

Faber is at an investment conference in Shanghai in May 1995. He has met an executive of a large American pharmaceutical company. The man says he has just sold his shares in his company and wants advice on what to do with the cash. Faber tells him that U.S. commercial real estate looks better value than equities.

The man replies that he has been soured against real estate. He had invested in the stuff from the early 1980s and consistently lost money. Faber knew that the U.S. real estate market rose steadily until 1988 or 1989, so how could he have lost money? Thinking about it, Faber realized that the man was a typical investor — and that means a loser. The typical investor always underperforms the averages.

Looking for evidence of this, Faber noted the results of a study of mutual funds by a research firm which analyzed the total returns of

219 growth funds over a five-year period ending May 31, 1994. The analysis compared the average fund's return with the return the investors actually achieved.

'The result of this analysis is hard to believe,' Faber later told a seminar in New York. 'While the funds returned 12.5 percent annually over the five-year period, the return to the individual investors was a negative 2.2 percent per annum. The reason for this performance divergence was that investors moved into funds late, long after the best gains had been made. At other times, they panicked and opted out of their fund during severe market declines. In other words, they make the classic mistake of buying high and selling low.'

What's worse is that they compound their error by not taking advantage when prices become cheap, he told the seminar. 'Investor reaction to falling prices doesn't seem to change. A bad experience leads them to back off and to avoid the entire asset class in which they have lost money. They continue to avoid it, no matter how good its value becomes.'

The gospel during the 1980s in the U.S., Europe, and in many other places was to invest in real estate. Those who did, had already missed the bulk of the boom. The same process could be seen again in the 1990s, only the gospel was to invest in equities, despite the fact that anyone who picked up a back copy of a financial magazine could see that the boom was behind them.

The Place is Full of Iditts

Wherever you hear brokers selling shares. Wherever you see a panel of people in suits talking about investments. Wherever you note a pundit predicting the future. Listen for the giveaway phrase, 'It's different this time.'

Investors stimulate each other into a state of excitement and become swept up in a wave of optimism. This leads them to talk about the dawn of a new era, a time of riches and plenty for everyone. This state of mind, which Faber calls 'new era thinking,' is the most dangerous form of the 'error of optimism.' People who fall into this state blind themselves to reason. By happy coincidence, those who proffer the It's-different-this-time argument can be known by the acronym, Iditts.

Faber's research showed that the rise of groups of Iditts displaying new era thinking is usually associated with new discoveries (the Americas, the gold deposits in California), the opening of new territories (the South Seas, the western territories of the U.S.), the application of new inventions (canals, railroads, the automobile, the radio, and so on), a dramatic rise in the price of an important commodity (rubber at the end of the last century, oil in the 1970s), outbreaks of peace (the breakdown of communism), or a time of strong economic performance.

But this is the bad news: Faber's research leads him to believe that waves of optimism tend to sweep through a country, or large swathes of the industrial world, not at the beginning of an era of prosperity, but toward the end of such a period. The best-known examples of such new era investment manias are the South Sea bubble of 1720; the various canal, railroad, and real estate booms in Europe and the United States of the 19th century; the Australian and Californian gold rushes; the late 1920s' U.S. stock-market run; and the Kuwaiti stock-market and real estate madness of the late 1970s. Faber believes that more recent examples of speculative waves related to similar Utopian thinking were the Taiwanese and Japanese stock-market booms of the late 1980s. He found it ironic that the words of these nations' many ultra-optimistic forecasters were often proved correct. It *was* the dawn of a new era — a period of company closures and economic hardship.

Faber felt strongly that a wave of new era thinking swept through the global investment community for much of the 1990s. The phrase, 'It's different this time' has been widely heard. Having said that, people have been upbeat, with some good reason. Many of the economic news events, after all, have been positive: the collapse of communism, the opening of a large number of new markets, the promise inherent in many new technologies, the benefits of the painful corporate downsizing and layoffs in the U.S., the shrinking number of major global military threats, the low inflation rate in the U.S. and several other major economies, the falling interest rates in many places, increasing globalization and free trade, and so on.

But this sort of general cheer and positive feelings made Faber uncomfortable. No, what he liked was a nice bit of negativity. He wasn't going to put his dollars into Wall Street, which had performed spectacularly well since 1990. What he was looking for was Contrarian Heaven.

Curiously, to find Contrarian Heaven, you don't necessarily look for dramatic crashes or bloodbaths. You look for quiet, forgotten, low-key markets. You look for the economic equivalent of Gerald Ford or Art Garfunkel. You look for things which it would never ordinarily occur to you to look for.

Faber had long been seeking such places, and one of his proudest discoveries was the Argentine stock market in the late 1980s. Volume was dismal, stocks sold below book values, there were hardly any initial public offerings (IPOs) or rights issues, foreign participation was absent, the stock-market capitalization as a percentage of the economy was low, few people wanted to get into the finance business, stockbrokers' offices were modest, and confidence was non-existent. Inflation was horrendous: in the 12 months ending November 1987, the year-on-year rise in prices was 93 percent. For the following year, the rise was 437 percent. When Faber visited the country at the end of 1988, the inflation rate was estimated at 600 percent. What was the public expecting in terms of returns from equities? Nothing. They'd given up waiting.

Great. Time to buy. Faber wrote to his clients in December 1988: 'In Argentina, the economic pendulum has swung towards the side of extreme undervaluation ... Buenos Aires, at one time possibly the world's most expensive city, has become unbelievably cheap. Apartments which used to sell for around US$1 million now sell for between US$100,000 and US$150,000, and an entire office block can be purchased right in the commercial centre of Buenos Aires for around US$1 million.' He had a more practical tip as well: 'Meat lovers can now purchase a huge beef steak, enough for two and as tender as Kobe beef, but with much more taste, for about US$5.'

What happened? Nothing, for a while. Then the Argentine share market started to move upward in 1989, and the index shot up more than tenfold by 1993. The index took investors on a wild and rocky ride through the 1990s, but Faber had correctly predicted when it would return to life after its long sleep.

The U.S. stock market after the Second World War was similarly forgotten, although 16 years had passed since the crash that led into the Great Depression. Market averages were still well below their 1929 highs, volume was low, and the awful memories of the early 1930s were still fresh in people's minds. Investors' expectations were very low. The end of the war did not bring about new era thinking, since there had been a boom, of sorts, from the war itself. After it ended, there was apprehension that the U.S. economy would slip back into another depression. In the financial writing of the time, Faber found no sign of the recent mantra, that equities were worth buying because they always outperform bonds and cash. Time to buy equities.

But what to buy? Real estate in the United States in the 1950s was a good buy, being clearly non-speculative. People bought homes in order to live in them, farmers bought land for the purpose of cultivating it, and investors acquired commercial buildings for their yield. These buyers were not focused on achieving capital gains or using property as a hedge against inflation.

What happened? This time, a new era really did dawn. The United States thrived in the 1950s. The soldiers came home, there was a baby boom, and everyone celebrated the new arrivals by going shopping. Economists were delighted: there were jobs for 95.5 percent of the population, inflation was 2.1 percent, and economic growth, at an average of 4 percent a year, was pleasantly healthy. In the peak years of 1947 to 1953, the average annual growth in real gross national product was 4.8 percent, close to what 'economic miracle' cities such as Singapore or Hong Kong were achieving in the late 1990s.

Another example: the commodity markets, especially gold and silver, were non-speculative in the 1950s and 1960s. Significantly, these markets were dominated by insiders and not outsiders, who participate in markets solely with the purpose of achieving profits from rising or falling prices. Your Aunt Myrna, who bought gold jewelry because she liked it, could have cashed out for a fortune in the late 1970s.

Art and collectibles were non-speculative markets as long as paintings and baseball cards were bought by genuine collectors. Faber could never think about art valuations without recalling an old schoolfriend, Ueli Hahnloser. Ueli's grandmother and great-aunts had studied in Paris in the early 1900s, and got into the habit of buying the cheerful, colorful, slightly blurry paintings that were the new fashion among artists. When Faber was at school, Ueli would boast that the paintings were becoming quite valuable. He wasn't wrong. Today, the Hahnloser galleries house one of the largest collections of Impressionist paintings in the world. The accidental nature of the purchase — they were bought not as investments, but because the young women found them cute — greatly impressed itself on young Faber's mind.

How do you spot a non-speculative market? A common feature of all of them is the almost total absence of leverage. Stocks, bonds, real estate, paintings, and gold are bought principally for cash and not on credit. Faber penned the following definition for his clients: 'A non-speculative market is a market for which capital gain expectations are low, and in which trading volume is comparatively light. Trading is dominated by a small group of people (insiders), and the public at large does not participate.'

Faber later quipped that the ultimate example of a non-speculative market was the paintings of Van Gogh during the painter's lifetime — only one was traded. Yet, ironically, it was Van Gogh's paintings which became a by-word for dramatic overvaluation during the 1980s, particularly in Japan.

Warning Bells

Let's look at this from another point of view. Equities seem to be on the way up. But you are nervous. You've heard a few people talking about the dawn of a new era. You've even heard a bullish financier, being interviewed on a business news television show, use the phrase, 'It's different this time.' How do you tell if equities are rising under their own steam, or are being lifted by an invisible bubble?

'For that,' says Faber, 'You need to check the warning signs. If it is a speculative mania, you are in trouble.' First, he says, you must classify your mania. Is it a mini-mania or a major mania? Faber reckons a mini-mania occurred in the United States in the early 1960s just before the Kennedy crash of 1962 (a sharp stock-market dip associated with U.S. President John F. Kennedy's policies). The objects of speculation were shares of electronics firms, bowling companies, and Small Business Investment Companies. Mini-manias, Faber explains, can be defined as speculative bubbles which can be popped without doing widespread economic damage. A bad cold rather than pneumonia, if you like. There is a sharp but brief sell-off, and the uptrend in the market resumes, but usually with different leaders. Other booms he classified as mini-manias were the 1983 craze for U.S. technology stocks, the 1987 global stock-market bubble, and the powerful 1993 boom in emerging markets. All came to sudden ends, which were painful for those investors who had become very deeply involved, but the rest of us survived.

Major 'investomanias,' Faber believes, are usually once-a-generation affairs, and lead to serious economic damage when they come to their inevitable close. The best you can hope for is that the damage is contained in one sector of the economy. Examples of major manias and their repercussions are clear: the late 1920s' stock-market mania was followed by a worldwide depression; the late 1980s' Japanese stock-market boom led to a lengthy and painful deflationary recession in Japan; and the abrupt end of the commodity bubble in the late 1970s caused serious hardship among the oil-producing regions of the world and a depression in Mexico, parts of the Middle East, and Texas. (All the major Texas banks either went bust or had to be restructured, as did a large number of oil drilling companies.)

The collapse following major investomanias 'shakes an entire generation's faith in the object of the speculation,' Faber says. 'Mini-manias may take place every few years. The uptrend leading to the mania may last as little as two or three years. But a major mania will represent the final stage or culmination of a very long-term secular uptrend, which may have lasted ten to 25 years.' So, while the late 1920s' stock-market bubble came after an uptrend which had lasted for slightly less than ten years, the U.S. stock-market mania of the late 1960s and early 1970s concluded a secular bull market which had gone on for close to 20 years.' The late 1980s' Japanese stock-market boom was the culmination of a largely uninterrupted uptrend which had begun in 1974, the Swiss investment advisor believes.

But it would be too simplistic to suggest that every long uptrend will be followed by an equally long downtrend. Other factors come into play. An important one for the careful forecaster is mood.

In the manic phase of a bull market, the mood is euphoric. Investors are caught up in a frenzy of buying. The longer the bull market has been in place, the more the uptrend will be regarded as a permanent feature of the new era. At this stage, traditional valuations are thrown out of the window — a clear warning sign that the end has come. Since investors are thinking in terms of 'a new era,' the future huge profit opportunities justify buying at any price. The optimistic mood is reflected by heavy public participation, risks are largely ignored, and the use of credit increases.

In this situation, crowd psychology takes over, and the critical faculty of the individual is paralyzed. Faber shuffled his chair from the history section of his bookshelves to the psychology section. He was fascinated to read the following in *The Crowd*, by Gustave Le Bon:

> A chain of logical argumentation is totally incomprehensible to crowds, and for this reason it is permissible to say that they do not reason or that they reason falsely and are not to be influenced by reasoning.[1]

In *The Principles of Political Economy*, J. R. McCulloch argues:

> ... in speculation, as in most other things, one individual derives confidence from another. Such a one purchases or sells, not because he had any really accurate information as to the state of demand and supply, but because someone else has done so before him.[2]

This appears to explain why the investor so easily overestimates the imagined demand, while underestimating the growing supply. Faber noted that in the oil boom of the late 1970s, it was never seriously considered that rising oil prices would bring additional supplies to the market, while energy conservation would curtail demand.

One of Faber's favorite books is Thomas Tooke's *A History of Prices*, which includes this paragraph:

> The possibility of enormous profit by risking a small sum was a bait too tempting to be resisted; all the gambling propensities of human nature were constantly solicited into action; and crowds of individuals of every description — the credulous and the ignorant, princes, nobles, politicians, patriots, lawyers, physicians, divines, philosophers, poets, intermingled with women of all ranks and degrees (spinsters, wives, and widows) — hastened to venture some portion of their property in schemes of which scarcely anything was known except the names.[3]

But again, let us not over-simplify. Over decades of watching booms and busts, Faber noted that the mood of investors during manias is not always euphoric or optimistic. Sometimes they can be fired into action through opposite emotions. Investors over-paid for gold and silver in the late 1970s not because they were optimistic about the future, but because they felt that the U.S. dollar would become worthless and inflation would accelerate. Booms in hard assets can be fueled by pessimism as much as optimism. Commodity booms are characterized by greed based on fear, he believes. In financial manias, the fear element comes from a different part of the psyche: 'The fear is that you don't make as much money in the market as your neighbors' investment club or your fellow fund manager.'

Another sign of the dangerous phase of investomania is the growth of contempt for cash. People actually don't like money. In the late 1970s, people seriously believed there was a danger that physical money would become worthless because of accelerating inflation. Thus, they rushed into (already over-priced) gold, silver, and resource stocks. Today, people believe that they will not be able to retire on their returns if they keep their money in savings accounts. So they buy equities. After all, equities always beat other investments in the long run, right?

In the 1970s, the International Monetary Fund (IMF) and the U.S. Treasury sold off a large proportion of their gold stocks. These sales clearly increased the supply, yet people didn't see this as negative. Each successful auction was followed by another buying stampede.

The desire to regard bad news as good news is a common, and sometimes hilarious, symptom of market mania. Is the market going up? 'Get in quick!' Is the market going down? 'It's a buying opportunity!' After the 1989 property crash in the U.K., the words 'buying opportunity' and 'good time to buy' were heard ad nauseam from the less respectable property commentators on a more-or-less weekly basis for the following seven years. For at least the first six of those years, it wasn't true.

All Together Now

Here they come. The shoe-shine boys, the nightclub hostesses, the taxi drivers, the woman from the dentist's who runs the neighborhood investment club, the soldier, the sailor, the candlestick-maker; they all want to 'get into the game.' That's fine. It's a free country, and some of them do a lot better than the professionals. Meanwhile, the professionals are also in a ferment. Men and women in suits organize trusts and funds and Eazee-Purchase savings schemes to accommodate the newcomers. Seeing the rush, the large corporations, despite their size and muscle, are driven by exactly the same thinking: There's a lot of money sloshing around there, Splotkin; let's organize IPOs and new issues so that we can play, too.

Faber finds these factors as predictable today as they were 400 years ago. He reckons the first true public companies, such as the Dutch East India Company, the infamous South Sea Company of bubble fame, and John Law's Mississippi Company, were more like investment pools than companies with a specific business purpose. Some had no defined purpose at all. One new issue launched during the time of the South Sea bubble declined to tell investors what it did; it was a secret. It described itself as: 'A company for carrying on an undertaking of great advantage, but nobody to know what it is.' Just hand over the loot, sirrah.

Faber traces the formation of modern-style investment trusts to the late 1920s — and we all know what happened in 1929. The next great wave of investment pool formations was in the late 1960s, where someone came up with the term 'mutual funds.' This was neatly timed just before the boom of the 1950s and 1960s came to an end in the early 1970s and was followed by the devastating 1973–1974 bear market. More recently, a huge number of similar pools have been formed around the world, where they are widely known as unit trusts.

People who make their money by advising investors are naturally glad to see so many people taking an interest in the field (and paying their commissions). The bad news is that the proliferation of investment groups tends to coincide with major market peaks. In other words, the herd mentality is the wrong mentality. Here we have another strand in Doom Thought. 'Basic economic theory suggests that demand falls as prices go up. But in the case of speculative markets, the opposite seems to be true,' Faber comments wryly.

When U.S. stock prices were low in the 1930s or the mid-1970s, hardly any new investment companies were founded. But in the 1990s, with U.S. stocks and shares available only at high prices, new investment groups have been springing up like mushrooms.

In the United States, investment clubs are easier to form and dissolve than investment companies, so the more informal groupings are more common. According to investment guru Robert Prechter, 987 clubs were formed in the United States in 1987, the year of the

Black Monday October crash (see Figure 3.3). Investing in equities predictably dropped out of fashion for a while, but came back in the early 1990s. More than 1000 such groups were formed in the United States in 1992. In 1995, interest among investors in pooling their funds together soared (partly stimulated by the success of one particular group, the Beardstown Ladies) and 5298 investment clubs were started. In 1996, it was estimated that such clubs were being formed at the rate of 50 a day. In 1998, there were an estimated 32,000 investment clubs in the United States.

Meanwhile in the glass towers, the business people spent much of the 1990s organizing an avalanche of new issues for the share markets. Again, this has historical precedents. A jump in the number of new issues was a characteristic of the industrialized world's canal, land, and railroad booms of Dickens' era. The new issue calendar was heavy again in the late 1920s, late 1960s, and in emerging markets in late 1993 — all danger periods. Energy and mining shares were issued during the oil and natural resource boom of the late 1970s. Technology stocks dominated the new issue lists during the 1983 technology craze. Junk bonds were the theme of the U.S. issues in the mid-1980s and biotechnology stocks in the early 1990s. All these tales had unhappy endings.

In the 1990s, many IPOs were grossly over-subscribed and jumped to high prices on their first day of issue — another clear warning of trouble. The more new issues concentrated in one industry (history gives examples of riverboat gaming, biotechnology, real estate investment trusts, country funds, and hi-tech companies), the more likely it is that such an industry is approaching a longer-term or cyclical high, says Faber.

Toward the end of a new issue boom, offer prices tend to become too high, and so many firms are rushing to the market that the 'quality' of companies going into public ownership deteriorates.

As is the case with so many other investomania syndromes, the line between boom and battyness is difficult to draw. But occasionally, it becomes plainly apparent to the most casual observer that something is not quite right. In the United States in 1998, an internet stock, Broadcast.com, was priced at $18 per share and

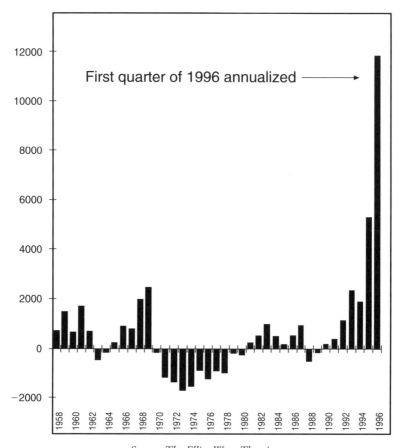

Source: The Elliot Wave Theorist.

Figure 3.3 Year to Year Investment Club Growth, 1958–1996

soared to $74 on the first day of trading, for the best gain of any initial public offering of more than $5 ever.

In Hong Kong during the early 1990s, single buyers would apply for more than the total number of shares available during an issue. This was just in case the issue was so over-subscribed that each applicant only received a certain percentage of the stocks he requested. In other words, the buyer was saying: 'You have six oranges for sale. Here's my money. I'd like to buy 18 of them, please.'

Investors, individual and corporate, get caught up in the buying frenzy. The mood of professional investors tends to be more cautious. However, that doesn't prevent institutional investors from participating in the boom, for several reasons. They are oriented to near-term performance; they are concerned about keeping up with rising indices; they have seen how money flows into the best-performing funds; so they feel they have to be in the sectors which have the strongest upward moves. Typical of an investomania, therefore, is another expression worth listening out for: 'We can't afford *not* to be in this market.'

In the late 1970s, many fund managers felt that oil and resource stocks were overvalued. But since, in 1980, only these shares moved up, funds had to buy them to show they were performing. Similarly, during the Japanese stock-market bubble of the 1980s, many foreign fund managers thought stocks were overvalued. But to be out of Japan would have meant to underperform international indices. As a result, foreigners participated in the investomania, albeit reluctantly. In the South Sea bubble of 1720, a banker remarked: 'When the world is mad, we must imitate them in some measure.'

Contagion spreads from investor to investor. As McCulloch noted, 'one individual derives confidence from another.' But it also spreads from one brokerage to another, across international borders.

The South Sea stock bubble which burst in 1720 coincided with the collapse of John Law's Mississippi Scheme in France, as well as with a period of widespread speculation in insurance shares in other countries of continental Europe. British investors had flocked to Paris to participate in John Law's companies, while continental investors, especially from the prosperous Netherlands, bought shares in South Sea stock.

In early 1873, a building and stock-market boom swept through Europe and the U.S. But when a crisis erupted in Austria and Germany, the panic spread to Italy, Holland, Belgium, and then to the United States. European investors, having been large buyers of U.S. railroad securities and land in the western territories in the early 1870s, were forced to withdraw their capital in order to repay loans at home.

The international propagation of a boom inevitably also leads to a crisis of an international character. In the late 1920s, European stock markets rose sharply (albeit less spectacularly than the U.S. market), and in the 1950s and 1960s, stock markets around the world performed well. But after the 1929 crash, and the crash of early 1973, all major markets declined. The advances in technology, particularly with reference to communication, increased the tendency of major investomanias to spread across borders.

In Faber's opinion, the first truly international investomania was the energy and gold boom of the late 1970s. Energy and resource stocks were bid up to (in retrospect) ridiculous levels in all major centers of the world, and the price of gold became a global fixation. Bucket shops dealing in gold and gold futures sprang up all over the planet. Speculators in remote parts of the world followed, minute by minute, the results of the gold auctions held by the U.S. Treasury and the IMF. In 1980, gold peaked at $850 an ounce, then fell to half that amount, and remained below $300 eight years later.

Another truly global investment boom concerned real estate in the 1980s. Real estate, everywhere, was perceived to 'always go up in the long run' and to have 'little downside risk.' In the process, it became grossly inflated.

Faber rates the financial asset bull market of the 1980s and 1990s as an equally global phenomenon. Taking 1982 as a starting point, stocks in industrialized countries have never performed better in history. Furthermore, stock and futures exchanges have opened for business in many former socialist countries. Never before in history has there been a proliferation of so many new financial instruments as over the past 20 years or so. Since Faber began working on Wall Street in 1970, he has seen the introduction of listed options, interest rates, currency and index futures, and also options on these futures, a wide variety of derivative products, swaps, and so on.

Today, the media broadcasts financial news into every corner of the world. Most major countries have sophisticated banking and custodial facilities. Foreign exchange restrictions are being lifted around the world. People who work in financial markets really feel they have moved into 'a new era.' Capital can now easily flow from one country, stock exchange, or favored sector to their equivalents elsewhere.

'We seem to be in a rolling financial orgy,' Faber says. 'People think the good times are like a rising tide, which lifts all boats, but at different times and with different intensity.' A tidal wave of speculation lifted the Japanese stock market in the late 1980s, then moved on to the emerging markets in the early 1990s, and seems to have now reached the shores of the United States. As the money flows, so do the booms and manias — and so does the contagion. Investors argue, 'They boomed last year. It's our turn this year.'

Signs of the End

They don't know what's what. They're outsiders. Their information is second- or third-hand. They don't understand the language. They don't understand the culture. They believe what they read. They believe what our investment advisors make up.

Foreign investors tend to buy when everything looks bright — in other words, at the worst possible time. They buy when markets reach their peak. Faber's studies lead him to believe that foreign investors are frequently responsible for the final spike in an end-of-a-boom market. They are responsible directly and indirectly. They increase their own purchases in the final phase of an investment mania, because they are anxious not to be any later getting into the game. Meanwhile, locals become accustomed to foreign money flowing in, and start to believe that the cash will continue to flow and rise in perpetuity. Locals expect foreign capital to boost prices, so they invest more themselves.

'I have never seen a boom during which investors didn't ardently believe that foreigners would drive prices higher,' mused Faber. During the gold boom of the late 1970s, the talk was of the Middle East's insatiable appetite for the yellow stuff; in the mid-1980s, people in the United States thought Japanese purchases of U.S. real estate would never end; during the 1980s' Japanese stock-market bubble, foreign investors were expected to buy in bulk because they were 'underweight' in Japan; and in the 1993–1994 boom in emerging markets, the countries concerned were expecting continuously rising foreign portfolio flows. Foreign demand is usually grossly overestimated during a boom, Faber says.

The Swiss investment advisor was interested to meet, in 1996, a portfolio manager who was bullish about the U.S. stock market because, according to him, foreigners were underweight in America. The manager thought they had not yet participated meaningfully in the market. He also suggested that there hadn't been much speculation in U.S. stocks as yet.

Disregarding that last comment, Faber was driven to investigate precisely what the foreign participation was in the U.S. financial markets. He found that in 1995, foreigners (financial institutions, including central banks, individuals, and corporations) bought more U.S. treasuries than ever before. In 1996, foreigners stepped up their purchases of U.S. equities. They bought record amounts of U.S. equities in the nine months preceding the summer of 1998.

This was consistent with his theory that foreigners buy near major highs and that the high of 1998 would be the final high. 'Foreigners would then be the last group of investors to be sucked into the U.S. equities market and propel stocks to their highs — their final highs — at the end of the 1990s,' he said.

Faber was amused to see his countrymen joining the rush. Swiss investors, after having been negative about the U.S. market for almost 30 years, had become major players in the overheated U.S. new issue market in 1996, he heard. 'Since the Swiss were the most active players in Japanese convertibles and warrants in 1989, this is not a good sign,' he chuckled.

The safer markets, which may be called non-speculative markets, may trade quietly with low volume in a narrow trading range for many years. Examples include the oil, gold, and silver markets in the 1950s and 1960s, and the Taiwan share market between 1975 and 1985. But in the more dangerous speculative markets, watch out for prices rising vertically — this often signals the end of the boom. During the manic phase, volume is unusually high, and daily price swings are wide and erratic.

The number of stocks leading the climb becomes small. Often, only a handful of stocks are still soaring, and continue to lift the index. Only the sharp-eyed observer notes that the broad market has become lethargic.

Everyone remembers the date 1929 as the year of the great crash in the U.S. share market, but Faber points out that if you look at the date when most stocks peaked, you'll find they did so in 1928. Similarly, most investment historians remember that the U.S. market made its high in January 1973, led by the 'nifty fifty.' But again, study reveals that the broad market had already started performing poorly in 1972. In Japan, it was really only one particular sector — banks and other financial issues — which pushed the market up to its final high at the end of 1989.

Thus, one of the most reliable symptoms of a boom coming to an end is the sight of speculators focusing on a few issues, usually in just one sector. Frequently, the last speculative move upward is accompanied by a surge in stocks of low quality and low price — the 'cats and dogs' — or of 'new era' stocks, like those of internet companies.

The peak is immediately followed by a sharp fall. That last vertical climb is followed by another vertical line — downward.

This News Just in

A lot of people are getting into stocks and shares. Let's launch a business magazine. Good idea! And so, *Business Week* was launched — in 1929, shortly before the great crash. It used much of its space in the issues of the following few years to discuss what had gone wrong. That wasn't the only example of awkward timing. In August 1929, John Raskop, chairman of the Democratic National Committee, wrote an article in *The Ladies Home Journal* entitled 'Everybody Ought to Be Rich' in which he urged everyone to save $15 a month and put it (through a soon-to-be-formed 'Equities Security Company') into the stock market. The late 1920s also witnessed the emergence of many stock picking letters and investment magazines.

In the late 1970s, a large number of books stressing the merits of investing in high P/E growth stocks were published. Winthrop Knowlton's famous book, *Shaking the Money Tree*, came out in 1972 — just ahead of the 1973–1974 bear market which devastated growth stocks. Then, later in the decade, a flurry of books appeared: *Crisis Investing* (1979), *New Profits from the Monetary Crisis* (1978), and *How to Prosper During the Coming Bad Years* (1979). All these books argued that the U.S. dollar would become worthless, that bonds were essentially certificates of confiscation, and that hyperinflation was around the corner and would push precious metal prices into the sky.

What happened? The U.S. dollar index had actually bottomed out when these books were published in 1979 and was on the way up. By 1985, it had almost doubled. Equities and bonds soared. The precious metals that some of these books urged readers to buy peaked in January 1980, and their value has fallen ever since.

Faber noted that during the 1970s, investment conferences and newsletters focused principally on gold, silver, oil, and energy-related stocks. It was a time when the 'gold bugs' enjoyed huge popularity and drew large crowds to their seminars which were held all over the world. Headlines and front covers of magazines regularly featured oil, OPEC, gold, the Hunt brothers, Saudi Arabian billionaires, the Shah of Iran, Texas, Denver, farmland, diamonds, the weakness of the U.S. dollar, stocks like Schlumberger, Halliburton, Dome Petroleum, Tom Brown, and the flow and power of petrodollars.

Turn on the TV? One watched either 'Dallas,' then the most popular show, or one switched to the news to follow the results of OPEC meetings and the latest commentary on the whims of Sheik Yamani and King Saud. 'Needless to say, Wall Street's oil analysts commanded a huge following,' says Faber. 'Where are they now?'

During the mid-1980s, business journals and books focused on mergers and acquisitions. Famous takeover artists, arbitrageurs, and their financiers such as T. Boon Pickens, Ivan Boesky, and Michael Milken became the pin-up boys of the financial and mainstream press. All this, just before the crash of 1987. 'What concerns me now is that Alan Greenspan is the Sheik Yamani of the 1990s, and optimistic strategists command a huge following,' Faber said in August 1998.

And the attention was not all focused on the United States. In the late 1980s, just before the end of the Japanese stock-market and real estate bubble, it was the time of 'Japan Inc.,' when books documented the superiority of the Japanese system and numerous research reports justified Japan's high stock valuations. These books hit the bookstore shelves just as the Japanese market peaked; it crashed at the beginning of 1990, and has yet to recover.

In the late 1990s, again, books about successful investment strategies, famous stock investors, and Asia are making the bestseller lists. 'Technology and the internet feature on the front pages of magazines as often as oil and gold did in the late 1970s,' Faber points out. Investment letters, business magazines, and business news channels are springing up like mushrooms all over the world. Particularly popular are books about how novice investors, such as the Beardstown Ladies, can make a fortune in the stock market. In a book called *Main Street Beats Wall Street*, we learn 'How the Top Investment Clubs are Outperforming the Top Investment Pros.'

The message from the business section of the book and magazine stores in the late 1990s is clear: putting your cash into equities is a rock-solid, cast-iron, sure-fire winning bet. 'Now, where have you heard that before?' asks Faber.

1   Gustave Le Bon, *The Crowd* (New York, 1947; first published as *Psychologie des Foules* in 1895).
2   J. R. McCulloch, *The Principles of Political Economy* (London, 1830).
3   Thomas Tooke, *A History of Prices* (London, 1838).

THE BUSINESS CYCLE
GETS A PUNCTURE

Circular Arguments

Business cycles have been around a long while. In fact, one of the earliest known cycles was recorded shortly after the world was created, and you can read about it in the Old Testament's *Book of Genesis*, chapter 41. There we read that Pharaoh has had a strange dream with numbers in it and is full of foreboding.

'No problem,' says his financial advisor, Joseph, son of Jacob (he of the technicolor dream-coat). 'It's just a business cycle, a phenomenon familiar to technical analysts and other persons on the more esoteric side of the predictions business. You will have seven years of plenty, followed by seven years of famine. Make your present commodity investment decisions wisely, and you'll be fine in the future.'

The advisor turned out to be exactly

right, although a modern economist may grumble that Joseph missed the Juglar cycle by a year or two. Instead of accepting a 3 percent front-end commission, the natty dresser was compensated with a new job in the Pharaoh's court.

Faber was prompted to renew his interest in business cycles by a confluence of events. At an emerging markets conference, one of the speakers showed the audience a graph of the Kondratieff wave (see Figure 4.1 on page 104). According to him, the Kondratieff long-term cycle had turned up very strongly in the early 1990s. He went on to compare the present — a time during which so many previously closed societies are opening up — with the entry of America into the global economy in the second half of the 19th century. This led him to very optimistic conclusions regarding future economic growth, especially for emerging economies. The speaker, needless to say, worked for a brokerage firm specializing in arranging deals in emerging markets.

Then, at a seminar in Italy, Faber met the economist Henry Kaufman, who delivered an academically brilliant paper about financial volatility. He said that the changing structures of our financial system (specifically: the proliferation of new marketable securities which have replaced non-marketable financial assets, the rapid expansion of the practice of marking to market, the tendency for professional investment managers to have near-term horizons, the internationalization of financial markets, and the increasing importance of the household sector as a sharer or risks) have become the 'drivers' of volatility. 'We won't return to those tranquil periods of the 1950s and early 1960s, as some suggest and many hope for,' he said. On the contrary, 'volatility might shift to the unpleasant side in the coming years.'

Shortly after attending this conference, Faber had a discussion with an investment professional. 'The business cycle may no longer exist,' the man said. 'The Federal Reserve Board and other central banks are now in a position to "steer" the global economy on a slow, non-inflationary 2 percent annual growth path.' Under this 'perfect world scenario,' he felt that gold prices could fall very sharply as there would be no need to hold the metal for investment purposes.

Gold is dead. (This paradise may have a rotten apple inside; some economists have said that an economy without cycles might be unable to grow.)

So the first speaker argued that the cycles showed good news; the second read them as bad news; and the third suggested that the cycles no longer existed. Clearly, there was a lack of consensus in the world of financial analysis on this subject.

The story in the Old Testament is firm evidence that the existence of agricultural cycles has been known since ancient days. (Remember, agriculture, for much of organized human history, has been the single Big Business, often employing 90 percent of a country's workers.) Until the 20th century, the main work on business cycles focused on the influence of the weather on agriculture and related economic factors.

The first great 'cyclist' was Clement Juglar, a French physician, who in 1860 identified an economic cycle that he believed lasted nine or ten years, and consisted of three parts: prosperity, crisis, and liquidation. Other economists built on his theories, eventually 'correcting' the length of his cycle to eight years. The initial years of crisis (which, of course, relate to European history only) have since been identified as 1825, 1836, 1847, 1857, 1866, 1873, 1882, 1890, 1900, 1907, 1913, 1920, and 1929.

Smaller cycles of 40 months (called Kitchin cycles after their discoverer) have been found that apparently fit in with and influence Juglar cycles, and the dual system of small and medium-sized cycles allegedly fits within the framework of much larger cycles, known as long-term waves.

The 19th century English economist William Stanley Jevons, who was intrigued by what he suspected was the regularity of the great English crises of the 19th century (he identified them, in line with Juglar, as occurring in 1825, 1837, 1847, 1857, and 1866), was 'perfectly convinced' that business cycles were caused by sun spots, on a ten-year basis. He wrote: '... these decennial crises do depend upon meteorological variations of like period, which again depend, in all probability, upon cosmical variations of which we have evidence in the frequency of sunspots, auroras, and magnetic perturbations.'[1]

Faber was intrigued to note that the influence of the weather on civilization was also observed by Karl Marx, who correctly assumed that 'the necessity for predicting the rise and the fall of the Nile created Egyptian astronomy and with it the dominion of the priests as directors of agriculture.' The weather theory was further extended by Ellsworth Huntington, who stipulated that 'business cycles appear to depend largely on the mental attitude of the community ... the mental attitude depends on health ... and health depends largely on the weather.'[2] The influence of atmospheric changes on behavior was further researched by an American, Edwin Grant Dexter, who wrote a pioneering work entitled *Weather Influences: An Empirical Study of Mental and Psychological Effects of Definite Meteorological Conditions.*

So what do modern business cycle theorists think about the relationship between the economy and the climate? They think it is hogwash. This may be the right thing to do in this technological era, when man has become at least partly in charge of his own climate, particularly when it comes to the production of food. On the other hand, the noted English economist Arthur C. Pigou claimed that the movement of business confidence in the human psyche was the dominant cause of the rhythmic fluctuations, so climatic changes could well have some influence there. Human beings in every country talk about feeling sunny as being a good thing, and feeling gloomy as being a bad thing. If there is a psychological factor in investing (and who can deny it?), there may well be a climate-related cycle influencing it. (See later in this chapter for more about Pigou.)

The list of business cycles that have been put forward in recent times by creative economists is remarkable. They range from long waves which sweep over much of the planet over the course of decades, to short, self-contained cycles that can be limited to a single country or industry. But the biggest question in the business cycles debate concerns the largest of the big waves.

A Secret in Siberia

For today's intra-day gamblers who are frustrated that the stock markets close for lunch, the thought of analyzing data about hypothetical economic waves that drift over several centuries is horrific.

On the other hand, if you can make money out of them ... why not take a closer look? The existence of lengthy agro-economic cycles has long been accepted as fact. During Faber's extensive reading of history, he has noted that the Mayans in Central America held a festival every 54 years, a festival to fend off calamities. That number, 54, seems to come up with unusual frequency in the study of long cycles. A cycle in wheat prices, also of 54 years' duration, can be traced back to the 13th century.

Faber noted that more recently, a 54-year cycle in wholesale prices has been observed by a number of economists. In 1947, Edward Dewey published *Cycles — The Science of Predictions*, which contained a diagram showing 54-year cycles of U.S. wholesale prices going back to 1790. It also included projections for the future. Faber was particularly impressed to note that the book clearly forecasts the next high for wholesale prices to be in 1979 — not a bad prediction, as commodity prices peaked in the 1970s, agriculture in 1973, and metals in 1980. (The next low, according to Dewey, is expected in 2006.)

As a result, many observers think the long wave in economic conditions, generally known as the Kondratieff wave (named after the Russian economist Nikolai D. Kondratieff), also follows a rhythm of 54 years. But Faber returned to Kondratieff's original writings and his interpretation of the text shows that the theory was more complex than is generally thought, and that the writer was careful not to suggest a precise number of years.

It was in 1922 that Kondratieff, then relatively unknown, first published his theory in an essay entitled 'Long Economic Cycles.' He postulated the existence of a long economic wave. He also saw the cycle as having three phases, but they were far longer and more dramatic in nature than Juglar's.

Kondratieff wrote:

> ... the further the investigation of recurrent capitalist crises proceeded, the more it became evident that a crisis was only one phase of an entire capitalistic cycle; that the whole cycle usually consisted of three basic phases — upswing, crisis, and depression; and that such crises could be understood only by studying all phases of the cycle ... in studying the dynamics of capitalistic society, I came across phenomena that were hard to explain without postulating the existence of long cycles in economic conditions.[3]

It is important to note that Kondratieff was not attempting to construct a comprehensive theory of economic waves, but merely pointing out something that he had observed. He had 'no intention of laying the foundation for an appropriate theory of long waves,' he wrote. He merely wished to demonstrate their existence empirically.

He did this by examining trends of commodity prices, interest rates, wages, foreign trade, production and consumption of coal, private savings, and gold production. He also looked at political events from 1790 to 1920. He came to the conclusion that 'the length of the long wave under observation fluctuates between 48 and 60 years.'

Unfortunately, Kondratieff was drawing his conclusions based on empirical observation of straightforward facts — an unacceptable method of working in a society which valued ideology above all things. The Bolshevik leaders, such as Lenin and Leon Trotsky, classified Kondratieff with 'unacceptable' socialist economists such as Karl Kautsky, J. Van Gelderen and Sam De Wolff, who were also publishing works on long waves.

Trotsky and Kondratieff held a debate on the question of stability in the capitalistic system. Trotsky insisted that 'universal crises' threaten the survival of capitalism. But Kondratieff, like Kautsky, suggested that crises were merely a phase within the capitalistic system, which was basically stable. The Marxists believed that the deepening recession in the United States after 1929 was the 'final crisis of capitalism.' Kondratieff said that capitalism would survive the crash. In terms of forecasting, Kondratieff's answer was bang-on correct; in terms of ideology, it was dangerously wrong. In 1930, on the orders of Stalin, Kondratieff was officially repudiated, arrested, and sent to a Siberian prison camp, where he died.

His name was largely revived through the efforts, five years later, of economist Joseph Schumpeter, who wrote:

> Historical knowledge of what actually happened at any time in the industrial organism, and of the way in which it happened, reveals first the existence of what is often referred to as the 'Long Wave' of a period of between fifty-four and sixty years. Occasionally recognized and even measured before, especially by Spiethoff, it has been worked out in more detail by Kondratieff, and may therefore be called the Kondratieff Cycle.[4]

Schumpeter broke down the Kondratieff wave into a number of mini-cycles of 'nine to ten years duration' named after Clement Juglar and further divided these into three 'Kitchin cycles' of about 40 months each.

Kondratieff studied the price movement of commodities, French *rente* (government bonds), English consols (British government securities without redemption date and with fixed annual interest), wages, coal production and consumption, production of lead and pig iron in England, and loan-to-deposit ratios in countries such as the U.S, England, and France.

All the data fitted his wave structures in a reasonably convincing way. But Kondratieff was nothing if not careful. In *The Long Wave Cycle*, he concluded:

> I consider it is impossible to determine with absolute accuracy the years of turning points in the development of long cycles, and have taken into account the margin of error in fixing such turning points (from five to seven years), which derives from the very method used in analysing the data; the following limits of those cycles can nonetheless be regarded as the most probable.

First Cycle:
1. Rising wave: from about 1789 to 1810–17.
2. Downward wave: from 1810–1817 to 1844–51.

Second Cycle:
1. Rising wave: from 1844–51 to 1870–75.
2. Downward wave: from 1870–75 to 1890–96.

Third Cycle:
1. Rising wave: from 1890–96 to 1914–20.
2. Probable downward wave: beginning in 1914–20.[5]

What causes an upturn, and how do you spot one? The obvious answers, which may be breakthrough inventions and new technology, are wrong, the Russian said. On the contrary, inventions are a sign of the downward wave. How can this be? Kondratieff explained:

> Scientific–technical inventions in themselves, however, are insufficient to bring about a real change in the technique of production. They can remain ineffective so long as economic conditions favorable to their application are absent. This is shown by the example of the scientific–technical inventions of the seventeenth and eighteenth centuries which were used on a large scale only during the industrial revolution at the close of the eighteenth century.[6]

In other words, inventions tend to pre-date their use in business by a number of years. 'The depressed state of economic life [in the downward wave] stimulates the search for ways of cutting production costs — the search for new technical inventions that will facilitate such cost-cutting.'

So the energy of the rising wave does not come from the scientific breakthroughs, but from some years later, when the new processes have been successfully assimilated into the production line and results can be seen.

Does the opening up of new territories cause a rising wave (as the 'new era' thinkers — see Chapter 3 — would like to think)?

No, says Kondratieff. The joining of new countries to the world economy 'cannot be considered an outside factor which will satisfactorily explain the origin of the long waves.'

> The United States have been known for a relatively long time; for some reason or other they begin to be entangled in the world economy on a major scale only from the middle of the nineteenth century. Likewise, the Argentine and Canada, Australia and New Zealand, were discovered long before the end of the nineteenth century, although they begin to be entwined in the world economy to a significant extent only with the coming of the 1890s.[7]

Do wars trigger the downward section of long waves? No, the Russian said.

> Much more probable is the assumption that wars originate in the acceleration of the pace and the increased tension of economic life, in the heightened economic struggle for markets and raw materials, and that social shocks happen most easily under the pressure of new economic forces.[8]

In other words, the greatest number of social upheavals, such as wars and revolutions, occur during the periods of the rising wave of each long cycle.

Kondratieff also highlighted two other factors. First, the periods of the downward wave of each long cycle are accompanied by a prolonged and very marked depression in agriculture. Second, during the period of a rising wave in the long cycles, the intermediate capitalist cycles are characterized by the brevity of depressions and the intensity of the upswings; during the period of a downward wave in the long cycles, the opposite is true.

Kondratieff also referred to data which had been compiled by Spiethoff (see Table 4.1) which shows that 'during the period of downward waves of the long cycle, years of depression regularly predominate, while during the period of rising waves of a long cycle, it is years of upswings that predominate.'[9]

Table 4.1 Pattern in the Long Cycles

Period	Number of Years of Upswing	Number of Years of Depression
The downward wave of the long cycle of 1822–43	9	12
The rising wave of the long cycle of 1843–74	21	10
The downward wave of the long cycle of 1874–95	6	15
The rising wave of the long cycle of 1895–1912	15	4

Source: N. Kondratieff, *The Long Wave Cycle,* translation by Guy Daniels, London, 1984.

So the waves are triggered by innovations that eventually gain widespread commercial application. Schumpeter considered the period between 1787 and 1842 as the first long-term cycle of our capitalistic age. It was a period of industrial adaptation to many new inventions, the construction of canals, roads, and bridges, and the expansion of banking — much of which can be summed up by the term 'The Industrial Revolution.'

The second Kondratieff wave (1842–1897) is associated with the age of steam and steel, and the third Kondratieff wave (1898–) with advances in electricity, chemistry, and motors. In Schumpeter's *Business Cycles* (published in 1939), no ending date was stated. There was left a conundrum for later economists to argue over.

Faber was surprised to find some of the reasoning of Irving Fisher, the great economist of the 1920s and 1930s, useful in his own interpretation of long business cycles. This was unexpected, because Fisher himself flatly disbelieved in cycles — or at any rate, he acknowledged that they may exist, but refused to find them in any way useful.

In his book *Booms and Depressions*, Fisher memorably compared the economy to a choppy sea, with the investor as a boat lifted and lowered by waves, and buffeted from side to side by crosswinds:

> Imagine, then, a rocking chair on the deck of a rocking ship, on a rolling sea. The ultimate chair is subjected to so many influences that its motion will not conform with any simple rhythm. The net motion will be made up of many rhythms and non-rhythms, and will, therefore, appear sometimes rhythmic and sometimes completely unrhythmic. At all events, no one would think of referring to it as 'the rocking chair cycle.'[10]

Faber noted that Fisher goes on to concede that the economy is subjected to a vicious spiral of expansion and a vicious spiral of contraction in a cumulative process brought about chiefly by the accumulation and liquidation of debts (debt deflation theory). According to Fisher, large debts tend to intensify the deflationary process, because the debt burden becomes heavier with the fall in prices which then leads to distress-sales which depress prices further, creating a downward spiral. Here we mangle our geometric metaphors, but this boom and subsequent downward spiral, seen in terms of values, becomes a rising and falling wave.

Many economists are surprised by Marc Faber's interest in the Kondratieff cycle, because it appears to demolish the Chief Bear's argument that a lengthy period of serious economic hardship lies ahead. The wave, they say, is due for an upturn. But that assumes that it really is time for the wave to swing upward. So, the 64 trillion dollar question is: what time is it on the Kondratieff clock?

Kondratieff and Schumpeter agreed that the peak of the third Kondratieff wave occurred in the 1914–1920 period. Subsequent events — falling commodity prices, depression in agriculture, falling interest rates, and the Great Depression — suggest that a downward wave followed until the late 1930s or early 1940s. Since commodity prices bottomed out in the 1930s and interest rates in the mid-1940s, Faber and other analysts have assumed that the upswing of the fourth Kondratieff wave began some time in the 1940s. This would also fit with the idea that the Kondratieff long wave lasts between 48 and 60 years. (The third Kondratieff wave began in the mid-1890s, and thus logically ended during the 1940s.)

Given the fact that commodity prices peaked in the 1970s, the plateau of the fourth Kondratieff wave is likely to have taken place some time between 1970 and 1980 (some 25–30 years after the trough of the wave in the 1940s). Falling commodity prices, real wages, and interest rates in the 1980s, and the depression in agriculture in the early 1980s, seem to confirm that a downward wave followed. This is likely to be bottoming out during the period from the mid-1990s to the early part of the 2000s (see Figure 4.1).

Faber was interested to note that other modern economists follow similar reasoning. J. Forrester of the MIT System Dynamics Group believes that the peak of the long wave was in the late 1970s and that the low point was in the mid-1990s. He expected a business downturn that 'shakes out the imbalances in our economic system.' This suggests that the new wave has already started. The June 1995 issue of *The Bank Credit Analyst* suggests that 'the US economy is embarked on its third long-wave expansion of the 20th century.' Brian Reading of Lombard Street Research talks about the 'Great World Boom of 1993–2013.' We are already on the way up, according to him.

These economists argue that if the peak of the fifth Kondratieff wave was in the 1970s and the trough in the late 1990s, strong economic growth should follow. This would do incalculable harm to Faber's repeated posturings that a fresh period of major downturn and deflation is just around the corner.

Faber can take some comfort in the fact that interest rates, real wages, and commodity prices are not behaving in the way they should, if we were in a new upswing. They should rise, as has always been the case during the start of a rising long wave in the past. Yet economists have been forecasting since 1996 that U.S. long bond yields will fall to about 4.5 percent by the end of the decade.

The Swiss investment advisor also defends himself by means of a dangerous tack — putting on the hat of the Iditts, and arguing that 'It's different this time.' 'Kondratieff based his theory principally on the movement of commodities at a time when, in most countries,

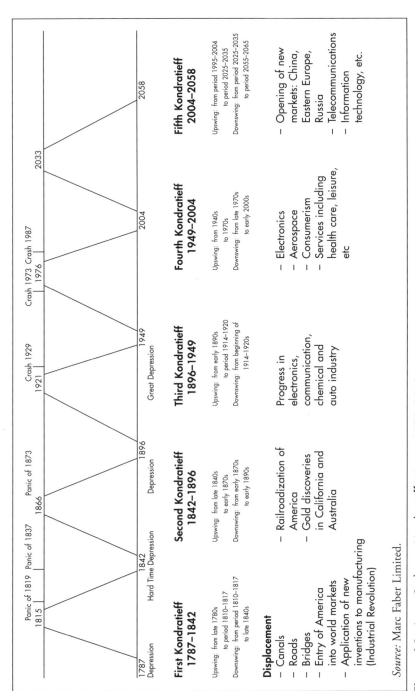

Source: Marc Faber Limited.

Figure 4.1 Long Cycles — Kondratieff Waves, 1787–2058

commodities played a much more important role in the economy than today,' Faber says. 'In 1900, in spite of all the industrialization which had taken place in the U.S. during the second half of the last century, employment in agriculture still accounted for over 40 percent of total employment. Today, employment in agriculture only makes up 3 percent of the total working population, while the service sector and government make up more than 70 percent. Thus, in the past, when commodity prices — especially agricultural prices — rose, it had a favorable impact on wages and on the economy as a whole. Today, this is clearly no longer the case in industrialized countries, where employment in agriculture is insignificant while the service sector and government dominate.'

Faber believes that the globalization of the economy and the absence of a gold standard (that is, now we have fluctuating, instead of fixed, exchange rates) greatly complicate the long wave theory, producing misleading results.

Kondratieff himself was also fully conscious that his observations would have to be revised, because 'each new cycle takes place under new concrete–historical conditions, at a new level in the development of productive forces, and hence is by no means a simple repetition of the preceding cycle.'[11]

The Swiss financier also takes issue with the assumption that the fourth Kondratieff downward wave began in the 1970s. 'Service sector and government employment continued to rise rapidly in the 1980s, and growth in Japan and the rest of Asia was impressive. Equally inconsistent is the rapid expansion of world trade in the past 15 years and the opening of new markets such as China and India, which, according to the theory, take place during rising waves.'

Faber reckons it is not possible for rising wave theorists to claim that we have been in a downswing since the late 1970s because, after 1982, he notes the absence of any kind of serious global recession — a key characteristic of downward waves. How can a whole major downward wave occur before our eyes, and nobody notice it?

'I believe that to put the peak of the fourth Kondratieff wave some time in the 1970s is a mistake,' Faber says. 'One could argue that the peak may have taken place somewhat later or that the effects of the downward wave have been postponed by the rapid debt growth, particularly in government debt, that we experienced in the 1980s.'

In the past, the intensity of the economic downturn was particularly strong at the beginning of the downward wave — but that was because of the collapse in commodity prices, when commodities were the key factor. Faber believes that today, the economy could be hardest hit toward the end of the long downward wave. He points out that this hypothesis is more consistent with the monetary over-investment cycle theory and Irving Fisher's debt deflation theory.

To further justify how 'it's different this time,' Faber chooses to replace agriculture in the original theories with financial markets as the dominant sector of the economy. While recognizing that the substitution may not be a perfect fit, 'today the financial markets seem to be far more important for the global economy than agriculture, especially since growth in recent years has been increasingly financed through credit expansion and rising stock prices.'

The present time then, in Faber's eyes, is the ending of the fourth Kondratieff wave, and it could cause rising financial asset prices to go into reverse. Would the impact on the economy be the same as in the last century when agricultural prices began to fall? If so, it would prove the correctness of Faber's substitution.

But Faber's key argument against economists who claim we have already entered another 'rising wave' scenario relates to the cycle of speculation. Speculative excesses and bubbles (real estate, commodities, tulips, canals, railroads, stocks, and so on) are always associated with peaks in the long business cycle — never troughs. Near business cycle peaks, speculation moves very quickly from one market to another, moving through international borders through real estate, collectibles, Japanese stocks, emerging markets, the yen, U.S. equities, and so on. This is clearly descriptive of recent years.

The opposite is true at long wave lows, when investors and business people are risk-averse and commit the 'error of pessimism.' Who would claim that pessimism ruled in the 1990s, when equities were continually setting new record highs? 'Now, of course, someone could object and say that there is no excessive speculation in financial assets but that stocks merely rose because of rising corporate productivity and an improved, inflation-free economic environment,' Faber says. 'I admit that how far along one is in a bubble is a subjective judgment, but look at the evidence of excess in the 1990s: record transaction volumes, the proliferation of leverage and all kinds of new financial instruments, the willingness to take risks, the growth of public participation, the number of new issues jumping to high premiums on the first trading day, and so on. These are certainly more symptomatic of speculative excesses than Kondratieff troughs in economic activity.'

Faber's reading of business cycles in the closing decades of the 20th century is as follows. The severe 1974 recession was the starting point for a Juglar cycle lasting eight years, until 1982. A powerful Juglar upswing got under way in 1982 which ended, again eight years later, with the mild 1990 recession. This Juglar was largely fueled by the rising U.S. budget and trade deficit, which shifted growth to Japan and the emerging economies.

When Faber first did a detailed examination of business cycles, in March 1996, he told his Asian clients that a big change was on the way. The 1990 Juglar upswing 'is likely to end some time in 1997 or 1998,' he warned them in April 1996. The Asian countries went through a major period of economic instability in the latter half of 1997 and sailed into depression-like conditions in 1998, which in its severity easily compares with the Great Depression of the 1930s in the U.S.

Faber reckons the buoyancy of the Asian emerging economies in the years before 1997 could be explained by 'pent-up demand' after the breakdown of socialist ideology in the late 1980s, and to some extent by the monetary over-investment theory, where there is excessive investing of fresh capital because of the ease of borrowing money and the accelerator principle. (The accelerator principle is the link between consumer demand and investment. An increase in demand for televisions, say, will eventually require increased investment in television factories. The accelerator principle implies that an increase in a country's national income will stimulate investment.)

Faber believes it is possible that the fifth Kondratieff downward wave has been so far atypical in the sense that economic under-performance in the industrialized countries was offset by a powerful up-cycle in the emerging economies. The problem, as Faber sees it, started to arise when the energy of the emerging economies came to an abrupt halt in 1997 or 1998. This occurred when the Juglar cycle, which began in the Western world in 1990, turned down.

Faber sticks rigidly to his guns in insisting that the turn of the century is going to be a time for a shakeout in the global economy. But what if he is wrong about the fifth wave? What if it has started?

'It's not impossible. Only the severity of the next recession will provide the answer,' he says. 'If we have already entered a Kondratieff upward wave, the recession will be mild and brief. If the downward wave is still in progress, the recession will possibly be devastating. I don't think we'll have to wait too long to find out.' Even if we are in the upward wave of Kondratieff, there is no guarantee that stocks would rise. By definition, an upward wave instead causes interest rates to rise.

We have already looked at psychological factors as a component of short business cycles. But Faber, with his nose in a book of political history, was intrigued to discover that human emotional factors could also be seen as an element of long wave theory.

The historian Arnold Toynbee remarks in his book *A Study of History*: 'The appearance of economic "long waves" might not be hallucinations but might be economic reflections of political realities.' Explaining the cycle of war and peace, Toynbee writes:

> The survivors of a generation that has been of military age during a bout of war will be shy, for the rest of their lives, of bringing a repetition of this tragic experience either upon themselves or upon their children, and ... therefore the psychological resistance of any move towards the breaking of a peace ... is likely to be prohibitively strong, until a new generation ... has had the time to grow up and to come into power. On the same showing, a bout of war, once precipitated, is likely to persist until the peace-bred generation that has been light-heartedly run into war has been replaced, in its turn, by a war-worn generation.[12]

This struck Faber as an analogy that could be applied perfectly to financial warriors: 'I suppose that the same "generation cycle" exists in financial markets. Investors who lost all they had in the 1929 crash and the subsequent depression probably vowed never again to touch stocks and remained conservative for the rest of their lives. Conversely, the vast majority of today's investors, having never really experienced a severe and long-lasting bear market, are much readier to take a risk.'

Tuning in to the Short Waves

Independent of the large waves are smaller business cycles. There are a lot of these. We have the under-consumption cycle, the under-saving cycle, the over-production cycle, the agrarian cycle, the psychological cycle, the over-investment (marginal efficiency of capital) cycle, the monetary cycle, the technological or innovation cycle, the demographic cycle, the political cycle, and the displacement cycle theories.

Faber reckons the under-consumption theory holds the most relevance for modern times. This is ironic, since most under-consumption theories have been dismissed as 'wholly unfounded,' to quote G. Haberler.[13] The one exception was John Hobson's analysis, which focused on production, consumption, and income inequality, and which Faber believes is worth looking at again.

This again turned conventional economics on its head. The favorite cry of the amateur capitalist is that wealth disparity is good. If incomes in society are close to one another, you end up with something like a socialist or communist system, and they simply don't work. Hobson showed conclusively that extreme wealth disparity leads to economic slowdown and, eventually, depression. You end up with a situation where those at the low end of the income scale would be glad to 'consume' the products of society but cannot afford to, while those at the high end have the ability to consume but have no need or desire. The whole thing seizes up.

The cycle flows like this: (1) The masses work to produce goods. (2) They also use their salaries to buy goods. (3) The bosses increase productivity and profits, but fail to pass on the increased income to the workers. (4) The amount of goods produced rises. (5) But the amount of goods purchased falls. (6) This dangerous disparity intensifies until the system breaks down. (7) The workers and the bosses end up in a state of depression. (8) So does the economy.

In support of his argument, Hobson produced a table (see Table 4.2) which shows an estimate of savings in relation to incomes in 1931. It was estimated that about three-fourths of total savings at that time came from the richest classes. Had this society moved 'towards equality of incomes,' the move 'would reduce the proportion of income saved to income spent.' People would be buying the goods produced, and the economy would have started moving again. Hobson's arguments appeared to be confirmed by the examination of the movement of output, costs, prices, wages, and profits in the U.S. during the period 1920–1930.

The findings of P. H. Douglas, in *Controlling Depressions*, seemed also to support this.[14] Hourly output in manufacturing industries increased by about 30 percent between 1922 and 1929. During the same time, hourly earnings of labor rose by only about 8 percent. The result was an increase in profits during this period of about 84

Table 4.2 The Economics of Unemployment: London, 1931

Families with	Average Income per Family	Average Spending per Family
Over £5,000	£12,100	£7,600
From £700 to £5,000	1,054	690
From £160 to £700	357	329
From £52 to £160	142	138
Under £52	40	40

Source: John A. Hobson.

percent which led to excessive expansion of production capacity (which, in turn, brought about an unbalance of production over consumption). According to Douglas, production as a whole increased by 37 percent between 1922 and 1929, while real incomes of urban lower-paid groups increased by only 18–20 percent (and much less for agricultural laborers). Corporate profits increased by 83 percent during this period. Douglas concluded that the purchasing power was simply insufficient to absorb the growing supply of consumer goods, which led to the collapse in 1929.

Other economists supported this view. A. D. Gayer came to similar conclusions in *Monetary Policy and Economic Stabilization*: 'The failure of the income of the final consumer in the end checked the process' of expansion in America in 1929. 'Relative to the means of the ultimate consumer, the vast expansion of capacity in durable goods industries and the huge volume of domestic and factory buildings erected were altogether excessive.'[15] Equally, A. B. Adams stated in *Our Economic Revolution* that: 'This lopsided growth in the division or distribution of national money income brought about a rapid development of industry, ending in our present condition, which is marked by excessive productive power and a deficiency of consumers' money income.'[16]

Faber became excited when, in Haberler's *Prosperity and Depression*, he saw under-consumption defined as:

> ... the process by which purchasing power is in some way lost to the economic system, and therefore fails to become income and to appear as demand in the market for consumer goods. Money disappears or is hoarded, and the income-velocity of money diminishes. In this sense, under-consumption is just another word for deflation. Deflation is, of course, a possible cause of the breakdown of the boom and the main cause of the depression; but, as such, is covered by the monetary explanation of the business cycle.[17]

This married well with Faber's own theories about the economic cycles taking place in the late 1990s: a clash of various factors leading to a major period of deflation.

By 1996, Faber had become convinced that economic data from the U.S. suggested a similar growth in wealth and income inequality as was experienced during the 1920s. There was trouble ahead.

Now, it could be argued that increased corporate profits will lead to increased capital spending and bring about a rise in employment and wages — thus boosting workers' spending power. Not so, say the under-consumptionists: the corporate profit explosion leads to massive new investments and in the first phase prolongs the prosperity period as it over-stimulates the construction of capital goods. But the breakdown inevitably follows when the production facilities which have been started during the upswing are completed and consumer goods begin to pour out.

Joseph Schumpeter, to whom we have already been introduced, believed that a boom finished when new productive processes are completed and additional finished goods flood the market.[18] In other words, sharply rising profits lead to excessive investments, which eventually lead to a collapse of the boom.

Faber believes that the under-consumption cycle theory has much in common with the over-investment cycle theory, which stipulates that 'credit expansion' is the real villain. The huge rise in profits (while wages lag) is harmful only in as far as the money tends to be used for inflationary credits, which in turn lead to over-investment. But regardless of the theory, the 'proximate cause of the breakdown is an insufficiency of demand as compared with the supply coming on the market.'[19]

Growing income inequality, high consumer debts, and an aging population aside, Faber found other reasons to be pessimistic about future consumption growth in industrialized countries. A significant portion of today's capital spending goes toward labor-saving investments, which further depress growth in the wages of the worker–consumer.

More bad news: these days, capacity is frequently expanded overseas where manufacturing is cheaper. As a result, labor in the U.S. and even more so in Western European countries hardly benefits from a capital spending boom. Again, one could argue that slowing consumer demand in industrialized countries will be offset by rising income in the emerging economies, to which new production facilities are frequently transplanted.

Cycling is All in the Mind

According to the French economist Y. Guyot, psychological factors are the driving force of economic fluctuations: 'In economy, as in all other social phenomena, psychological factors play an important part. It is because they have not been sufficiently taken into account that we have had so many erroneous explanations of commercial crises.'[20]

In essence, the psychological theory holds that in a period of growing prosperity and rising corporate profitability, each entrepreneur is likely to over-estimate the profits to be obtained by himself as compared with others.

Arthur C. Pigou, the protagonist of the psychological trade cycle theory, points out:

> When an error of optimism has been generated ... it tends to spread and grow, as a result of reactions between different parts of the business community. This comes about through two principal influences. First, experience suggests that, apart altogether from the financial ties by which different businessmen are bound together, there exists among them a certain measure of psychological interdependence. A change of tone in one part of the business world diffuses itself, in a quite unreasoning manner, over other and wholly disconnected parts ... Secondly ... an error of optimism on the part of one group of businessmen itself creates a justification for some improved expectations on the part of other groups.[21]

Pigou's theories, although he wrote his seminal works in the 1920s, have much in common with Faber's own beliefs about errors of optimism and crowd psychology. Importantly, in 1927, in *Industrial Fluctuations*, Pigou put forward his theory of 'noncompensated errors.' This says that if individuals behave in a completely autonomous, independent way, their various errors will offset each other — a free market principle working in the human organism. But a curiosity of human society, particularly in the investment field, is that humans will imitate each other. Errors, instead of being compensated for, multiply, until friends and colleagues are all caught up on the wrong path. Add today's instant global communications into the equation, and you can see how human society makes its own economic disasters.

Crowd psychology was positively dangerous, said F. Lavington: 'The rational judgment that the greater their number the greater will be the risk is likely to be submerged by the mere contagion of confidence which persuades him that the greater the numbers the more safely he himself may venture.'[22]

There are other factors involved. Some economists stress that the longer the time interval between the decision to make an investment and the final result, the greater the possibility of a mistake. Lengthy production processes (Schumpeter talks about the 'period of gestation' — the period from the time products are produced to the day when they are ready for delivery) tend not only to facilitate the miscalculation of total demand, but also, because of competition, lead to the miscalculation of market share. 'Today,' Faber notes, 'Every PC manufacturer expects his market share to increase.' There is no way they can all be right.

The Cardinal Sin: The Error of Optimism

The number one sin, in Faber's book, tends to occur with most distressing effect when new concepts or ideas arrive on the business scene. Some of the most pronounced boom and bust periods in history were caused by excessive expansion of new industries (canals, railroads, supertankers, radios, autos) or the opening of new territories (the South Seas, America's western territories, Latin America in the second half of the last century). Well-documented is the enthusiasm which was created by the railroads in the last century, and their subsequent expansion into new territories which led to repeated erroneous forecasts regarding their future profits and later to great losses.

The errors of optimism are actually plural in nature. Besides over-estimating the overall demand and their expected share of the market, entrepreneurs are also likely to under-estimate their costs. Then it all comes crashing down. Why does it always end so painfully? Look at it this way. The atmosphere of profit and greed leads to the error of optimism. But when a crisis of confidence occurs, the investor is gripped by fear — the error of pessimism, if you like.

As Pigou writes: 'This new error is born, not an infant, but a giant; for an industrial boom has necessarily been a period of strong emotional excitement, and an excited man passes from one form of excitement to another more rapidly than he passes to quiescence.'[23]

It is almost impossible to study the psychological view of investors without a comic vision coming into one's head. The investor is always portrayed as a person who goes from extreme confidence to sheer panic. A look at the way any stock market moves reveals the accuracy of this portrait — soaring markets do not level off, but rise vertically and then fall vertically. Spikes are the norm, not the exception.

Other business cycle theorists argue that while psychological factors play an important role in reinforcing the expansion and contraction phase, they cannot by themselves be held responsible for economic fluctuations. The thinking is this: moods of optimism and pessimism among investors tend to be caused by economic factors, and should therefore not be seen as the sole cause of economic turns.

There is Such a Thing as Too Much Money

According to the monetary over-investment business cycle theory, every credit expansion must lead first to the sin of over-investment and then to a breakdown. According to W. Röpke, 'the credit expansion setting the boom going proceeds by way of the interest rate being "too low".'[24]

How low is too low? Röpke means that the rate of interest is below the 'natural rate' which, according to K. Wicksell, is the rate 'at which the demand for loan capital just equals the supply of savings.'[25] The follow passage from Röpke particularly impressed itself upon Faber's mind:

> The too low interest rate invites a general increase in investment which then leads to the mechanism of the boom drifting on towards its ultimate debacle ... The expansion of credit in the boom expressing itself in the too low interest rate leads to an over-expansion of the economic process and by introducing a general over-investment disrupts the equilibrium of the economic system. It allows more to be invested than is saved.[26]

This credit-driven imbalance is a key factor, but there are others. Poor decisions about where the credit should go are a major factor, Röpke said. His study of the 1929 crash produced a host of examples.

> This period which has been followed by the severest crisis in history shows, on the whole, a price level which was slightly sagging rather than rising. How, then, can there have been inflation? ... owing to decreasing costs following on technical progress, prices would have fallen if an amount of additional credit had not been pumped into the economic system. Hence there was inflation, even if only of the relative kind.
> But it can be perfectly well argued that the quantitative effect of this inflationary credit expansion was considerably aggravated by an abnormal qualitative distribution of credits. One case is the great expansion of instalment credits which gives the impression as if the Federal Reserve system was trying to administer the heroin not only per os but also per rectum ... Another instance is the real estate market which was grossly over-supplied with credits. The worst and most conspicuous case, however, was the stock-market speculation which was the leader on the road to disaster.[27]

Faber found that these and more recent writings about monetary over-investment theory confirmed his own deductions (highlighted in his writings in November 1989) about the inability of the

Japanese economy and its stock market to end its boom in a soft landing, the way most other analysts were expecting.

With Japan's recent history in mind, he was amused to read what theorists had to say about the ensuing depression period. Can the recession and the deflationary trend be corrected by massive reflation? F. Hayek, referring to the then ongoing depression, provided the following answer:

> To combat the depression by a forced credit expansion is to attempt to cure the evil by the very means which brought it about; because we are suffering from a misdirection of production, we want to create further misdirection — a procedure which can only lead to much more severe crisis as soon as the credit expansion comes to an end. [28]

Faber found interesting modern parallels to Röpke's theory that 'too low interest rates' leads to a disruption of the economic equilibrium which is frequently aggravated by an abnormal qualitative change of credits. This was precisely what Faber's American counterpart, Kurt Richebacher, was writing about in late 1995 concerning financial trends in the U.S., where 'the credit machine is running full speed without any constraints.'

To make his point, Richebacher produced the following statistics in his 1995 *Richebacher Letter*:

> In the United States, total outstanding non-financial debt has more than tripled since 1980, from $3.9 trillion to $13.5 trillion. In absolute terms, debt growth of $9.6 trillion has contrasted with simultaneous nominal GDP growth of $4.32 trillion. From the end of 1989 to mid-1995, GDP growth of $1.77 trillion was matched by non-financial debt growth of $3.32 trillion. And these figures do not include the trillions of dollars borrowed and lent for speculation in the domestic and international money markets.

Furthermore, credit growth seems to have accelerated in 1995. In the first half of that year, nominal GDP growth of US$127.7 billion was accompanied by debt growth in the non-financial sector of

US$415.5 billion, resulting in a debt-to-GDP ratio of 3.25 to 1, which is 'the biggest ever "overhang" of credit expansion relative to GDP growth as the national account measure of economic activity.' According to Richebacher, borrowings by the non-financial sector (government, businesses, and consumers) were running annually at more than US$800 billion, compared with business and personal savings totaling only about US$330 billion. He concludes that 'given such a tremendous excess of credit demand, the equilibrium interest rate probably is somewhere between 8–9%.'

What Richebacher is suggesting is that the current interest rates are significantly below the Wicksell 'equilibrium' or 'natural rate' at which the demand for loan capital equals the supply of savings.

Rapid credit growth combined with a recent surge in corporate profitability (besides the ease of borrowing money, which is another driving force of the over-investment trend) have led to strong capital spending growth in the U.S. over the last few years. The economist Gary Shilling has shown that real producers' durable equipment (PDE) spending on new machinery and equipment has risen significantly above levels predicted by his hitherto very accurate model which predicts PDE based on industrial production and final demand. Now, one could argue that this time around, high capital spending will not lead in the traditional way to over-investments by adding too much capacity.

After all, much of the increase in capital spending has been directed toward cost-cutting and labor-saving capital equipment, especially computers and communication equipment. However, the following should be considered: computers have a low multiplier effect. (They involve a low input of labor and materials — particularly when compared to the construction industry — and much of it is sourced from overseas.) Furthermore, spending on computers is designed to automate, thus putting additional pressure on the already weak labor market. Therefore, while in the 'classical' theory, over-investments lead to excess capacity, in the late 1990s over-investments (at least in the U.S.) bring about weak income growth and under-consumption (or consumption which is only supported by growing consumer indebtedness).

Faber wrote the following to his clients in 1996:

> It would appear that the present labor-saving capital spending boom is leading to growing income inequality. While real compensation per hour for all workers has continued to rise since the early 1970s (although much more slowly than in the sixties), real compensation per hour of production and non-supervisory workers (which make up 80% of the workforce) have been falling alarmingly. In addition, while domestic capital spending may be directed more toward cost cutting than toward capacity expansion, one should not forget that the surge in foreign direct investments in emerging economies is rapidly expanding consumer good manufacturing capacity — but outside the U.S. and other industrialized countries. This is a trend from which unskilled labor in the industrialized world will continue to suffer.

Someone who questions the validity of the under-consumption and over-investment theory with regard to the present could, of course, argue as follows. It is true that the workers' share of GDP has been declining, and that in order to maintain their standards of living, consumers have had to go deeper into debt. However, look at how much more wealth has been added to the household sector as a result of the sharp appreciation of the stock and bond market. (In 1995, household wealth increased by US$3 trillion, while debts grew by US$352 billion.)

Faber reckons this argument is flawed. The sharp increase in wealth has gone to the households with incomes of $75,000 and over (which have a high savings rate), while the households with incomes below $40,000 (with negative savings rates) are unlikely to own a lot of financial assets. Thus, one can safely assume that the surge in the U.S. capital market (and elsewhere) has actually widened the income gap further. It is not looking like a recipe for happiness.

1   William Stanley Jevons, *Investigations in Currency and Finance* (London, 1884).
2   Ellsworth Huntingdon, *World Power and Evolution* (New Haven, 1919).

3 Nikolai D. Kondratieff, *The Long Wave Cycle* (translated by Guy Daniels; New York, 1984).

4 Joseph Schumpeter, 'The Analysis of Economic Change,' *The Review of Economic Statistics*, Vol. 17, No. 4, May 1935.

5 Kondratieff, *The Long Wave Cycle*, op. cit.

6 ibid.

7 ibid.

8 ibid.

9 ibid.

10 Irving Fisher, *Booms and Depressions* (New York, 1932).

11 Kondratieff, *The Long Wave Cycle*, op. cit.

12 Arnold Toynbee, *A Study of History* (London, 1954).

13 G. Haberler, *Prosperity and Depression* (New York, 1946).

14 P. H. Douglas, *Controlling Depressions* (New York, 1935).

15 A. D. Gayer, *Monetary Policy and Economic Stabilization* (New York, 1935).

16 A. B. Adams, *Our Economic Revolution* (New York, 1935).

17 Haberler, *Prosperity and Depression*, op. cit.

18 See also A. Aftalion, *Les Crises Periodiques de Surproduction* (Paris, 1913).

19 Haberler, *Prosperity and Depression*, op. cit.

20 Y. Guyot, *Principles of Social Economy* (London, 1884).

21 Arthur C. Pigou, *The Economics of Welfare* (London, 1920).

22 F. Lavington, *The Trade Cycle* (London, 1922).

23 Pigou, *The Economics of Welfare*, op. cit.

24 W. Röpke, *Crises and Cycles* (London, 1936).

25 W. Wicksell, *Vorlesungen uber die Nationalokonomie*, Vol. II.

26 Röpke, *Crises and Cycles*, op. cit.

27 ibid.

28 F. Hayek, *Monetary Theory and the Trade Cycle* (London, 1933).

VANISHING CITIES

What They Don't Want to Hear

Dr Doom is on stage. His speech is entitled 'The Rise and Fall of Great Cities.' It is a cheeky title for a speech to be delivered this month in this city. He is in the ballroom of a hotel in Hong Kong, two weeks before it ceases to be a British colony and is handed over to China.

It is impossible to look at a title like that without being put in mind of the troubles which potentially await Hong Kong; an obvious point, but one which is now rarely made. Over the past year, the Hong Kong press, previously free and lively, has become increasingly reluctant to say anything even slightly negative about the situation. Publishers are worried that they will lose their advertisers; journalists, their jobs; locals, their prospects; foreigners, their work visas. Now, two weeks before the big day, the business community is almost unanimous in its conclusion: the reunification with the motherland will be a great and glorious day for Hong Kong, a city on the south coast of the Chinese mainland. So why is Marc Faber rocking the boat?

Polite applause greets his ascension of the stage. The tall speaker angles the microphone up slightly, narrowly resists the temptation to tap it to see if it is switched on, and starts speaking. After a brief introduction, he gets to the subject at hand.

'Having lived in Hong Kong since 1973, I have had the good fortune to see the meteoric economic development of many cities and countries. Twenty-five years ago, countries like Taiwan, South Korea, Singapore, and Malaysia were still relatively poor. Today, they are rich countries, and their capitals are large, modern cities with infrastructure one would not have dreamt of then.'

There is a palpable feeling of relief in the audience. This is the same good, positive stuff they have been hearing from other sources: Asia, land of economic miracles, the miracle is just beginning, the forthcoming global triumph of the tiger economies, with China soon to be the biggest tiger of them all, etc, etc. Yes, that always goes down well.

Faber continues: 'Similarly, we may underestimate how quickly cities in formerly closed societies may develop and in some cases displace present centers of prosperity. I am here thinking particularly of Hong Kong.'

Several members of the audience noticeably stiffen. Their instant hostility is visible in the way their lips tighten. Some roll their eyes: here goes the mad Dr Doom again. Reporters, sitting at the side of the auditorium, pick up their pens and tape-recorders, their instinct for controversy overriding their knowledge that their editors will be reluctant to print such views at this time. The slower news-hounds prod their neighbors: did he really say Hong Kong would be displaced as a center of prosperity?

Faber continues: 'Could the opening of China do to Hong Kong, what the opening of the sea route to Asia under the Portuguese at the end of the 15th century did to the thriving cities along the Silk Road? The change brought about the end of several great cities. I speak of former centers of prosperity such as Turfan, Khotan,

Kashgar, Samarkand, and Bactra.'

Some of the pens on the press benches stop scribbling. Their holders whisper to each other. Turfan? Kho-what? How do you spell it?

Faber speaks at length about the great cities of the past, how they had become powerful, what their populations were at their height, and what eventually brought them down. He speaks about the trade, the products, the services that expanded them, and the wars that tore them to pieces. But what was initially stunning wasn't the drama and tragedy of the stories. It was the names. Many of them were names that most people in the audience had simply never heard. Faber was saying that the greatest cities in the world had vanished, not just physically, but from the general consciousness of humanity.

The Swiss investment economist's list of most populous cities in the pre-Christian era included such names as Akkad, Lagash, Ur, and Thebes. Others on the list were vaguely familiar, but reminded listeners of fiction, rather than fact. There was Nineveh, off the coast of which Jonah had been eaten by the whale; there was Babylon, used as a metaphor for evil by the writer of the Psalms. Could these really have been great business cities, antiquity's equivalents to London or New York? As Faber moved on through history, the list of names in the past two millennia included some familiar ones, such as Constantinople and Baghdad, but also many unfamiliar ones. Where on earth was Ctesiphon? Or Changan? Could they really have been the largest cities on earth at one time?

Only when Faber came to the great cities of the most recent 1000 years were there some slightly more familiar names. He listed, as cities which temporarily wore the crown of most populous center in the world, Cordoba (largest city in AD 935), Merv (largest city in 1145), and Fez (largest city in 1170). Today, none remains even in the role of national capital, he said. The mighty really do fall.

Faber backtracked over his list for his audience — which was mystified but listening intently — and filled in some much-needed detail. Ctesiphon was in Persia, Faber explained, and was the largest population center in the world in AD 340. It was captured by the Arabs in 637, and by 750 it was a deserted ruin. The stones of the city were taken to a small Sasanian village called Baghdad, where they were used to build Madinat al-Salaam, which meant the 'City of Peace' (now, ironically, the home of Saddam Hussein). 'It is hard to believe that the world's biggest center could completely vanish in less than 120 years,' said Faber. 'The equivalent today would be the total disappearance of a city like New York.' He paused. 'Or Hong Kong.'

This wasn't what the audience wanted to hear. They scowled. There were smiles from the press bench at the discomfiture of members of the financial establishment in the audience.

Faber then moved on to the subject of China, and the audience shifted in its seats. Some looked rather comforted. Now here was a subject that this rude barbarian was unlikely to know much about. He will probably regurgitate the same old stuff about the fall of Shanghai after 1949.

'The largest city in China in ancient times was Ao, which had a population of 32,000 in 1360 BC,' said Faber.

The man sitting in front of me (I had opted for the front stalls rather than the press bench) leaned over to the Chinese–American financier sitting next to him. 'Where's that?' he whispered.

'Uh, I don't know. I don't think he's pronouncing it right,' the suit replied.

'The cities which next took the crown of most populous cities in China in the pre-Christian era were Anyang, Loyang, Lintzu, Yenhsiatu, and Changan,' continued Faber.

'Where are those cities? North or south? What are they called now?' whispered the man in front of me.

His advisor looked uncomfortable. 'I don't know.'

'In the T'ang dynasty under the emperor T'ai Tsung, who lived from AD 627 to 650, the country became quite wealthy and its capital, Changan, became a showpiece in terms of elegance and riches,' said Faber. 'Silk, then selling in Europe for literally its weight in gold, was a common dress for half of Changan's population. The use of fur coats was widespread. But in the eighth century, a Tartar invasion sacked Changan. It was subsequently rebuilt but didn't regain its former glory. Under the Sung dynasty, the empire's capital moved to Kaifeng. Some estimate its population to have reached 1,200,000 in the 11th century. But when Kaifeng was destroyed by invading Mongols, the capital was relocated south of the Yangtze river to Hangchow. Hangchow had been an important commercial center since the T'ang dynasty and gained in importance following the construction of the Grand Canal which connected it to Peking.'

This was turning into a lesson in Chinese history. What was surprising was how unfamiliar it was, even to us in that room. With such a strong focus on finance, politics, and ideology in Hong Kong, even the China scholars in that room knew little about the history of the cities of the great land mass of which we were part.

Hangchow, Faber said, had splendor and good administration, and this was documented by Marco Polo, who stayed in the city at the court of Kublai Khan. He quoted the Italian traveler: 'The streets are all paved with stone and bricks ... there is an abundant quantity of game of all kinds ... the number of bridges amount to 12,000 ... in other streets are the quarters of the courtesans, who are here in such numbers as I dare not venture to report.'

The audience were starting to relax at this point. Positive stories about the glories of China were much more in accordance with the ruling ethos about what was expedient to discuss in public in Hong Kong at the time.

Faber continued: 'Let me make one general observation about the history of China's largest cities — which were also commercially the more important ones. They were all in the north. None of these cities was located further south than Hangchow — a fact that may have some relevance for making projections about the future regions of wealth in China.'

The point Faber was making was missed by nobody in that audience in the city at almost the southernmost tip of China. The financial advisor sitting one row in front of me winced.

Without a Trace

Faber spoke often and in detail about his theories of great cities from 1997 onwards. His work was built on wide reading. This ranged from Tertius Chandler's *Four Thousand Years of Urban Growth*,[1] to Edward Gibbon's *The History of the Decline and Fall of the Roman Empire*.[2] During his studies of the subject, Faber became a great fan of the historian Daniel J. Boorstein.

But while historians tend to focus on the individuals, the history-makers of each period, Faber looked at the trade flows and how prosperity seemed to visit certain societies but not others.

It was a detailed but fascinating study for an economist to do, and Faber was delighted to find that he was following a path that had already been laid down 25 centuries earlier. He discovered this quotation from Herodotus, written in the fifth century BC: 'The cities that were formerly great, have most of them become insignificant; and such as are at present powerful, were weak in olden times. I shall, therefore, discourse equally of both, convinced that human happiness never continues long in one stay.'

On the day of Faber's June 1997 speech in Hong Kong, an expanded version of the talk was released in book form to his clients. Although he is a good speaker and has an impressive vocabulary in English and several other languages, he is an economist, not a writer. Much of *The Rise and Fall of Great Cities*, issued as a 20,000-word monograph, is an unappealing string of unpronounceable names, interrupted by more names in parentheses. Here's a sample sentence:

> Assyrian rule in West Asia (a territory which encompassed greater Mesopotamia and Egypt) did not last for long and was overthrown by the Babylonian king Nabopolassar (Nineveh was destroyed in 612 BC upon which Assyria ceased to exist) and his son Nebuchadnezzar, who conquered Egypt and Jerusalem (leading to the Babylonian deportation of the Jews).

Dull stuff, which was a shame, because the latter parts of the monograph contained some fascinating arguments.

After his speech, Faber went for a break at the Foreign Correspondents' Club of Hong Kong. Although it is 2.30 pm, many of the older members were still at the bar, drinking their lunch.

Faber was teasing them. 'So, stocks always go up in the long term, right? If this is true, then any investment in the ancient commercial centers of Tyrus, Sidon, or Carthage would be a good one, right? Say you invested only $1 and achieved a rate of only 3 percent a year. Today, your $1 would be worth ...' Here he grabs the back of his bar bill and starts scribbling. The final figure is $142,000,000,000,000,000,000,000,000. He flaps the paper. 'Lot of money, right? That's the theory. In actual fact, can any of you even tell me where Tyrus, Sidon, or Carthage is now?'

There was a line of silent, blank faces at the bar of the FCC. Now this is not saying much, because there is always a line of silent, blank faces at this bar, and several members might be unable to recite their own office addresses, let alone locate Carthage.

But an experienced speaker can perform perfectly well without the benefit of sentient listeners, so Faber soldiers on. Today, he is on a roll; and besides, this is important. This is a key part of what is sometimes known as Doom Thought — the amorphous conglomeration of all his pessimistic theories. We all know about wealth generation, and we as a society talk about it endlessly — but we brush aside the merest intrusive thought about wealth destruction, refusing to acknowledge that it is as inevitable as its sunnier counterpart. Faber continues to talk about Tyrus and Sidon to the blank faces at the bar. 'History shows that things go wrong. It must happen. Established economic equilibrium is disturbed from time to time.'

Faber's study of the history of cities has proved to be a good way of making this point. Nothing makes the destruction of wealth more stark than the realization that entire cities of hundreds of thousands of people and buildings can vanish without trace, due to economic and political changes.

Many of Faber's best examples are once-wealthy places which people today have never heard of, which lends weight to his hypothesis. Ouro Preto was Brazil's largest city in 1750 because of its nearby gold deposits. Manaus, another Brazilian city, was rich beyond the dreams of many of its inhabitants at the end of the 19th century because of its temporary monopoly on rubber production.

Both cities went from rich to poor when their respective booms came to an end.

But even if you look at the most familiar cities, history is often surprising. Think of big cities in the United States, and you think of Los Angeles, New York, and Washington. In fact, America's initial centers of prosperity were Boston, Philadelphia, New York, Baltimore, Salem, Charleston, Newport, Providence, New Haven, New London, and Norwich. Boston was bigger than New York until 1760.

Many people see California, and particularly Los Angeles, as a huge, jam-packed, pop-culture capital of the world. Yet the state of California was barely inhabited in 1800. One hundred years later, Los Angeles had started to grow but was nowhere in the list of the top ten cities in the United States. Today, California has a population of close to 30 million, and Los Angeles has more than 12 million people, second in population only to greater New York, which has 17 million.

The speed of economic development of the United States and its key cities in the 19th and 20th centuries is unprecedented. In 1800, the United States was a country with a total population of less than six million, of which 95 percent lived in rural areas. By 1900 it had a population of more than 76 million and an industrial output exceeding that of Britain and Germany combined. The United States is the original economic miracle, make no mistake, says Faber.

That afternoon, some of the foreign correspondents, not bound by the fears of the Hong Kong press barons, decide to interview him and go into his theory of great cities in more detail. Faber starts by giving a potted history of the world, focusing on the booms and busts of major cities.

Alexandria: After being founded in 322 BC, Alexandria was able to take advantage of the Romans' rapidly expanding East–West trade. It benefited from being on the best trade routes. It was also a manufacturing center itself, producing cloth, oils, perfumes, and creams. It had its own ship-building industry. Alexandria sounded like capitalist heaven. The Roman emperor Hadrian praised Alexandria's pace of life and commercial activity, where 'even the blind people work' and where 'money is their God, worshipped by Jews, Christians, and all other religions.'

What went wrong? Alexandria's decline began with its partial destruction by the invader Marcus Aurelius, and was accelerated by the breakdown of the Roman Empire. Yet it was many centuries before its commercial life suffered a serious blow. It finally lost any claim to the title of the greatest center of commerce in history with the discovery of the sea route around the Cape of Good Hope in 1497.

Antioch: Two thousand years ago, Antioch became the Romans' most important military base in the east. From there, Rome conducted all its operations in Mesopotamia. It also became famous as a center of Christianity, and is featured in the biblical writings of St Paul.

What went wrong? Antioch was sacked and plundered by invaders several times through the centuries, notably by the Persian leader Khosrau I in AD 540. Khosrau transplanted its population to a new suburb of the Persian capital Ctesiphon, then the world's largest city. Antioch was totally destroyed by Timur in 1401. A traveler in 1432 found a ghost town containing only 300 inhabited houses — the sort of population that would barely fill a village these days.

Rome: Rome was not a meaningful producer of any goods. But its rulers had organizational genius. They also had prodigious military skills, a talent at setting up systems of law and order, and an ability to administer an empire with a skill which some people think has never been surpassed. Rome also had a well-functioning capital market. About the time of Christ's birth, Rome was the biggest city in the world. Also worth noting is the fact that it had an insatiable appetite for luxury goods, and became the world's biggest consumer market — comparable, to some extent, to today's United States.

What went wrong? Rome's lack of self-sufficiency meant that practically all goods had to be imported from its territories or from neighboring countries. It also had a huge trade deficit which eventually led to hyperinflation, currency depreciation (the silver content of its coins was steadily reduced), decay, and loss of power. Further blows were dealt to Rome when it was sacked by the

Visigoths, Ostrogoths, and Vandals in the fifth century. From a peak of about 500,000 people in the first century, its population fell to 50,000 in the year 600, and bottomed out at about 30,000 in 1300. 'Imagine what a 90 percent fall in population does to property prices in a city,' said Faber, rubbing his hands together like a Victorian villain.

Changhan: In China, the tendency was for the political capital to become the country's largest, most prosperous city. In the T'ang dynasty (AD 618–907), the country was quite wealthy. In 637, its capital, Changan, was considered the most populous city in the world.

What went wrong? Bad neighbors. In the eighth century, a Tartar invasion sacked Changan. The city was rebuilt, but it never recaptured its former glory. Today, it has been forgotten.

Baghdad: Baghdad was the most populous city in the world in 775. Some scholars believe it was the first city to achieve a population of more than one million.

What went wrong? Toward the end of the ninth century, Baghdad's fortunes began to decline. The city was badly damaged in a civil war from which it never fully recovered, and the caliphat (the Islamic ruling team) became increasingly embroiled in factional fighting. By 1000, its population had declined to around 150,000, and in 1258 it was laid waste by the Mongol warrior Helagu, who overran Mesopotamia and killed Baghdad's entire population. Today, it is a sprawling but poverty-stricken place.

Cordoba: In AD 1000, Cordoba, in Spain, was the world's largest city in terms of population, with 450,000 people. Moorish Spain was Europe's most populous nation.

What went wrong? Cordoba's success didn't last long. Strife between Berbers, Arabs, Jews, slave officials, Christians, and Spanish converts to Islam weakened the authority of the Omayyad caliphs. In the 11th and 12th centuries it came under the rule of the Almoravids and later the Almohads. Already long past its glory, Cordoba was reconquered in 1236 by the Spanish king Ferdinand III of Castile, an event which accelerated its decline. By 1300 its population had shrunk by 90 percent to 40,000.

Venice: Urban centers in France and northern Europe in the ninth and tenth centuries became prosperous and gained an appetite for luxury goods and spices from Asia. The Italian coastal cities of Venice, Amalfi, and Genoa took advantage of this demand. They called on ports in Egypt, Palestine, North Africa, and Constantinople to load cargo for northern Europe or to be sold at the trade fairs held in Champagne and Brie. The Italians had sophisticated banking, insurance, and accounting systems. Double-entry bookkeeping was first used in these cities, and in 1157 Venice issued the first government bonds.

What went wrong? The circumnavigation of the Cape of Good Hope and the opening of a new trade route to the Orient by Vasco da Gama in 1498 hit Venice like a *coup de foudre* (bolt of lightning), says the philosopher–historian Montesquieu. Faber thinks this may be somewhat of an exaggeration, since Venice remained an important trading city for most of the 15th century. But the long-term impact was, as Montesquieu memorably remarked, that Venice was *'jetée dans un coin du monde ou elle est restée'* (thrown into a corner of the world where it has remained). Problems were exacerbated by wars against the Turks, the loss to the Turks of Cyprus in 1571, and the extremely costly loss of Candia (now Crete) after a 20-year siege in 1669. Today, Venice is popular with tourists, but no one would call it one of the world's great centers of commerce. Amalfi and Genoa are even less significant.

Antwerp: By the mid-16th century, Antwerp had become arguably the most prosperous and influential city in Western Europe. It was a major trading and financial center. Some scholars think that, during the 'age of the Fuggers' (the Fuggers were a banking family), Antwerp became the center of the international economy, dethroning Venice and edging out Lisbon. The trade flows were in its favor, at the expense of rival port Bruges. The Portuguese had decided to ship their pepper to Antwerp instead of Bruges; and German merchants had moved to Antwerp, which was closer to their home market than Bruges.

What went wrong? The first blow came in the form of the Spanish state bankruptcy of 1557 (followed by further Spanish defaults in

1575, 1596, 1607, 1627, and 1647). The Fuggers, operating from Antwerp, had been the main lenders to Spain and its royal family. Antwerp was sacked by unpaid Spanish mercenaries in 1576 and suffered disturbances because of religious wars. Then there was the problem of intolerant rulers. After its recapture by Spain in 1585, many Jewish and Protestant families chose to move to Amsterdam, where 'no man has any reason to complain of oppression in Conscience.'[3] Antwerp survives as a port city, but it is no longer a prime port, being far outclassed by Rotterdam.

Potosi: Potosi, in Upper Peru (now Bolivia), was founded on Spanish silver mines. By 1600, its population had reached 105,000, making it by far the biggest city on the South American continent.

What went wrong? The silver production of the main mine reached its peak in 1590, after which output fell rapidly. Today, Bolivia cannot by any means be described as a big player in international commerce.

Haiti: Although Haiti was never one of the most important countries in the world, it did go through a momentous rise and fall. It was France's most prosperous overseas territory in the 17th and 18th centuries. It was responsible for three-fourths of France's colonial trade, which is remarkable considering that France had many West African colonies, plus the Canadian territories and Madagascar.

What went wrong? A history of mismanagement has made Haiti one of the world's poorest countries.

Manila: In 1898, the Philippines had been ceded by Spain to the United States, along with Puerto Rico and Guam, following the Spanish–American War. Manila had become an economically important (and comparatively rich) city in Asia in the 16th and 17th centuries, because of its role as an entrepôt for the silver trade. Silver mined at Potosi was shipped from Acapulco to Manila, where it was exchanged for Chinese porcelain, pearls, precious stones, and luxury cottons from India. Under American rule, Manila had also become politically important. As recently as the 1970s, its stock market had been bigger than Hong Kong's.

What went wrong? Poor management of the economy by a

succession of leaders, notably Ferdinand Marcos, who managed to enrich himself and his family by impoverishing his countrymen, led to the Philippines being dubbed 'the sick man of Asia.'

Vijayanagar: Vijayanagar, founded in 1336, quickly became the richest city in India, and the second largest in Asia. Its circumference was estimated at 60 miles, and it was said to contain 100,000 houses. Its population was estimated at 500,000 in 1500. The city was, according to the Portuguese missionary Domingos Paes, 'the best provided city in the world.' The Persian traveler Abdu-r Razzak lauded the city for its commercial morality which was based on barbarous severity (including hanging a man on a hook through his chin until he died). It had a well-financed police force; and prostitution was regulated and a source of royal revenue. Faber was intrigued by the official role of the brothels. 'Opposite the mint is the office of the prefect of the city, to which it is said twelve thousand policemen are attached; and their pay ... is derived from the proceeds of the brothels. The splendour of these houses, the beauty of the heart ravishers, their blandishments and ogles, are beyond description.'[4]

What went wrong? The Muslims invaded. Hindu leader Rama Raya took his force of 500,000 soldiers, 32,000 horses, and 551 elephants to fight at Talikota in 1565. But the Hindus were defeated and their king was beheaded. The Muslims pillaged and burned down Vijayanagar. It was left 'as if an earthquake had visited it with not a stone upon a stone.'[5]

Angkor: In 1200, Angkor, along with Pagan in Burma, was among the Orient's largest and most important cities. The ambassador of Kublai Khan (1215–1294 — a grandson of Genghis Khan) reported that the Khmer capital had a strong government and had become wealthy from rice-paddies and hard work. The king had high moral standards, having five wives: 'one special one, and four others for the cardinal points of the compass.'[6] There were some 4000 concubines in case the king wanted to point in the direction of a more precise compass reading.

What went wrong? Angkor's glory came to an end with invasions from the Thais and the Mongols, who destroyed the irrigation systems upon which Angkor depended. Thereafter, the capital was shifted to Phnom Penh in 1484. The flourishing city was wiped out so thoroughly that, for several hundred years, no one knew where it had been. It was only rediscovered in 1858 by a French explorer. Today, it is one of the world's most impressive historical sites.

What Makes a City Rise or Fall?

Before answering this question, Faber asks you to think again about how you define a city. How many neighbors do you have? Five thousand? If so, you live in a village. A hundred thousand? You live in a town. A million? You live in a city. Ten million? You live in a super-city.

But this configuration, which we take for granted, is extremely recent in application. For much of human history, most of the urban centers known as cities contained the populations today's citizen would expect in a village or a town. Athens, at the height of its glory in 430 BC, contained 155,000 souls, fewer than Plano, a small city in Texas, has today. As recently as 1700, Mexico City had a total population of just 85,000 (the 1990 population of Naperville, Illinois). Mexico City is now a super-city with an administrative region covering 20 million residents.

What caused the dramatic growth in urban centers to occur where it did? And why did some become wealthy while others languished? Faber's studies suggest different answers for different cities, with a variety of key factors credited for the growth. However, the one key factor that applied to most of the cities he has studied is the traditional mantra of the estate agent: location, location, location.

But that answer begs a question. Located where, or next to what? For a start, near water. The earliest centers of prosperity developed in regions which were naturally fertile or which could be made fertile. Proximity to natural waterways, so that irrigation systems could be used to cultivate the land, was a key factor. Very early civilizations developed in Mesopotamia between two great rivers, the Euphrates and the Tigris; in China, development was along the Yellow river, and in Egypt along the Nile valley. Early civilizations based their economies on agrarian production. The farmer was king, and water was his resource.

When international trade began to flow, cities tended to develop along the routes favored by the traveling merchants. This gave rise to such great cities of the past as Turfan, Khotan, Samarkand, Bukhara, Bactra, Petra, Merve, Kashgar, Taxila, Mathura, Pataliputra, Babylon, Seleucia, and others.

As the shipping industry became increasingly powerful, port cities emerged as key commercial centers. Examples from the ancient world include Tyrus, Tripoli, Sidon, Carthage, Gades, Athens, Marseille, Syracuse, Rhodes, Alexandria, Odessa, Aden, and Ormuz. In more recent centuries, cities which grew powerful through their port facilities included Venice, Famagusta, Genoa, Constantinople, Kaffa, Lisbon, Bordeaux, Bruges, Lubeck, Bremen, Danzig, Riga, Hamburg, Antwerp, Cadiz, and Barcelona.

When new areas of land were made known to the ruling powers, ports acted as gateway cities, and this ensured speedy growth. In the Caribbean, Havana grew up as the Spanish gateway to Latin America. In South America, coastal cities which grew up as gateways included Cartagena, Salvador de Bahia, Rio de Janeiro, and Acapulco.

The growth of port cities occurred all over the world. The Asian counterparts of Antwerp and Bruges were Malacca, Goa, Batavia, Surat, Hangchow, Canton, Shanghai, Amoy, Foochow, and Nagasaki. The history of North America also shows port cities as the first important centers. These included Salem, Boston, Baltimore, Newport, New Orleans, Quebec, and Montreal. New York, with its prime port position facing Europe and its network of inland waterways, seemed destined by location to become America's largest city. The African continent also provides examples. Flourishing cities developed along the coast at Zanzibar, Mombasa, Luanda, Cape Town, Tangier, Algiers, and Tunis.

Proximity to coastal waters has remained an important factor up to relatively recent days. During the Industrial Revolution in Europe, proximity to resources and waterways was crucial.

But what is a port without traffic? If an ambitious ruler of an undistinguished country builds a large container transhipment facility, will they come? Or are the ships the key factor, rather than the port?

Faber noted that the discovery of the trade routes around the Cape was a major blow to the importance of the Mediterranean port cities. In more recent times, the opening of the Suez canal had a devastating impact on the finances of the transit port island of St Helena.

The growth of trade in the United States is a fascinating example of how well-located port cities grow if they can become stops on a worthwhile trade route. The east coast cities of the United States grew quickly, and the country was perceived as being located on the opposite side of the Atlantic from Europe. Yet the remarkable growth of the west coast in the past century can be credited to the fact that cities there were in prime positions for taking advantage of the under-developed trade flows across the Pacific Ocean. It had been slow to develop, but had proved worth waiting for. Today, the United States' largest port is not on the Atlantic coast, but the west side's Long Beach. 'Had there been a huge desert between the west coast of the U.S. and Asia, instead of the water which allowed for inexpensive transportation, trade between Asia and the U.S. would not have taken off in the same way,' said Faber.

A location near water is a key factor, but there are others. Faber noted that prosperous cities often developed in resource-rich regions. It has already been mentioned that the now-forgotten Potosi was South America's largest city at the beginning of the 17th century. The 'gold-rush towns' in the U.S. are examples of how a resource can trigger a boomtown, usually temporarily. Modern cities such as Houston and Dallas can also, to some extent, be counted as resource-driven cities. They joined the list of the United States' largest and most economically important centers on the back of their proximity to oil.

Can a great location on a growing trade route guarantee the enduring success of a city? In human terms, the answer is probably 'No.' Growth cycles are too unpredictable to be able to say that a city will flourish for sure during one person's three-score years and ten. But from the point of view of a historian looking backward, Faber noted that certain locations have produced impressively long-lived centers of commerce. 'Since antiquity, there has always been an important city near the Nile delta,' says Faber. 'First Memphis, then Thebes, then Alexandria, and later Cairo.'

Byzantium, which became Constantinople and is now Istanbul, has always been a key city, thanks to its location between East and West, and between the Mediterranean and the Black Sea. Faber noted that there has always been an important city at the straits of Malacca: first Malacca itself (a port city in Malaysia), then Penang, to the north, and then Singapore, slightly south. In northern China, important cities always developed on the coast between Ningpo and Tianjin.

So, you have built (or moved to) a city which has a major seaport, a good location on international trade flows, and is near an area which is under-appreciated but resource-rich. What other factors do you need to sort out in order to create a center of prosperity?

Faber identified several factors. The first comes straight from business school: good administration. This in itself is not easy to define. Snapshots of the Singapore and Hong Kong business districts show them to be almost identical, and newspaper and magazine publishers regularly mix them up. But the style of administration of the two cities, at least until the handover of Hong Kong from Britain to China in 1997, couldn't have been more different. The British Hong Kong government maintained the ultimate laissez-faire system, letting Adam Smith's invisible hand act as the main mover in the markets. The Singapore government, although still capitalistic, has kept a tight hand on its population, engaging in strong economic management, social engineering, and censorship of free speech.

Faber believes that these two cities have not really taken different routes to prosperity. Rather, it is what the two cities share that has led to their success. To succeed, a system must be fair to all market participants. This means there must be clear civil and commercial laws (including well-defined accounting standards, property rights, well-regulated but free markets for goods, services, and labor, an efficient financial market, bankruptcy laws, fair taxation, and so on). The rule of law must be established, strictly enforced, and administered in an impartial way. It is worth noting that the judicial processes of both Hong Kong and Singapore are closely modeled on the British system. Hong Kong's legal system is 'arguably the finest in Asia,' according to a 1997 editorial in the *Far Eastern Economic Review*.

The importance of law is shown by a comparison of two other very different historical expansionist groups. Faber believes that the rise of Rome in the pre-Christian era, and the more recent dominance of the British Empire, shared an important factor: both sets of colonialists had sophisticated legal systems, and, in the British case, the judiciary seemed to be genuinely impartial as to whether litigants were British or foreign. 'Impartiality and independence of the judiciary may actually be a more important factor for a city's success than is generally given credit for,' says Faber.

Of course, cause and effect in these situations are not clearly defined. In many instances, it may well be that the wealthy who have made money and gained power under arbitrary circumstances may wish to introduce a fairer law-based system to protect themselves and their children — in which case, good administration follows a period of prosperity rather than ushers it in. An example Faber uses to support this argument is Henry Morgan, one of the most infamous pirates of classical legend, who later in his life became a respectable businessman and was knighted. 'There are modern equivalents, too. Think of all the great gangsters, drug dealers, and smugglers who send their children to American business school to turn them into decent citizens,' says the Swiss financier.

Faber was pleased to find that it can be argued that history reveals tolerance as a significant factor in regional prosperity. Cordoba, under a relatively tolerant Muslim rule, became rich, but the city disintegrated under the rule of the Spanish with their infamous Inquisition. Alexandria, Venice, Genoa, Lisbon, Amsterdam, London, and Hong Kong all offered minority groups a more-or-less level playing field. All became great merchant cities of history.

'A dynamic society arises where there is also intellectual tolerance, freedom of conscience, social mobility, freedom of ideas, and the expression of ideas which may be hostile to established beliefs or to the government,' says Faber. 'Where intellectuals, scientists, and philosophers were persecuted, imprisoned, tortured, or murdered, they fled. But it is their know-how on which progress depends.'

In such cases, the creativity sometimes simply moves to another city. As an example, he points out that the Huguenots left France in 1685 when the Edict of Nantes, which had given them civil and religious liberty, was repealed. Many of them moved to Switzerland. The French Huguenots were famed for their watch-making ability, and their new home became (and still is) the world leader in the supply of mechanical watches.

'The caliber of teachers and pupils in higher learning institutes depends on a political system's tolerance,' says Faber — an unpalatable truth in modern Asia. To substantiate this claim, he compares North and South America in the period between the 16th and 19th centuries. The north was relatively poor in natural resources, but open-minded, creative, and innovative. The south, governed largely by the heavy-handed Spanish, was remarkably rich. Today, their relative positions have been reversed.

Faber pooh-poohs the bleatings of tough Asian leaders who try to persuade their listeners that freedom is a bad thing. Today, liberal Western or Western-style regimes are rich. Totalitarian communist regimes are poor. It is as simple as that. 'It is interesting to note that, Japan aside, Asia has no world-class universities,' says Faber.

Can a city's mindset, philosophy, or religion lead it to prosperity? The economist Max Weber thought that Protestant ethics were conducive to capitalist achievements by stressing high work ethics such as thrift, punctuality, austerity, and dependability. The trouble is, the same attributes are labeled 'Asian values' in the East. Roman Catholics and followers of Islam similarly claim these qualities for themselves.

Earlier this century, economists wrote books explaining how Confucianism had prevented capitalism from getting a foothold in China. In recent years, politicians from places which are hostile to political freedoms have been arguing that Confucian values are to be credited for their capitalistic success.

Faber finds this argument extremely far-fetched, especially with regard to China. China has been the one country to cling to (some) Confucian values, and has remained, even up to the present, a relatively poor country. In traditional Chinese society, merchants are classified as belonging to the lowest class. Yet in a successful capitalist society, merchants play the key roles and become the most powerful citizens. Singapore's *capitalism* has made it rich, not its imagined Confucianism.

Faber concludes that morality and self-discipline, in the context of a free society, are conducive to prosperity; it can hardly be argued otherwise. But zealous fanaticism, as demonstrated by the Spanish Inquisition and 20th century communism, is destructive to economic development.

A second factor in the growth of cities is good infrastructure. If a fair-handed judiciary and a creative, liberal atmosphere can be seen as good social infrastructure, then the ambitious city-builder needs to reach the same standards with his physical infrastructure.

In times past, this has meant the need for good roads, bridges, ports, access to fresh water through aqueducts and canals, and a working system for the distribution of fresh food. During the time when Rome ruled supreme, its talent with physical infrastructure was legendary.

In most modern cities, usable roads and the supply of food can be taken for granted. Today's equivalent needs for a successful city, Faber believes, are a cost-efficient and technologically advanced communications system, uninterrupted power supplies, easy access to an airport, good recreation facilities, comfortable living conditions, and, preferably, a pleasant climate.

As usual, the validity of an argument is best tested by examining the exceptions to it. There is little doubt that well-established, trustworthy property rights contribute to the long-term prosperity of a city. Yet there are cases in which the absence of such laws may have occasionally led to speeded-up growth in the short term. Mining cities are an example. 'I am also thinking here of Shanghai's recent explosive growth,' says Faber. 'With well-established property rights, it would never have been possible to put up so much new infrastructure in such a short period of time.' But anyone tempted to use this as an example of the benefits of China's tough government should flip back a few pages in their history books. 'Shanghai decayed a great deal under communist rule. It would not have done so quite as much if the city had had the rule of law and established property rights.' Faber added one more point, one suspects aimed particularly at his audience in complacent Hong Kong. 'The introduction of a good legal infrastructure usually has some beneficial effects on an economy. But the removal of good legal practices in a system has always had a devastating impact on confidence and economic development.'

Is muscle a factor? Do you need military power or a strong political leader to make your chosen city prosperous? A superficial view of history suggests that the answer is 'Yes.' Look at the early explorers and conquerors. Faber reckons the Assyrians, the Romans, and the Mongols became rich largely because they invented an early, pre-capitalism technique of takeovers and management buyouts. 'Their specialty was asset stripping,' he says with a laugh. 'Some colonizers were good at downsizing, sometimes accidentally, such as when the Spanish brought influenza to the New World and killed large numbers of natives.' Others were good at corporate restructuring. The Romans, for instance, used military methods to conquer their neighbors, but when they got there, they inevitably spread their efficient management skills, particularly their administration and legal systems.

Faber sees Timur, the 15th century warrior who rode through his world conquering one city after another, as a kind of early superstar hedge fund manager. He was smart, well-educated, courageous, and had a 'killer instinct' — a phrase much favored by trainers of financial traders today.

But a closer examination of history reveals that muscle has not been absolutely necessary, and has become less important as time has gone by. In some of the earliest recorded history, we read about the Phoenicians, who thrived through their skill as sailors. They were great shipbuilders, and are credited with the discovery that the Pole Star could be used in navigation. The Phoenician cities of Byblos, Sidon, and Tyre thrived in the 15th century BC. They founded the first global trading empire by eventually establishing hundreds of trading settlements, including Cathage and Utica. They are believed to have circumnavigated Africa in about 600 BC and even reached England. They were not in any way conquerors or a military force, yet they built the world's first 'global' trading empire.

More than a millennium later, from the 11th to the 16th centuries, the Italian trading cities of Genoa, Amalfi, Florence, Pisa, and Venice were major economic centers. They did this through commerce, with no military or political expansionist ambitions. Venice at one stage was a military power, but it became one only because it had to protect its wealth. 'Their wealth was not derived from military power, but the other way around. The same is also true of the United States. They became the dominant military power in the world because they had technology, organization skills, a strong sense of unity — patriotism — and could afford to maintain a large army,' says Faber.

The Hanseatic League was an early trading organization encompassing 100 cities in Germany, plus outposts and trade connections throughout Europe. It held trade fairs beyond Europe's borders in places as far afield as Scotland and Novgorod. It achieved all this in the 14th century, without the use of an army or navy.

Modern places which have created vast fortunes without recourse to significant military might include Switzerland, Singapore, and Hong Kong.

There are some interesting side issues here. Faber's reading of history leads him to believe that two psychological elements — he calls them the NTL (nothing-to-lose) factor and the momentum factor — have been an aid to growth.

Poor and oppressed people with no opportunities to better themselves are driven by a nothing-to-lose mentality, and thus may take greater risks and fight harder for the available prizes. People who have succeeded one or more times in achieving some sort of expansion may feel they are on a winning streak, and may be driven on by momentum to a string of victories. Faber believes such factors were responsible for the rise to power of the Huns, the Tartars, the Mongols, and the Romans; and for the rise of Hellenistic Greece under Alexander the Great, France under Napoleon, and Nazi Germany under Hitler. But Faber warns that this type of aggressive expansionism doesn't appear to create lasting wealth. A parasite which feeds heavily on rich carriers risks eventually killing the carriers and then may attract its own parasites.

Soldiers may not be a vital ingredient, but what about scientists? If you make sure your city contains lots of inventors, will their creativity turn it into a center of prosperity? Faber found the history of invention and its relation to economic growth fascinating. Early societies were responsible for the development of the sail, the wheel, chariots, and irrigation systems. The Romans made great advances in the development of roads, bridges, and aqueducts, as well as showing the benefits of a good system of law and order. During the Western European Dark Ages, the Islamic societies developed mathematical skills, including accounting, which eventually were widely used by the rest of civilization. The Italian city-states were great innovators of commercial and financial techniques. British cities, and later the cities of the United States, produced new goods which were popular around the world, and in more recent times so has Japan.

But the work of inventors is not enough to make a society rich. China excelled in having inventors producing new products long before the rest of the world caught up. But it lacked an environment that fostered the commercial exploitation of its innovations. You need both.

In contrast, 19th century America had the perfect environment for business to thrive. There was an air of freedom, a capitalistic mentality, free markets, and a population of immigrants, freed from the conventions of their home towns and motivated by the drive to make new lives for themselves. The new Americans created centers of prosperity on a scale which had no precedent in history.

Does this perfect city have to be a big city? Or could it be a relatively small place? Faber stops and thinks. 'I'm not sure there is an answer to this question. Which perform better, large companies or small companies? You can't say. Similarly, there may be times when large cities do better, while under some circumstances small cities may have an edge.'

Faber's findings show that rich places also frequently grow into physically large, heavily populated cities, with Babylon, Alexandria, Rome, Constantinople, Cordoba, London, Hangchow, and New York as examples. But at the same time, history has examples of many small cities which became prosperous while remaining small: Amalfi, Cadiz, Goa, Batavia, Geneva, Abu Dhabi, and Monaco.

In this context, there is one recipe that seems to work. You could benefit greatly if you live in an independent or semi-independent city-state at the edge or in the middle of a huge empire. Examples from history are Bruges and Antwerp in their early days, Venice, Genoa, and Singapore. 'And, of course, Hong Kong,' Faber adds. 'Prior to the handover.'

But with this comes a warning. Cities which flourish under this rather parasitic system run the risk of becoming vulnerable to the victim from which they feed. One or more counterbalancing powers (or strong allies) are of crucial importance for the survival of autonomous small cities and small neutral countries such as Switzerland, Singapore, Brunei, or the United Arab Emirates. Hong Kong before the handover had two contrasting influences. Now it has only one. Faber says: 'The lack of a powerful counterbalancing power, and the absence of its own military force, are the Achilles' heels of Hong Kong after the handover.'

Why do great cities fall? In some cases, there is nothing the city's economic advisors can do about it, however good their technical analysis. Pompeii was totally destroyed by the violent eruption of Mount Vesuvius in AD 79. Other cities were wrecked by human violence in the shape of invading hordes: Nineveh, Babylon, Seleucia, Carthage, Rome, Pagan, and Angkor Wat are examples.

Other great cities fell more slowly. Venice declined in the 16th and 17th centuries, but remained reasonably prosperous until the 18th century, long after its commercial importance had diminished. Today it survives as an aging but attractive tourist center.

Faber found that cities which did not suffer dramatic ends from natural disasters or wars, fell from grace in much the same ways as stock-market index counters. First, there is a rise which is accompanied by cycles of rapid growth and is interrupted by small recessions. Then the cities go into decline, but this fall is sometimes punctuated by periods of seeming recovery.

Cities which became rich through warfare — in other words, most cities in antiquity, although thankfully fewer in modern times — also tended to lose their wealth through wars. The economist could conclude that war is, therefore, an important factor in the loss of a city's or country's wealth. But Faber found such an obvious conclusion too superficial. Why do organizations which are good at winning wars suddenly start losing them? There must be underlying factors at work which lead to this loss of military competitiveness. 'The loss of wealth through war can be seen as a symptom of a process of destruction and may not be the initial cause,' Faber says. After all, companies go bankrupt today, but you wouldn't list competition as a bad thing which causes companies to go under.

To what extent will the rise and possible fall of our hypothetical city be a cyclical thing? Will it just decline by itself?

There is an attractive poetic justice in the concept that success and wealth contain their own seeds of destruction. But it's more than just a nice idea. Faber reckons he has the evidence. Now he gets excited. He can talk forever about the sins and mistakes made by rich cities. He reckons that it is true that as cities become rich and powerful, they inevitably become arrogant, overconfident, and complacent; they also tend to overspend. In other words, they suffer the same shortcomings as many individuals who become rich. Furthermore, such cities tend to concentrate overmuch on the business that made them rich and neglect to safely diversify their interests. Wealthy cities tend to have surplus funds to invest. This excess liquidity leads to a high domestic price level, which makes them unable to compete with their neighbors. The tendency, too, is for these funds to be invested in increasingly less profitable ventures. Thus, profit margins fall.

They then commit still worse sins. Rich cities (and rich individuals) invariably invest in foreign countries about which they know little (consider the Romans, mentioned above). This makes them vulnerable to problems from outside. Also, the poorer neighbors start to become envious, and predators start to try to bleed what they can from what they see as an easy target. Faber believes that psychological pressures are against the rich, in that hardship has a unifying effect, while wealth often leads to internal factional strife.

'Wherever we live, whatever we do, and whoever we socialize with, it is obvious that with success a certain arrogance, self-righteousness, overconfidence, and complacency arises,' he says. 'Very successful societies, and all the cities I have studied, were at some point the Microsofts of the urban universe, and became overconfident. Having become so incredibly successful, they developed a nothing-can-go-wrong attitude and committed gross errors of optimism. In some cases, they consequently overspent and overinvested.'

Faber considers the Roman Empire the perfect example of a well-ordered organization that lacked a good financial controller. Its initial success was partly due to its superior infrastructure. So, what did the Roman executives do? They built similar bridges and roads in regions where the maintenance costs were far higher than the economic benefits. They turned a money-making idea into a loss-making one.

And when the money coming in started to dwindle, they were already in trouble. The Romans had developed a strong appetite for luxury goods from foreign countries, creating a trade imbalance. They began to spend more than they made, and the resulting trade deficits led to a depreciating currency. What was the answer to the problem? They decided, just like modern presidents of companies (and sometimes presidents of countries), to expand their way out of trouble. The Romans thought that the acquisition of new territories would lead to an increase in tributes (their name for profits) which would bail out the creaky system. The problem was, however, that the corporation failed to make any highly profitable acquisitions when they needed them. They conquered, or tried to conquer, new lands, such as Persia, but only managed to get themselves into more trouble. In the meantime, Rome itself suffered from internal strife, which weakened the empire even further.

Many cities fell because they failed to diversify their interests.

They had become rich because of one or a small number of products or services. They were either trading, manufacturing, or financial centers, or had built their wealth on conquests. But markets for all products eventually become saturated. This is even true for professional conquerors. When you have conquered all your neighbors, what do you do then? You're stuck. Furthermore, competition in one or other form inevitably develops and lowers your profit margins just when you least expect it — perhaps one of your neighbors finds out that he is good at conquering, too. And most frightening of all, the demand for a popular and successful product can — for whatever reason — suddenly disappear. Venice had a great business as a processing center for international trade. Suddenly, the Portuguese find a new route around the Cape of Good Hope, and Venice's profit margins immediately slump. Potosi and Manaus, mentioned above, failed spectacularly to diversify, although it should have stood to reason that their resources would eventually be depleted.

When a city becomes a center of prosperity, there are cyclical elements that have to be dealt with. All rich cities have had to cope with the problem of rising prices which lead to a loss of competitiveness. Both Rome and, later, Spain suffered from high inflation. These empire's armies (you can see them as shop-floor staff) became more expensive than those of their enemies (equivalent in business terms to competitors). Spain lost a great deal to pirates, who could be seen as competitors with a lower cost structure who entered the market and cut the profit margins.

It is remarkable how similar the sins of the fathers of the great cities are to those of the modern investor. Whereas the modern investor whose friend has made a profit in an Asian fund will put his cash into a similar emerging markets fund, our forefathers would hear about the discovery of places of wealth and they, too, would venture with their ships into these new lands. 'In antiquity, this tended to happen through unfortunate conquests,' says Faber. 'It's funny, but right up to the modern day, the idea of new markets has always had a particular appeal.' Some modern investors prefer to entrust their funds to bonds. Faber reminds his history students wryly that Antwerp and Genoa lent their surplus funds to Triple-A rated governments which eventually defaulted.

Faber saves his grimmest warnings for cities which make their fortune as financial centers. 'Financial centers simply do not control their own destiny. They are controlled by their debtors. Without a powerful military, they can, in the worst case, never enforce their claims. This is something Hong Kong may be forced to discover one day.' The financial center has other problems. It takes a few years for most industries to run down and die. But it only takes a few seconds for finances amounting to billions of dollars to be spirited by electronic transfer out of one country and into another.

Today's wealthy districts (Kuwait and a few other places aside) don't have to worry about marauders entering and razing their city to the ground. But their prospects can vanish just as fast. A neighboring territory can suddenly offer tax holidays and special deals, and the money you had your eye on will suddenly flow next door.

When a wealthy city becomes unstable, the minorities are often thrown out. This is a predictable but unfortunate response. The majority unwittingly frequently cuts off its nose to spite its face. Very often, the minorities are merchants or are in the banking business, and are people the community cannot afford to lose.

Obvious examples of displaced groups in history include the Jews, Huguenots, Indians, and Armenians, but this applies to many group of foreigners who are economically useful and maintain their identity as foreigners in their adopted home. And it's not just in times long past. Many people were expelled from Uganda in the 1970s, and ethnic Chinese locals were targeted for trouble in Indonesia in 1998.

The nature and networking of these international groups makes them more mobile, so it is relatively easy for them to pack up and go. In some parts of Europe during the Middle Ages, Jews were not allowed to own property, so their own countrymen made them even more mobile.

What makes a great city last? The Huns, the Tartars, and the Mongols had only a brief moment of glory, whereas the Roman and British empires stretched over centuries. These empires had discipline, legal and commercial infrastructures, strong administration skills, a talent with education, and military power.

But strong-arm rulers, societies which only had informal and arbitrary government structures, didn't have the same resilience. Their success tended to depend entirely on the genius of their leaders. Therefore, when Alexander the Great, Attila the Hun, Genghis Khan, Timur, Akbar, and Kublai Khan passed away, their respective empires and cities fell apart as quickly as they had risen.

What of the future of great cities? Huge changes are afoot, there is no doubt at all about that. The key change is that location, the major factor mentioned above, will no longer be as important. What happens when aircraft offer transport deals as cheaply as ships? What happens when billions of dollars of business are being done in cyberspace? Today, who cares (or knows) whether you are in a port city or not?

Faber believes that airport hubs will rise and seaports shrink in importance. The proximity to water will no longer be significant, while being adjacent to main markets could become a vital factor — particularly when you consider that the life cycle of products is becoming short, through accelerated technological obsolescence. This factor has certainly benefited Mexico in recent years, which can quickly ship goods made to new specifications to the United States.

Faber believes that cities which are close to higher learning institutes (universities, technical colleges, research institutes) may well thrive.

Now, here's the scary bit. Faber's study of great cities has revealed to him and his students just how dramatically the wealthy centers of the world can rise and fall. But the rate of change is likely to accelerate. At the time of the Portuguese expansion in the Orient, it took two-and-a-half to three years for a ship to transport goods from Portugal to South-east Asia and back. At the beginning of the 18th century, sea voyages from Europe to China and back took about two years. Even as recently as the middle of the 19th century, ships took more than four months to sail from London to Shanghai.

Table 5.1 America's Ten Largest Cities, 1850–1986 (in 000s)

1850		1900		1930	
New York	516	New York	3437	New York	6930
Philadelphia	340	Chicago	1699	Chicago	3376
Baltimore	169	Philadelphia	1294	Philadelphia	1951
Boston	137	St. Louis	575	Detroit	1569
New Orleans	116	Boston	561	Los Angeles	1238
Cincinnati	115	Baltimore	509	Cleveland	900
St. Louis	78	Cleveland	382	St. Louis	822
Pittsburgh	47	Buffalo	352	Baltimore	805
Buffalo	42	Cincinnati	326	Boston	781
Washington	40	San Francisco	343	Pittsburgh	670

1950		1986	
New York	7872	New York	17807
Chicago	4921	Los Angeles	12373
Los Angeles	3997	Chicago	8035
Philadelphia	2922	Philadelphia	5755
Detroit	2659	San Francisco	5685
Boston	2233	Detroit	4577
San Francisco	2022	Boston	4027
Pittsburgh	1533	Houston	3566
St. Louis	1400	Washington	3429
Cleveland	1384	Dallas	3348

Notes:
1. Philadelphia, the second-largest city in 1850, had dropped to number four by 1950.
2. Baltimore, New Orleans, Cincinnati, St. Louis, Pittsburgh, Buffalo, and Cleveland, all among the ten largest cities in the 19th century, had disappeared from the list by the second half of the 20th century.
3. Los Angeles, not on the list until 1930, is now America's second-largest city.
4. Detroit and Cleveland, the most prosperous industrial cities in the 1920s, experienced a relative decline thereafter.
5. Before 1800, America's largest cities were: Boston, Philadelphia, New York, Baltimore, Salem, Charleston, Newport, Providence, New Haven, New London, and Norwich.

Source: Marc Faber Limited.

But after the opening of the Suez canal in 1869, travel time from London to Hong Kong was reduced to just 40 days, with a further three days to Shanghai. Today, ships can cover this distance in about 25 days, and Boeing 747s fly from London to Hong Kong in just over 12 hours. Voice and message communication has become instant. Electronic bank transfers can take place in a fraction of a second. As a result, changes in the economic landscape of the world will occur much faster.

This speeding-up of the cycles of cities can be seen in the recent history of the United States. Table 5.1 shows the growth of American cities over the past 140-odd years. In 1850, urban real estate prices on the east coast were some 100 times higher than in urban centers on the west coast. But in 1950, this price differential no longer existed because the American economic geography had totally changed. In Hong Kong, huge 'new towns,' housing hundreds of thousands of people, are thrown up in a matter of months.

Faber believes that countries which began to open up following the breakdown of communism in the late 20th century can industrialize and become important commercial and financial centers in 20 years or less. Already, today, the total stock-market capitalization of China, at US$172 billion, is larger than Hong Kong's was in 1992. Hong Kong, although a major financial center, had a stock-market capitalization exceeding US$50 billion for the first time only in 1986. In 1997, real estate prices in Hong Kong were eight to ten times higher than those in Beijing and Shanghai. But what about in ten years' time? It appears exceedingly unlikely that the differentiation can be maintained.

What is clear is that world trade flows are about to go through a period of dramatic change. 'In the next ten to 20 years, the changes we are going to see in terms of new centers of wealth will be mindboggling,' says Dr Doom. 'Only investors who understand this will be able to capitalize on the changes.'

1   Tertius Chandler, *Four Thousand Years of Urban Growth* (New York, 1987).
2   Edward Gibbon, *The History of the Decline and Fall of the Roman Empire* (London, 1780).

3   William Temple, *Observations upon the Provinces of the United Netherlands* (1720; reprinted Cambridge, 1932).
4   V. A. Smith, *Akbar*.
5   Will Durant, *The Story of Civilization* (New York, 1954).
6   H. Candee, *Angkor the Magnificent* (New York 1924).

6

AN ACCIDENTAL MIRACLE

Discovering Asia

The early 1970s saw Faber move across three continents. While working in New York for the American broker White Weld an opportunity arose for him to be posted back home, to work in the Zurich office of the firm, advising financial institutions in Switzerland and the Netherlands. He accepted, and found himself slotting in very easily. Europe was a mature market with a measured pace of life. In Amsterdam, Faber would visit his clients on a bicycle.

In the spring of 1973 his immediate boss, John Bult, offered Faber the opportunity to be transferred to the firm's Far East operation. He would be based in Hong Kong, but would have to travel around Asia, servicing clients in Japan and elsewhere.

On a 'sniffing around' mission before formally accepting the new posting, Faber was flown to Japan for two days and introduced to several Tokyo firms. The experience was unsettling. Tokyo seemed very alien to a young European, and the people were impossible to communicate with.

He then flew to Hong Kong, where he was looked after by Rudi Bischof, a Swiss national who worked for Schroeders in the territory. The new arrival's first experience of Hong Kong — cramped Kai Tak airport, and a journey through some of the world's most densely packed tenements in Kowloon's Mongkok area — was not an enticing introduction to the city. But when Bischof later collected him from his hotel in a red, open-topped Spitfire, and drove them over the Peak to the tranquil, wooded slopes of Repulse Bay, Faber was enchanted by the dramatic beauty of the settlement off the South China coast. They stopped at a sandy beach and spent the afternoon water-skiing. Faber began to think that he could live in Asia after all.

After two days in Hong Kong, he went to Bangkok and then to Pattaya for a break. There, he saw another side of Asia. He became friendly with an attractive young woman who ran a nightclub, and found himself sitting on the beach listening to a Thai fortune-teller. 'You are going to move to Asia and you will never leave,' the man said. Faber realized the man was probably a charlatan, attempting to maximize his customer base, but a little node of superstition in his heart was touched. Maybe he should take this as a sign?

Why not? He flew back to Zurich to accept his new assignment. Compared to Asia, life in Switzerland had been safe, disciplined, and intensely boring. 'It's run like a high-class country club,' he told his friends. He wanted something different. Faber arrived in Hong Kong in August 1973, aged 26. Asia was the opposite of Switzerland: it was young, dynamic, and deliciously chaotic.

Since he had lost the clientele he had built up in Europe, Faber had in effect taken a pay cut. But it didn't seem to matter. Asia was cheap. With the exception of Japan, prices were extremely low compared to those he had left behind in Zurich and New York. A luxury apartment in Hong Kong could be rented for about US$800 a month. (By 1998, the same apartment would rent for between

US$8000 and $10,000.) The flagfall on a Hong Kong taxi was less than 20 U.S. cents (compared to the 1998 level of US$2). There was no subway train system; most of the cross-harbor traffic took place by ferry or sampan. Prices were so low that Faber found himself repeatedly asking whether the prices were in Hong Kong dollars or U.S. dollars. At the time, the exchange rate was US$1 to HK$5.

The rest of the region was little different. On his first visit to Taiwan, Faber found an old crumbling airport with very few buildings nearby. Tun Hua North Road, now a thriving business center, had just one sizable building, the Mandarin hotel, in which he stayed. Taipei was 'a bit of a dump.' Confidence was so low that U.S. dollars sold on the black market for a 20 percent premium. The Taiwanese were obsessed with the threat of a communist takeover by neighboring China.

But the night-life was wild. Rich Chinese traveled from all over Asia to spend weekends at the luxurious President hotel with its renowned Champagne Room nightclub where they patronized 'Asia's most beautiful girls.' In the famous Singapore Ballroom, an orchestra played the tango, the waltz, and the cha-cha-cha.

In economic terms, east Asia was small potatoes. Indonesia had no stock market yet, and the entire stock-market capitalization of Hong Kong and Singapore was only about US$2 billion and US$1 billion respectively. South Korea was so poor that its banks had problems raising money in the Euro-dollar market.

The financial sector was small and old-fashioned. There were no fax machines or cellular phones, listed options had not yet been introduced, the word 'derivatives' didn't exist, the *Asian Wall Street Journal* wasn't yet in circulation, and, even in large cities such as Jakarta and Manila, the telephones rarely worked.

Faber had few rivals. There was only a handful of American brokerage houses in Hong Kong apart from White Weld — Merrill Lynch, E. F. Hutton, Bache & Co.; and only a small number of British brokers, including W. I. Carr, James Capel, and Vickers da Costa, had offices in the territory. While the British firms were placing Asian stocks with British institutions, the business of American brokers was exclusively the sale of U.S. stocks to Asian investors. In the 1970s and early 1980s, American portfolio investors had practically no investments in Asia, apart from a few Japanese stocks.

Unlike many other Westerners, Faber quickly made friends among the Hong Kong Chinese. On the day he arrived in Hong Kong, he had gone to tea at the old Luk Yu Tea House and been introduced to a well-connected local broker named Raymond Hung. Faber later taught Hung's family to water-ski, and a strong friendship took root.

Hung introduced Faber to Tony Fung of Sun Hung Kai Securities, the son of a well-known business family in the city. They became close friends, and Faber used to stroll in and out of the Fung house as if he was a family member. 'Without Tony and Raymond, perhaps I wouldn't have stayed in Asia,' he said later. 'It's not easy to break into the Chinese community.'

The parents of Faber's new friends were sophisticated enough to realize that the world was rapidly becoming cosmopolitan. They encouraged the friendship, believing that a friendly contact with an understanding of how finance worked in Europe and the United States would be of great value in the near future. Sir Run Run Shaw, the film mogul, was known to be suspicious of foreigners, but his nephew Vee King Shaw became a close friend of Faber's.

At a cocktail party Faber attended in 1973, he met a Chinese tycoon named Chan and made a bet about the U.S. prime rate, which then stood at 12 percent. 'I wager it will fall to 6 percent next year,' he said. 'What? Impossible,' said the older man. By 1974, the prime rate had fallen to 6.5 percent. The tycoon, far from being aggrieved at the virtual loss of face, started steering his equities business through Faber's office.

Life was interesting. Hong Kong, Faber told his friends back home, was like the harbor of San Francisco, the bazaar of Marrakesh, the greed of Lebanese Beirut, the low-tax status of Monaco, and the night-life of Paris all rolled into one.

One morning in 1976, Faber was having a Chinese lesson at his apartment when the doorbell rang. At the door was a tall, stunningly attractive Thai woman named Supatra Srinark. She was a friend of the woman who was temporarily occupying Faber's guest room. 'I'm sorry, she's not here,' he told her. By the time he closed the door, the image of the 23-year-old visitor was implanted in his brain, never to leave.

They were soon dating. Supatra was a bombshell. She looked like a nice, demure, quiet Asian girl. But she was temperamental and strong-willed. She had been working as a flight attendant in the first class section of Cathay Pacific Airways when one day she was abused by a difficult and unpleasant female passenger. Supatra kept up her dazzling smile, but wreaked a terrible revenge on the woman. She slipped a *bombe* — a dome-shaped European ice-cream cake — into the woman's Louis Vuitton handbag.

The sabotage was eventually discovered. When the incident was investigated, Supatra admitted the deed and accepted her dismissal. It had been worth it.

Faber was delighted by this outrageous tale — and by everything else about Supatra, who was from a small town near Bangkok. The two were married on February 28, 1981. Tony Fung was his best man. Today, they have one child, an attractive teenager named Nantamada, which means 'love of the mother' in Thai. Faber and his wife are both strong-willed individuals, and have retained independent streaks. Supatra has become well-known in Hong Kong as the proprietress of 'Supatra's,' an upmarket Thai restaurant in the center of town.

More Money Faster Than Ever Before

Between 1973 and 1978, Faber spent a lot of time in Japan and was immensely impressed by its economy and hard-working people. He also regularly visited Taiwan and South Korea and felt that these two countries had economic potential similar to Japan's, but starting from a much lower base. He therefore invested some of his savings with South Korean and Taiwanese brokers. When people asked him how he would ever get his money out of these countries, since both had strict foreign exchange controls, he replied that he intended to leave it in these promising economies. Things would change.

The popular investment themes in the early 1970s were steel mills, ships, and shipyards. Every country wanted to own its own steel mills, equipped with the latest technology, and the larger the better.

And tycoons were especially gung-ho about the shipping industry. Shipping magnates such as Y. K. Pao, C. Y. Tung (father of Tung Chee-hwa, the first Chief Executive of Hong Kong following the resumption of Chinese sovereignty over the territory in mid-1997), and Robin Lo were among Asia's richest and most respected businessmen at the time, and were regularly featured on the front pages of business magazines. Every wealthy family wanted to own some ships. This ship-owning mania was whipped up by local and international banks, anxious to get their cut by lending people the vast sums involved. Many banks established finance companies for the purpose. At the time, shipping loans were considered to be as profitable an investment as Brady Bonds were later to be in the 1990s, and were regarded as totally risk-free. This ship-owning investment boom led to huge orders for new ships from which shipyards in countries like Japan and South Korea benefited grandly — but temporarily.

The 1970s weren't easy years for Asia. The oil crisis and the 1974 recession hit most Asian countries hard. Many steel mills became white elephants and tanker charter rates began to fall, leading to huge losses for ship owners and their lenders. But recovery followed, with resource-rich countries such as Indonesia and Malaysia, which had oil, experiencing a mini-boom late in the decade. Ironically, the greatest oil stock boom took place in the Philippines, a country without any oil. 'But Philippine geologists' findings have to be taken with a grain of salt, as investors in BRE-X Minerals now know all too well,' says Faber. However, mining and oil stocks aside, Asian investors weren't particularly interested in equities. Their attention was focused on copper, gold, and silver. In bucket shops all over Asia, gold was traded day and night.

During the gold mania of the late 1970s, Faber left White Weld and was running Drexel Burnham Lambert's Hong Kong operation. At night, when the local London gold market was active, his office resembled a casino. Crowds of gamblers would come to the premises and trade the precious metal markets ferociously — usually with borrowed money at maximum leverage. This led to huge losses for Hong Kong-based commodity brokers when the market collapsed.

'In those days, nobody paid any attention to the now-popular indicators such as Initial Jobless Claims or Change in Nonfarm Payrolls. What everybody anxiously awaited were the results of the U.S. Treasury and IMF gold sales,' recalls Faber. 'They wanted to know how much of the gold had been taken up by Middle Eastern investors and central banks. Commodity brokers and gold dealers made fortunes.'

In Asia at that time, the dream of young financial types was to land jobs as brokers in commodities futures. Few people thought it worthwhile to train as fund managers, research analysts, equity strategists, or bond or stock salesmen. There were no Asian equity strategists and just a handful of fund managers in firms such as Wardley, Jardine Fleming, and Schroeders. All this was to change.

During the 1982 global recession, a number of Asian countries suffered very badly. The petro-dollar flows dried up; and the real estate market in several cities, including Singapore, collapsed. But then strong U.S. consumption growth brought about an explosion in the volume of Asian exports, and the region really took off. 'Between 1985 and 1990, Asia was truly running on all four cylinders,' says Faber. 'The Japanese economic miracle was at its height and seemed unstoppable.' Also, because of Asian export growth averaging around 25 percent a year, the Asian region was flushed with liquidity. Much of this came from Asian countries' large trade and current account surpluses.

Not surprisingly, Asian stock markets soared. It was a heart-pumping, dream of a time to be in business in Asia. 'If ever there was a "best of all possible worlds" in finance, then we had it in Asia in the late 1980s,' the Swiss economist says. The liquidity-driven Japanese boom had spilled over to South-east Asia, whose exports at that time didn't have to contend with competition from China, Mexico, or Latin America.

Significantly, at the same time, South-east Asia gained the benefit of rapidly rising foreign direct investments. Where else could investors put their money? There were few other opportunities in the emerging markets. The Iron Curtain still existed in Europe, China hadn't yet been identified as an Eldorado by consultants of large multinational companies, and Latin America was just coming out of its early 1980s' depression and hyperinflation period.

The Door Opens a Crack

China's 'Open Door' swung ajar in the late 1970s, and Marc Faber was one of those who slipped in quickly to take a look around. What he saw amazed him. All the clichés of Chairman Mao's celestial kingdom were still intact — the squads of people in blue uniforms, the grey cities unadorned with billboards or any form of advertising, the huge population of bicycles on roads built for cars, the mile after mile of paddy fields worked by laborers wearing cone-shaped hats. China wasn't so much a different type of economy, as a bizarre, real-life fairy tale. One-fifth of the world's population were caught up in a huge experiment in which all the tenets of modern economics — the theoretical, the partially tested, and the completely proven — were denied. It was like a huge control group for an experiment intended to show what happens if a society is structured so that Adam Smith's 'invisible hand' is totally powerless. It was peaceful, slow, calm, rural — and terrifying.

As a historian, Faber immediately realized that there was no question as to whether China would join the modern world. It was inevitable that it would. The only issues worth focusing on were how it would come about and what the results would be. He knew, too, that it would all happen much faster than people expected. Ironically, it was a line of Adam Smith's that ran through his mind: 'Little else is requisite to carry a state to the highest degree of opulence from the lowest barbarism, but peace, easy taxes and a tolerable administration of justice.'

With this conviction that China would flourish, Faber pledged to undertake a study-visit every two or three years, a pact he still adheres to today, more than 20 years after his first glimpse of the closed kingdom. With each visit, he has become more bullish about the economic potential of China — and has added more warnings to his list of the difficulties of succeeding there. For as Faber came to know something of the depth to which China's ludicrous economic obstacles were entrenched, he realized the amount of change that would have to take place before its economy could link into the fast-globalizing financial system.

The first thing to do, he decided, was to mentally cut China up into a lot of small pieces: 'When one is talking about China, it is important to understand that at present there isn't really *one* China. Each region, province, city, and even village may be subjected to very different and distinct historical, economic, political, and social conditions.'

As usual, Faber parted from the conventional wisdom, which says that Guangdong, the province in the far south directly bordering Hong Kong, is the key region and the most likely candidate to become a successful Asian tiger economy. 'Foreign businessmen should think twice before investing in southern China,' he wrote to his clients in 1994.

Instead, he has been particularly bullish about several other parts of the country, notably the north-east, the area stetching from Tianjin and Beijing in the west, to Liaoning, Jilin, and Heilongjiang in the east. These provinces, which border North Korea and far east Russia, are rich in resources, and will benefit over time from increased trade within the region, and investment from Japan and South Korea.

But there was one city in China which stuck out as a winner: Shanghai. One particular visit, in 1994, stands out in Faber's mind. Following a previous visit to Shanghai in 1990 he had described the city as 'an obsolete, run-down metropolis.' In 1994, he found it transformed. The roads, the buildings, the traffic-clogged streets were no different. It was the atmosphere that had changed — the number of building sites, the buzz among financial people, the expressions on the faces of the people. 'It was a boomtown in the process of becoming Asia's most important commercial and financial center after Tokyo,' he wrote in a newsletter on his return.

When he first visited the country's largest broker, Shanghai International Securities, in early 1990, it employed about 50 staff. There were only about 12 security houses in Shanghai. By 1994, there were more than 500 security houses, and Shanghai International Securities alone had more than 1200 employees spread across 22 branches in Shanghai and another 20 or so in the other provinces. 'Never before have I seen a city change so much for the better, economically speaking, in such a short space of time,' Faber wrote.

He identified eight factors which made him particularly excited about Shanghai.

First, its geographical location sets it up for a boom. It is situated at the mouth of the Changjiang (Yangtze) river delta, and is China's main transportation hub. It is by far the largest port in China, handling a huge percentage of its total freight volume. The state news agency, Xinhua, has claimed Shanghai is the world's third-largest port. Even if one takes their reports with a pinch of salt, it is likely to be sizable.

Second, Shanghai is surrounded by the four population-rich and rapidly growing provinces of Jiangsu, Anhui, Jiangxi, and Zhejiang. These provinces have a combined population of more than 210 million. Combined with Shanghai, the industrial output of this region is more than three times that of over-hyped Guangdong province. Faber says: 'I have little doubt that Shanghai is in the process of becoming to these provinces what New York is to much of America: a major commercial, communications, transportation, and shopping center.'

Third, the location is important for external reasons, too. It is close to Japan and South Korea, both of which are eager to invest in and do business with China. Direct flights between Seoul and Shanghai take about two hours. Flying time between Shanghai and Tokyo is three hours. Shanghai is closer in air terms to both Europe and the United States than Hong Kong is.

Fourth, Faber, like many people in the region, believes the Shanghainese have their own special brand of financial magic. After 1949, many fled from that city to Hong Kong — and it is no coincidence that historians trace the birth of the Hong Kong miracle period of economic growth directly to the setting up of certain industries (such as textiles) by the Shanghainese immigrants from 1950 onward.

Fifth, there is a greater tradition of education in Shanghai than in the rest of China, with more students enrolled there than anywhere else. Of the 14 million inhabitants, there are more than 120,000 students. Compare this with Guangdong's 65 million population and less than 100,000 students.

Sixth, the overseas Shanghainese are a wealthy group living principally in Hong Kong and Taiwan, and most are eager to take advantage of their native city's economic revival and have begun to invest in it.

Seventh, Shanghai is well connected to the Central Government. Both Jiang Zemin, China's President, and its Prime Minister, Zhu Rongji, are former mayors of Shanghai.

And lastly, the Central Government has designated Shanghai as China's future financial center. When Faber visited the Shanghai Stock Exchange in early 1991, just after its official opening in December 1990, he found only eight stocks and 22 bonds listed. The stocks had a market capitalization of less than US$1 billion and foreigners had practically no access to the market. After his 1991 visit, he wrote: 'I wouldn't be surprised if within ten years the market capitalization of Shanghai exceeds that of Hong Kong.' By the mid-1990s, other analysts were agreeing with him.

The Swiss economist is ever mindful of how dramatically and swiftly the fortunes of individuals and cities can change. In relation to his theories projecting growth for Shanghai, he points out that the New York Stock Exchange in 1835 consisted of just 38 banks, 21 railroads, and 33 insurance companies. It was much smaller than the European exchange of Leipzig. Where is Leipzig? You have probably never heard of it, which is the point he wishes to make.

Faber believes that an increasing amount of direct investment will bypass the traditional route through Hong Kong and will go straight into China — with Shanghai being the most obvious target.

That's the good news. Now for the bad news. Shanghai, Faber admits, still suffers from many of the structural problems that plague the business scene in the rest of China. And these are not inconsiderable.

For a start, it has been clear for several years that Shanghai, like several other major cities in China, is gambling on a property boom. The whole city is one big building site, and even the most bullish Sinophile must have some doubts as to whether all these offices and residential complexes can be filled by people willing to spend enough money to make them a going concern.

Not only are there too many property developments, but they are over-priced. By the mid-1990s, corporate office rents in Shanghai and Beijing had risen to more than twice the level of those in Taipei, Singapore, Bangkok, and Sydney. Shanghai rents made Manhattan seem a bargain — there has to be something wrong here.

Not only will property be shaky in Shanghai, but the retail sector looks doomed to suffer for several years, Faber believes. There are simply too many retail and commercial outlets opening up. He visited a branch of Giordano, a successful Hong Kong garment chain store, and found the prices similar to those in Hong Kong — a surprise, since the purchasing power in Shanghai is a fraction of that of Hong Kong.

It is not just private businesses that are set to suffer. In the mid-1990s, more than 50 percent of the industrial production of Shanghai was from the infamously ill-managed state-owned enterprise sector. The obvious answer in almost any other country would be to trim staff and make it profitable. This is never considered an option in China, for ideological reasons.

With high costs and high inflation, Shanghai will no longer appear as an attractive place for industry, so it will have to undergo a transformation to become a services center, in much the same way as Hong Kong changed in the 1980s.

Faber believes that none of these problems are insurmountable, and that Shanghai will rise to become the dominant city of Asia (see Chapter 9).

But there are other parts of China worth watching. In 1991, Faber took a car journey along China's first motorway, the Dalian–Shenyang highway, the first leg of which had just been completed. During the trip, a thought impressed itself on Faber's mind: to be slow off the mark can be good. Countries which started to modernize late, did so much faster than the front-runners. Places such as Dalian and Shanghai were transforming themselves at speeds ten times faster than their counterparts in the West had done.

This principle was clearly documented by Brian Reading of Lombard Street Research of London, an analyst whose work has greatly impressed Faber. Reading calculated that Britain led the world into the industrial age from 1780 onward — and its real per capita GDP growth from then to now has averaged 1 percent a year. The United States and Germany, which began their industrialization 50 years later, have averaged 1.75 and 2 percent, respectively. Japan, which didn't start industrializing until 1875, has averaged 2.75 percent since then. South Korea and China, which began their industrialization processes in the early 1950s and 1960s, respectively, have achieved 5.5 percent and 5.75 percent growth a year.

'Fast growth comes from starting behind the world leaders and catching up,' Reading had said when presenting a paper on this subject in London in 1993.

It would be wrong to assume that this principle can cause the whole of China to modernize at high speed, but it is certainly likely to speed up the development of those parts of the country that were already well-placed for growth.

Dalian, Faber reckons, is a good bet. It has excellent port facilities, with practically no competition for goods going in and out of the heavily industrialized and resource-rich Manchurian hinterland. Its airport is likely to become a regional hub within north Asia. Flights to Beijing, Shanghai, Harbin, and Tianjin all take about 90 minutes. Flying time to Tokyo is three hours. Flights to Seoul will take about one hour, and to Taipei, two hours. He believes Dalian will eventually connect wth Russia's Vladivostock, which will be no more than two hours away.

Faber hasn't been the only one to note the attractiveness of this particular city, although it is virtually unknown in the West. By 1994, there were already more than 3500 foreign-funded enterprises in Dalian, a large proportion of which were Japanese. Matsushita, Canon, Toshiba, Seiko, and others have made sizable investments in manufacturing facilities in Dalian.

The other salient fact is that it *looks* nice. It's no tropical paradise, but it's all relative. China's north-eastern cities tend to be ugly industrial places with high pollution. Dalian has a seashore and a scenic peninsula. A golf club and a yacht club have been constructed with fine views. Many Hong Kong groups, such as New World, the Kerry Group (of Shangri-La hotels fame), and Cheung Kong have hotels or real estate developments there.

Many Japanese banks, as well as Hong Kong's Bank of East Asia, have already set up branches in Dalian, as has the Hongkong and Shanghai Banking Corporation.

So, several places in China have good prospects. So what? Can foreigners make money in China? According to the depressing talk in the bars frequented by old China hands in Beijing and Hong Kong, the answer is 'No.'

Faber admits that the difficulties must be recognized. There is a lack of legal infrastructure, the bureacracy is a nightmare, the rules and regulations keep changing, the tax laws are constantly altered, and 'an army of government officials from all kinds of ministries and government bodies keep showing up for monetary contributions.'

What about benefiting from China's economic growth through share-purchases instead? Faber shakes his head. 'The shares that have been made available to foreigners were all greeted with great hoopla — even among the Hong Kong Chinese, who should have known better. But they have proved disastrous.'

Faber adds, 'So far, it is mostly unattractive companies which have been listed on China's exchanges or placed overseas, while the attractive businesses, companies run by smart local and a few foreign entrepreneurs, haven't yet been permitted to raise public funds. In this respect, the Chinese government has been very smart and behaved like true capitalists. Before selling new and desirable merchandise, it got rid of the unwanted, obsolete, and old inventory to ignorant foreign buyers.'

Nervous Neighbors

At a Swiss Business Council meeting in Hong Kong in 1997, Marc Faber sat in the audience and listened to Rita Fan, the unpopular President of the Provisional Legislative Council, the team of pro-Beijing people appointed to replace the British-era legislators deemed to have been elected with too much democracy.

First, Fan attacked the electoral reforms of the last British Governor, Chris Patten. Then she bitterly criticized Martin Lee Chu-ming, the popular leader of the Democratic Party. Thereafter, she reassured the attendees that under the new administration 'freedom of speech and expression,' 'freedom of conscience,' and 'freedom of the press' would be safeguarded. But then she went on to lambast a 'Swiss who makes negative comments about Hong Kong in the Swiss press.' There was probably no one in the audience who didn't know who she was talking about.

In the question-and-answer session which followed, Faber found it difficult to refrain from questioning Fan about this obvious inconsistency — free speech is allowed, but not for a person who dares to criticize Hong Kong.

On June 27 of that year, the *South China Morning Post*, Hong Kong's largest English-language newspaper, published a supplement entitled 'New Era Business.' On page 4, a Chinese government official predicted that under Chinese rule Hong Kong's economy would have a better future. On page 6, a professor whose work was sponsored by a property company projected Hong Kong as a new Tokyo or a new London. On page 21, Robert Ng, chairman of Sino Land, was quoted as saying that Hong Kong was 'the center of the universe.'

Faber waved the supplement from the podium where he was giving a speech to the business community. 'This 28-page-long supplement doesn't contain one seriously cautionary or even negative comment.' Nowhere in the 28 pages did it say what it really was — one long advertisement, rather than a serious news report.

Could Hong Kong really be the new London or new Tokyo? 'As early as the 18th century, London was an unusual city, because more than 10 percent of Britain's population lived there, and the same proportion lives there now,' says Faber. 'More than 10 percent of Japan's population lives in Tokyo, and more than 40 percent of Japanese live in the Tokyo–Yokohama–Nagoya–Osaka–Kobe belt — a region which generates more than 60 percent of Japan's GDP.'

Hong Kong, he points out, has less than 0.5 percent of China's population. It isn't the capital of China. It doesn't have the industries of the Ningpo–Hangchow–Shanghai–Nanjing–Tsingtao–Weifang–Tianjin belt. And Hong Kong's language differs considerably from Mandarin, the language of the powerful and elite in China.

'Unlike Tokyo and London — or, for that matter, Shanghai — Hong Kong doesn't have the quality and the quantity of these cities' higher learning institutes: universities, technical colleges, medical and art schools, research laboratories, and naval and military academies. It doesn't have those cities' libraries, museums, temples, stadiums, churches, theaters, opera houses, scholars, intellectuals, artists, and scientists — all factors that make a city a truly great city,' says Faber.

But there are three factors which, above all, spell disaster for Hong Kong. An increasing amount of trade which went through the city now finds its way into and out of China through other routes. Second, it was obvious from the mid-1990s that Hong Kong's property market was due for a major crash. And third, the Hong Kong dollar, which is pegged to the U.S. dollar, makes the city one of the most expensive places in the world to do business — and that has to be bad news in the present climate.

The relationship between China and Taiwan is one of the thorniest in modern politics. China's leadership considers Taiwan to be a province of China. Faber believes there is little historical justification for this, and points out that so revered a Chinese statesman as Mao Zedong has stated on the record that he didn't believe Taiwan was really a part of China.

'For China, an independent Taiwan isn't acceptable for strategic reasons,' says Faber. 'A hostile power could use Taiwan as a base to control shipping lanes in the Strait of Taiwan. Also, an independent Taiwan would set a precedent for other provinces, such as Tibet and Muslim Singkiang, to seek independence as well.'

In China, Western parliamentary democracy is denounced as fake and an instrument of capitalistic exploitation. Readers of the *People's Liberation Army Daily* are urged to 'stick to the leadership of the Communist Party' in order to avoid 'social turmoil.'

In Taiwan, President Lee Teng-hui has proven that people of Chinese race are not unsuited for democracy, putting the lie to the claims of many of Hong Kong's leading businessmen.

'Totalitarian or military rule, or the so-called controlled democracy, may have been the best option for most countries in the early stages of independence,' admits Faber. 'But now, economic reforms, the market economy, and capitalism require market institutions with dependable rules and laws. Capitalism also requires individual freedom and independent thinking — something democracy is in a better position to accommodate. Thus the move toward democracy in Asia seems to be, from a historical perspective, an irreversible trend.'

Faber isn't surprised that the transition from a political system which resembles feudalism to sovereign power with liberal representative governments has created strong tensions. He believes that countries whose governments resist such changes may face a politically and socially more uncertain future.

7

WHAT REALLY HAPPENED
ON BLACK MONDAY?

The Good Old, Bad Old Days

Wall Street is buzzing. Ferraris and Porsche Targas are backed up in a line behind the yellow taxis. Almost all the trophy cars are red.

This is the late summer of 1987 and these are the good times. They are also the bad times. People here are being arrested and thrown into the slammer for doing things which they would have received a pat on the head and a fat bonus for a few years ago. The art of making money by networking, swapping hot gossip, buttering up useful contacts, was drummed into the heads of trainee traders as the most important thing they would ever learn — but it has now been outlawed under the name 'insider trading.' It was so unfair. At least, that's how many brokers felt, and even the editorials of the heavyweight magazines agreed there were areas in which there was no clear right and wrong in the issue. A *Business Week* article put it clearly: 'Many situations, however, fall into a vast gray area in which it can't be proved that someone with inside information is seeking to defraud investors. The result: People can't be sure whether they are committing a crime or just being astute.'

Marc Faber is walking along the shoreline at Battery Park watching the boats. He knows full well that trading on inside knowledge has always been a part of a broker's life. But at the same time, he is aware of the ironies of the situation. All brokers spend their time swapping stories and tips and rumors which drive markets. If a story you made up over your breakfast donut turns out to be true, does that make you an insider trader?

Faber chuckles as he recalls his own experience as a genuine insider trader of the worst sort. It was in the 1970s, when he was working as a broker in New York. He was dating a secretary at another finance house. She phoned him one afternoon and whispered down the phone that something exciting was happening. A certain company would be taken over that very day — probably within the hour. And yet nothing was going to be announced until everything was signed and sealed. Was this information useful to him?

It certainly was. Faber took it as a hot tip on which to cash in. He thanked her and immediately got her off the phone, so that he could dial his broker to buy as many shares in the company as he could afford at the time. When the bid was announced, it turned out to be a not-very-attractive share swap, and the stock price dropped. 'I must be the only person who lost money on an accurate insider tip,' he used to tell people.

Having been forced to think about the issue because of its high visibility in the mid-1980s, Faber decided he didn't like any sort of insider trading — not for any ethical considerations, but because it was an act of cowardice. He wrote in April 1988:

> I regard white collar crimes committed by highly paid executives as about the most despicable of crimes, since they

> involve very little risk. If Dennis Levine [a high-profile Wall Street executive jailed for insider trading] had been poverty-stricken and had walked into a bank and committed a robbery, I would at least give him some credit for his courage and boldness ... insider traders committed fraud not out of necessity but out of sheer greed.

Ever the historian, Faber was intrigued by the idea that there may even be a business cycle in major financial frauds. Such events occurred in 1873, the 1920s, the late 1960s, and in the 1980s. Each wave of fraud coincided with a booming stock market. A standard image of these occasions: persons formerly considered rich and respectable being led away in handcuffs.

Faber thought it too simplistic to blame greed alone for the financial scandals of the 1980s. 'After all, people are always greedy, not just during a boom,' he says. But there is a degree of exhilaration whipped up when money is moving around that makes people excited and careless. They see people making millions of dollars at high speed. In the 1980s, it was the takeover artists, the Wall Street gamblers, the arbitrageurs. Other people decide they want a piece of the action, and the rules start to get bent.

There were other reasons for the liveliness of the financial markets in the mid-1980s, not all of them good. Particularly worrying, in Faber's view, was the fact that it had become really easy to gamble on the markets with other people's money. No longer did you have to find a rich uncle. The development of index futures contracts (betting on where the Dow, or another stock-market index, would be at a certain date) went hand in hand with a huge growth in borrowing. With this type of deal, investors' minds were focused on a transaction sometime in the future — a transaction which, thanks to human nature, always consisted of a vision of themselves cashing out with a large profit.

Near the market's 1980s' peak, even a small investor could have controlled over $150,000 worth of stocks by buying just one S&P 500 index futures contact, for a margin deposit of as little as $6000. In Hong Kong, near the market's 1980s' top, the Hong Kong index futures contract had a value of about HK$200,000, but investors only had to stump up a cash deposit of HK$10,000 to $15,000 — so 95 percent of the money was someone else's.

Of course, futures contracts were often portrayed as good tools for hedging (organizing counterbalancing gambles to offset the effects of negative changes in the value of your main holdings). In Faber's view, this actually added to the problem, since it gave investors a false sense of security. The system only worked well if your downside and upside forecasts were roughly correct and the proportions were correctly balanced. This was rare. 'While such a strategy may work for a few relatively small investors, it clearly can't work if all investors implement it at the same time,' he told his clients.

Faber was bearish on financial markets in the mid-1980s. He recalled how he had stunned an audience in Australia by playing the role of Superbear to the hilt at a presentation in December 1986. 'Sooner or later, the current financial mania will stop in very much the same way all excessive speculation ends,' he had said. 'With a collapse or bust which invariably follows the boom. It is a sudden fright and occurs quite often without much cause. It involves a rush from less to more liquid assets, and results in sharply declining prices. Panic and distress follow, as speculators want to get out at any price ... stock prices will decline by at least 50 percent — more likely by 70 percent — from their highs.'

Then he made them smile by pointing out that Wall Street may be due for a tumble, but Asia was on the rise. After the coming crash, 'one U.S. dollar will no longer buy 160 yen; rather one yen will buy 160 dollars. Democracy in the West will be threatened.'

Men in suits will no longer shuffle figures on screens, but will actually have to do something to earn their living, he continued. 'People will work again. Index futures, currency options, Reuters screens, and financial conferences will no longer exist. Budget deficits will belong to the past, and a gold standard will again be in place, with one ounce of gold equal to US$3000.'

This was tongue-in-cheek, of course, but there was a serious message underneath: the financial picture is due for a dramatic change. Wall Street will crash. But Faber painted an attractive scene for investors in the Asia-Pacific for the years ahead. 'The societies in Asia will rise. Japan, Taiwan, South Korea, and Singapore will provide the technology, China and India the labor, Indonesia, Malaysia, and the Philippines the natural resources, and Australia, the beautiful beaches, casinos, and good oysters.'

A hand went up in the audience. What will trigger the crash, and when will it happen? 'As was the case with the Great Depression in the 1930s, no one will know exactly why the collapse of 1987 or 1988 occurs,' Faber had replied. He had made similar warnings in his letters to his clients in 1986: 'From a business cycle point of view, it is not an opportune time to purchase financial assets. We recommend a high level of liquidity.'

He was encouraged in his view by the distaste for cash which was evident everywhere. Also in late 1986, he told his clients: 'It seems as if cash is an untouchable commodity. Customers who have cash are compelled to rush into department stores to buy useless items. Cash holders are outcasts and are laughed at by the stock speculators who perform so well. I believe that in 1987, a diversified cash portfolio may outperform stocks and bonds.'

After his stern warnings of 1986, Faber toasted the forthcoming crash of 1987 on New Year's Eve and waited for it to happen. But instead the market soared, and kept on rising. Nineteen eighty-seven was a boom year. By the fall of 1987, Faber was having a seriously bad year. The promised crash had simply not materialized. He later explained to his public exactly how wrong he had been:

> As far as the first half of 1987 was concerned, I was totally wrong. The year opened with a salvo. In New York, the market soared from 1890 in late December 1986 to 2428 in early April, without any significant correction. Other markets performed even better ... After a brief correction in the April to June period, the markets soared once again to new highs in August. On August 25, 1987, the U.S. market hit a peak of 2722, having risen 43 percent since the beginning of the year.

The numbers don't lie. He had been wrong.

It wasn't just Wall Street that was booming. From the end of 1986 to their respective highs of 1987, Mexico's stock market rose a stunning 692.4 percent; Europe climbed slightly more sedately, but still with real muscle, with Norway leading the pack with its index up 65 percent and the U.K.'s FTSE Index climbing a muscular 45 percent. At least he had been right about one thing: the Asian markets had performed wonders for those who had invested in them. Taiwan was up 349 percent, Thailand up 126.79 percent, South Korea up 92 percent, Singapore up 68.9 percent, Hong Kong up 53.8 percent, and Japan up 42.5 percent. Even the 'sick man of Asia' was thriving: the Philippines' commercial and industrial index was up 115 percent, and the mining index was up a remarkable 268 percent.

But still, most of the investors who really trusted him were sitting on cash deposits which were doing nothing. Faber, convinced he would be proved right sometime before the end of the year, continued to compile lists of signs that the boom was about to end and a crash was imminent. Again, the lesser indices provided clues that the main indices appeared to have missed.

By the autumn, Faber noted that the Dow Jones Utilities Index had topped out in late January and failed to follow the industrial averages in making new highs in April and August. Although the industrial averages moved up sharply through 1987, there were notably fewer shares involved in the advance. He was particularly intrigued by what he found when examining a list of the ten-day moving average of stocks making 12-month highs on the New York Stock Exchange. The list shortened itself continuously as the market rose (see Table 7.1).

Table 7.1 Ten-day Moving Average of 12-month New Highs

	Feb 1986	Jan 1987	April 1987	Aug 1987
Dow Jones	1709	2101	2369	2722
	335	157	129	108

Faber also looked at other indicators, including some of the more esoteric ones favored by the more geeky technical analysts. One such chart, known by the delightfully Professor Brainstormian name of 'the short-range oscillator upside-downside volume and advance decline line,' had clearly peaked between January and March. 'If ever I have seen clear early warning signals, I see them here,' he told friends.

Yet, other investment analysts were saying that the minor indications of a topping out might be there, but the major signs of a crash were missing. Even Faber had to admit that the speculative excesses that signified grossly overbought markets were not immediately in evidence.

Other investment advisors were unashamedly bullish. The American Robert Prechter had become a big name by 1987. He had predicted a major rise in stock-market prices through the 1980s, and had named 1988 as the year when the Dow would peak at 3600. At the time, this seemed ridiculously high. Only when the Dow topped 1900 and moved into 2000 at the beginning of 1987, did people change their attitude to Prechter. By August of that year, Prechter's view was no longer the outside chance, but the established wisdom. 'Prechter's opinion has now come to represent the majority view (69 percent of a Financial News Network audience poll think the Dow will get to 3600 in 1988),' reported Dick Davis in his August 24 newsletter.

Other newsletter writers were also forecasting a continuing climb. 'What we said last time still goes: We still see absolutely no reason to reverse our long term bullish view,' wrote Stan Weinstein in the *Professional Tape Reader* on August 28, 1987. The people who know, he pointed out, were also buying. 'It's also bullish for the major trend that Corporate Insiders are selling relatively little stock. When most bear markets start, they are selling quite heavily.'

Faber had had discussions with many professional money managers in New York, and the recurring theme was 'the market simply doesn't want to go down.' They weren't foolish enough to believe that it would go on rising forever. But it definitely had another year or so's worth of upside, they said. By the autumn of

1987, there seemed to be a general consensus that the worldwide equities bull market would run for another six to 18 months, with a recession tipped for 1989. There was another reason why you could relax: 1988 was an election year in the United States and the stock market had a strong tendency to rise in election years. Hang on in there, financial advisors told their clients. Stay out, Faber told his clients, but with increasing fear that he may be wrong.

The bulls had an argument which they kept repeating: there was no evidence that excessive speculation was taking place. In 1983, there had been the craze for technology stocks, which had ended in disaster. Today was different. A huge range of small investors were buying shares in mutual funds, a relatively safe investment, and professional fund managers — people who presumably knew what they were doing — were channeling this money into the stock market. The rising market was based on the fact that the economy was doing well. Much of the investing today was overseas, with the financial scene becoming truly global. Dozens of unit trusts focused on countries thousands of miles away had been launched. The risk was thus spread. It all fitted together neatly enough. Where were the speculative excesses? There were none.

To Faber, it wasn't surprising that people preferred to take a positive view. Here, in Battery Park, business was booming. Cafes were opening up serving expensive mineral waters and fancy Californian cuisine, pricy gyms and health clubs were all the rage, and dealers in fancy cars thought they had died and gone to heaven. Not only were there spectacular yachts moored in the harbor, but some even had their own helipads.

In the glass and stone canyon of Wall Street, traders had become the gods of the finance houses. The way they swaggered, they felt themselves to be masters of the universe, taking the role that commodities dealers had taken in the 1970s. Since the whole financial services industry had expanded so quickly, there were just not enough bright young things to go round. Brokerages had taken to poaching each other's staff. In 1987, the salary for young traders was often in the range of US$200,000 to $500,000 a year. They joined with golden handshakes and left with golden parachutes.

Standing on the curb at Battery Park, Faber noticed that the limousines parked in front of Wall Street's glass cathedrals had become longer, and their users had grown younger. That's when he realized what was wrong. It was no use looking for specific examples of excess. The entire global equities investing scene itself had become one huge speculative excess. The crash was coming. It had to.

A Delayed Disaster

There has always been a venue for Hong Kong's two major foreign populations to meet. The public and press refer to the groups as the 'expats' and the 'amahs,' but the distinction appears to stand largely on racial grounds. In more honest parlance, Caucasians and Filipino domestic servants are both simply migrant workers. In the late 1980s, there were some 100,000 more men than women in Hong Kong. There were also tens of thousands of domestic helpers, a group which was more than 90 percent female. Naturally, all these spare men and spare women would find a place to get together. In 1987, the place was an underground dive called The Neptune.

Newspaper reporters through the years have made much of how Marc Faber has been known to hang out in the sleazy bars of Wan Chai late at night, as if he is a woman-hungry sailor on shore-leave. The truth, as always, is more prosaic. Faber's uncomfortable 24-hours-a-day work schedule means that the only places open when he enjoys what the rest of us would call an 'evening' drink (in the early hours of the morning) are the bars of Wan Chai.

Fictions such as *The World of Suzie Wong* have left most people thinking of Wan Chai as a red-light district. In fact, Hong Kong has two brothel quarters, but neither is in Wan Chai. They are Mongkok and Sham Shui Po, on the other side of the harbor, and they are designed for locals, not tourists. The 'girlie' bars that remain in Wan Chai are now outnumbered by the shops selling Italian marble toilet tiles, as the successful growth industry in the area has been the supply of materials for the construction and interior design industries. The former topless bars are now sad, under-populated venues where tourists wander in and are fleeced by *mamasans*, who arrange hookers at enormous prices for curious visitors.

But few local residents, Chinese or otherwise, would dream of entering any of them. Instead, they use the other types of bars in Wan Chai for social drinking and dancing. The Neptune and the other bars of that ilk were not primarily brothels. They have always had multiple purposes. They serve as bars; they work as discotheques; they are pick-up joints; and a little, informal prostitution goes on from time to time.

It is this second breed of bar which Marc Faber favors: the drinks cost a reasonable amount, and the atmosphere is relaxed. Several of the men are there, not to pick up women, but to have drinks and unwind after a long work shift. And some of the women are there to spend a little money, rather than to make a lot of money. You can have a drink at any time of the night, and you can talk.

On this particular Monday night in 1987, Faber is not much in the mood for talking, but sits alone at the bar deep in thought. Normally, he goes to the bar to clear the cobwebs of his work-day out of his mind, but not tonight. The events of the past few days have been too dramatic.

In fact, the whole month had been one of rising tension for him. During September, Faber made a close study of a number of key stocks. He was particularly struck by one trend: a curious weakness in U.S. retail stocks, which had failed to repeat their highs of earlier in the year. He wrote a technical report to his clients:

> What is striking is that a number of retailers (Limited, Gap, etc) have broken down below their May/June lows and have in the process formed well-defined double tops ... it would therefore appear that substantial downside risk still exists and we would advise our clients to sell retail stocks now or on any rebound. While it is useful for the investor to recognize that retail stocks have topped out, it is even more important to realize what this decline of retail stocks is signaling from the economic point of view. Usually, when retail stocks rise, it heralds an improvement in consumer spending; but when retail stocks fall sharply, it indicates that the consumer is tired and is running out of money.

Faber highlighted some other bad news points: brokerage stocks were suffering badly, with Salomon, for example, down from $60 to $30. Important shares such as IBM, General Motors, International Paper, DuPont (all companies sensitive to the economy as a whole) were performing poorly, with their stock prices lower than at their March or April highs. Also negative was the collapse of some leading stocks in their respective industries: Cray Research, and companies such as Limited and Telex, were examples. Airline shares also had very poor chart patterns. Drug stocks, along with the tobacco issues, were showing signs of weakness and added vulnerability to the market.

Still, the bigger names in the forecasting business remained bullish. George Soros, the legendary financier who had made a fortune with his Quantum Fund through the 1970s and 1980s, was featured on the front cover of *Fortune* on September 28. The headline was memorable: 'Are Stocks Too High? New Ways of Valuing Shares Give Some Surprising Answers — George Soros, Who May be Wall Street's Most Successful Investor, Thinks the Volatile Market Could Climb a Lot More.'

On October 5, Faber had a surprise ally: Robert Prechter, the superbull, had suddenly turned bearish and put out a 'sell' for anyone trading the Primary or smaller trend.

> We see a hundred market letters and magazines in this office every week, and after months of cautionary rhetoric, suddenly every other publication we read is calling for 'Dow 3000 by year-end.' Rest assured I would be very happy to see it; in fact I hope to see it, but the minimum target of 2700 which had been on the front page of *Elliot Wave Theorist* since April has been achieved, and lots of company is something I am not accustomed to and do not prefer to have.

Martin Zweig, in the October 9 *Zweig Forecast*, was also opening himself up to the possibility that something bad just might be lurking around the corner, although his tone remained bullish:

> The overall pattern of recent weeks is not unlike that of 1929, 1946 or 1962, just before stocks crashed. Still, it's hard to stop a bull market, and even with all the reversal days, bearish interest rate trends, lagging secondary stocks and record low divided yields, the bull might right itself and go even higher.

Not all tipsters were hedging their bets. Faber had recently picked up the *Hong Kong Stock Market Weekly Review*, published by James Capel's office in the territory, dated October 12–16. Here was a fine example of delicious, unapologetic bullishness:

> Buy
> Buy More
> Increase Weighting
> Fill Your Boots.

The analyst who wrote the text under this headline was anxious to share his favorite fantasy:

> In the hurly burly of daily trading it is easy to lose sight of what is real and what is not. Strategies can be warped by immediate concerns instead of being shaped by longer term trends. We invite investors to share with us a vision of what is possible and to put the market risk into proper perspective ... the risk is also much less than commonly supposed. Thus our resounding recommendation: BUY.

When there was a sharp fall of 108 points in the Dow Jones Industrial Averages on Friday, October 16, there was confusion. Stan Weinstein, in his October 16 issue of the *Professional Tape Reader*, became distinctly negative:

> The consensus is that this 'surprise decline' is the long awaited correction and is a great buying opportunity. We disagree. First, we don't feel that this sell off came totally out of the blue in a wonderfully healthy market; and secondly, we still feel that caution makes a whole lot more sense than does bargain hunting.

Faber took the tumble as a sign of the end for both the 1980s' boom and the worldwide boom. He wrote to his clients on October 17:

> We feel that investors should now lighten up on stocks and markets which have not yet declined ... we believe that the sharp fall in New York has signaled a change of direction in share markets from up to down and from an expanding economy to a depression. Another characteristic of the first decline from a top is that, at the onset, investors remain extremely complacent and naively continue to believe that the decline merely represents a correction within a rising market. In such a situation, hardly anyone realizes or wants to admit that the trend has changed from up to down.

Still, Faber did not see a major crash as immediately imminent, and expected one further rise before the major crash. 'At current levels, we no longer advise our clients to sell indiscriminately, but to wait for a rebound.'

On the morning of Monday, October 19, he had opened his *Wall Street Journal* to find conflicting views on what the Friday fall really meant. There was no clear consensus. Analysts had polarized into the positive and negative. One article in the *Journal* began with these words: 'The stock market's rout last week may signal opportunity, according to W. Parker Hall III, the new manager of Vanguard US Growth Portfolio.'

The paper's lead article neatly summed up the atmosphere as one of uncomfortable uncertainty, but not by any means panic. 'What Next — The Plunge in Stocks has Experts Guessing about Market's Course,' said the headline.

> As trading approached the closing bell Friday afternoon, a trader in stock-index options on the American Stock Exchange floor shrieked, 'It's the end of the world!'
> Not quite. By 8pm at Harry's Bar, the Wall Street watering hole, hordes of yuppie brokers and traders clearly were preoccupied with getting dates for the evening rather than with the market carnage.

The article gave both sides of the argument:

> Although no one is forecasting a crash like that of 1929–30, there's a growing consensus that the bull market is seriously, if not mortally, wounded. Nevertheless, some see the next 300 point move in the industrial average taking the market back up to the 2500 level rather than down to 1900 ... and if US stocks looked cheap to foreign investors when the industrial average was at 2700, optimistic analysts contend, they should be even more appealing now.

In the media the same day, Merrill Lynch bosses William Schreyer and Daniel Tully expressed their 'confidence in the financial markets and the underlying value of financial assets in this climate.'

Faber was on the wrong side of the planet, away from the heart of the action, so he had to wait until 10.30 that night, Hong Kong time, to see what the Dow would do when it opened. First, trading seemed to seize up on many New York Stock Exchange issues. Brokers said it was caused by an imbalance in the orders being placed. The S&P 500 contracts opened at a sharp discount. People who were 'long' in the futures market were no longer confident of a climbing market and wanted to get out. Insurance programs were selling contracts as fast as they could. This fall triggered stock-selling programs. Everything was starting to collapse.

Faber watched the screen with his mouth open and a phone hanging on his shoulder. It was 1.30 am and the Dow had fallen a painful 150 points when Faber decided to call it a day. It was going to be a nightmarishly volatile day on Wall Street, but that had only been expected.

He was in no mood for dancing as he headed for The Neptune. He drank the health of the industrial averages, and then headed home to bed. From force of habit, he slipped his and his wife's phones off their hooks before retiring for the night and falling into a deep sleep.

Faber was woken the next morning by a loud knocking at the bedroom door. His domestic servant called his name, saying there was a phone call for him on the kitchen phone. Faber was amazed.

The two main phone lines in the house were both off the hook, and the third phone, used only by the servant, was a number that even he didn't know.

'Marc, it's Robert. Robert Bovet.'

'Where are you?'

'Geneva. Have you heard what's happened in New York?'

'Tell me.'

'It's down 508 points.'

'Yeah, *right*,' said Faber sarcastically.

'I'm not joking, Marc. I have a client who needs to sell some Nikkei Index futures on Simex in Singapore to hedge a 30 million-buck Japanese share portfolio. I need your help.'

That was when he realized Bovet was being serious. For several moments, Faber was speechless. 'Jesus,' he said. 'Yes, of course I'll help.'

Faber immediately phoned Edmond Yeung, the Japanese index futures trader at his office, telling him to sell Nikkei futures on the client's behalf. He told him to sell 30 contracts at any price, about 10 percent of what Bovet's client wanted sold. Faber expected volatility in the Nikkei futures market, and didn't want to dispose of the lot at what might be a bad opening price.

He phoned other market watchers and received the full, shocking news about Wall Street's worst day ever. The market had fallen from 2246 to 1738.4 in what could only be described as panic selling at a level never seen before. There was an almost equal frenzy to buy bonds. The fall in the Dow was equal to 22.6 percent — more than twice the percentage fall seen in the worst days of the Great Crash of 1929.

An hour later, Faber was in his office and received the second shock of his day. Nikkei futures were undergoing a staggering degree of volatility. The contract had closed the previous night at 25,210, but had reopened that morning at just 10,000. It had then dropped to an unbelievable 5000 before bouncing to 14,000 and then ending the session up again at 18,200. Unlucky investors who had sold Nikkei futures at the opening had to take a US$30,000 loss per contract by the end of the trading session. Faber was grateful that he had not put all Bovet's client's contracts out for sale at the opening price. The level of volatility was mind-blowing.

Another client of Faber's was rather luckier. He had obtained a buy execution on Nikkei futures at 9000, and then watched it double. He made a clear capital gain of US$1 million in a single day.

But the occasional triumph was far outweighed by the slaughter. The portfolios of the vast percentage of investors around the world, both professional and individual, were in tatters.

While America dubbed the occasion 'Black Monday,' for the Japanese and other people based in Asia, it was a case of 'Terrible Tuesday.' On the face of it, the carnage in Tokyo didn't seem as bad as that in New York. The Nikkei Index fell 3836 points to 21,910.08, a fall of 15 percent, in light trading. But this was misleading. Unlike London or New York, the Tokyo Stock Exchange imposed a daily limit averaging plus or minus 15 percent on price movements of individual shares. Most shares simply could not move on October 20, since the difference between buyers and sellers was too great. In fact, the real news in Japan was seriously bad by any account. The value of shares on the Tokyo exchange was slashed by more than 60 trillion yen (US$421.1 billion at the exchange rates of the time) on October 20 alone. Shares had never fallen so far or so fast in Japan.

In Hong Kong, the stock market was shut for four days, in a move that was widely criticized. The man who made the decision, Ronald Li, was accused of running the exchange like a club for friends, and was eventually jailed.

And what of George Soros, who predicted that the new ways of valuing shares showed they could climb much more? He didn't have a good week. On October 22, he decided to liquidate a large block of index futures. A report on the sale in *Barron's*, dated November 2, 1987, tells the whole painful story: 'The other pit traders, picking up the sound of a whale in trouble, hung back, but circled the prey. The offer went from 230 down to 220 to 215 to 205 to 200. Then the pit traders attacked. The Soros block sold from 195 to 210. The [downward] spiral was ghastly.'

Soros was estimated to have lost US$200 million that day alone. His Quantum Fund suffered a total loss of US$840 million over a two-week period, wiping out 32 percent of its net asset value.

Faber's favorite story of the 1987 crash was that of David Bloom, an accidental contrarian investor. This 23-year-old fraudster pretended to be an investment advisor in New York. He collected more than US$10 million from friends and associates. Although Bloom never intended to invest in equities, he hired two employees who sent regular but fictitious portfolio statements to his clients. The money he collected was used for the purchase of a house in East Hampton and for an art collection. Faber commented, 'Luckily for Bloom and his clients, the art and property markets didn't fall during the crash and therefore his clients' funds performed much better than if he had invested them in equities.'

8

THE CREATURE THAT
ATE TIGERS

—·—··—··—··—··—·····—·—··—··—··—·—·—·

Preparing for the Pacific Century

In 1960 the typical urban Asian woke up
to the sound of the jackdaw. In 1990 he
woke up to the sound of the jackhammer.
The whole region appeared to have gone
construction-mad. Buildings were thrown
up at record speeds. And they weren't just
quick-fix boxes. We're talking serious
skyscrapers here. Kuala Lumpur, Singapore,
Tokyo, and Hong Kong all had world-class
monolithic towers, buildings which
genuinely seemed to have their heads in the
clouds — a seeming message, perhaps, for
the people who built them. To the rural
citizen taking his cassava crop to market in
town, the main cities of Asia appeared to
have become massive building sites. Who
was financing all this? That didn't seem to
be a problem. Tycoons borrowed money
from willing foreign investors and queued

up at auctions to buy land. How could poor Asians afford to buy the resultant condominiums? Easy. They didn't cost anything. Someone or other will provide 100 percent financing — just sign here, thankyouverymuch.

Japan may have stalled in 1990, but its problems seemed to have no effect on the rest of Asia, which had gone pell-mell in the direction of any sort of growth at any sort of price.

And why not? Citizens felt they had every right to preside over an orgy of property development. East Asia had shouldered its way into a prime position on the world stage in remarkably little time and fully deserved its rewards. The region had done well in the 1970s, and business had accelerated in the 1980s. By the early 1990s, economies had been growing at 7–8 percent a year for about a decade. Just 30 years earlier, much of what had been written in the West about Asia focused on the region's perceived problems: What can be done about the poverty? How were they going to feed their already-too-large populations? How can we stop them having babies?

These issues dropped out of the spotlight in the 1980s and a different theme emerged. First, the world decided that it wasn't bad, but good, to find 'Made in Japan' on the back of products, particularly electrical ones. Then the world learned about the four tiger economies — Hong Kong, South Korea, Taiwan, and Singapore — which had speedily achieved GDP rates comparable to those of the rich industrialized countries. Then these countries' poorer neighbors — Malaysia, Indonesia, and Thailand — started to attract attention, because they, too, seemed on their way to becoming tiger economies. Then, of course, there was China, a country that only seemed to have started to exist in the Western consciousness after Japan dropped out of it in 1990. After opening its doors in 1978, the world's most populous country had gradually started to follow the same road of Western-style market liberalization as had its smaller neighbors. And it was surely destined to become the largest tiger of them all. 'Emerging markets' was the investors' battle-cry of the early 1990s, and East Asia was where the best ones were located.

That was the time when Asian business people claimed the

future. The forthcoming 100-year period was dubbed 'the Pacific Century' (although those who were particularly bullish on China and bearish on Japan argued that it should be called 'the Dragon Century').

Nineteen ninety-seven dawned with the Asian business community in a state of relaxed confidence. 'Asian nations look set to play a leading role in world trade in 1997, following successful reinforcement of their position as the world's most dynamic traders in 1996,' said the section on trade in the *Far Eastern Economic Review*'s *Asia 1997 Yearbook*. Nineteen ninety-six had been the year when world trade in goods and services hit the US$6 trillion mark for the first time, and the most robust performers were the Asian nations. Not only did they deserve a pat on the head, but they were models that others could follow, the writer said.

> Armed with a new-found confidence, Asians took centre stage at the World Trade Organisation, the Geneva-based global trade watchdog: Singapore hosted the WTO's first ministerial meeting in December. And Asia's striking economic success prompted other international agencies such as the United National Conference of Trade and Development (UNCTAD) to recommend that the region's policies of export-orientated industrialisation should become a model for other nations seeking rapid economic development.[1]

Certainly the figures spewed out of the region's central bank computers in 1996 looked good. Business was expanding in both imports and exports, although the latter seemed to be growing faster than the former. Asia had exported 9.5 percent more and imported 13 percent more in 1995 than in the previous year.

Although export growth was considered most important, commentators took the expansion in import growth as good news too: it was all trade, after all. The more vigorous of the Asian economies showed import growth of 14.5 percent or more. Imports into South Korea and Malaysia grew by almost 20 percent. These compared with a world average of 8.5 percent growth in imports.

The European Union's import and export growth figures, in comparison that year, were a feeble 7 percent and 7.5 percent, respectively. The United States showed an unexceptional rise in imports of 7.5 percent and an 8.5 percent hike in exports.

What about the other emerging markets? Asia's performance was notably better even than these. Latin American exports grew by 11.5 percent that year, while imports rose a modest 4.5 percent. Central and Eastern European states also emerged as strong exporters, registering growth of 9.5 percent, but their import growth was smaller, at 6.5 percent. Yes, in 1995 and 1996, the Asian miracle was proceeding nicely.

For much of the 1990s, many popular economic commentators were not just enthusiastic about Asia; they were positively worshipful about it. And they seemed to have the evidence to back themselves up. In 1960, the East Asian economies, including Japan, contributed only 4 percent of the world's output. By 1995, they contributed 24 percent, the same amount as the U.S., Canada, and Mexico, reported John Naisbitt in *Megatrends Asia*. 'By the century's end, if current trends are played out, they will be responsible for one third of world output,' he added.[2]

That book was one of a dozen written about the economic miracle region, with names such as *Asia Rising* and *Pacific Destiny*. There was no shortage of dramatic statistics to back up the claims of a miracle. And there were no obvious reasons to think that the miracle wouldn't go on — if not indefinitely, then at least for the foreseeable future.

Economists did the math: since the economies of most Asian countries were growing at between 7 and 10 percent a year, this would mean that they would double in wealth in ten years at the slowest, or seven at the fastest. China, the biggest of them all, was registering GDP growth of 12 percent a year in the early 1990s.

It wasn't just the building sites all over the place that were evidence of the Asian miracle. Life in some of the poorest parts of Asia had changed dramatically. Most notably, China, locked into the past until the end of the 1970s, had finally started to catch up. A survey in 1995 showed that 85 percent of households had a television and 35 percent a washing machine. These people, together with a growing number of Indians, Indonesians, Malaysians, and other Asians, were joining the consumer society.

Certainly you could feel the difference in Chinese cities, just as you could in Vietnam or Sarawak. There were traffic jams in Shanghai's Nanjing Road — and the vehicles backed up for miles were cars, as well as bicycles. Gone were many of the soulless, product-less Friendship Stores. The new shops in Shanghai (and Beijing and Guangzhou) were similar to those in Hong Kong: American-style supermarkets, drug stores, and boutiques. The shops in Nanjing Road stayed open late into the evening, and an estimated 1.5 million visitors looked in every day.

And what did people in China buy goods and services with? Credit cards were used by several million people — a tiny number by the standards of other large countries, but remarkable for China. By 1994, eight million cards were in circulation there, and the People's Bank of China announced its plans to have 200 million cards in circulation by the year 2000. India had 1.75 million credit-card holders by 1995.

'The Asian middle class, not counting Japan, could have between 800 million and 1 billion people by 2010, resulting in a stunning $8 trillion to $10 trillion in spending power,' wrote Naisbitt. 'That's in the neighbourhood of 50 per cent more than today's US economy. It took Britain's middle class nearly a century to evolve. In Asia today, that process is being accomplished in little more than a decade.'[3]

But could Asia keep up the pace? The *Asia 1997 Yearbook* said that economic activity had slowed a little in 1996, but wasn't about to come to a halt.

> World investors are still voting with their capital, ploughing funds into China, Indonesia and Malaysia at a record pace. Even long-time laggards like the Philippines are earning the moniker 'tiger', and getting glowing reviews in the world press.[4]

The success of Asia was made more emphatic by the poor performance of some other areas. Japan was stuck in recession, and

Europe was in a slump, hit by high unemployment and other problems. The United States was booming, but was a mature economy, unable to offer the high returns promised by enterprises in Asia. Eastern Europe and Latin America were improving, but they seemed not to have the money-making energy that Asia had.

Financiers naturally consider the risks before investing. But Asia seemed a safer bet than many others. Trustworthy records of solid growth stretching back for ten or 20 years were at hand. Many Asian currencies were pegged to the U.S. dollar, so currency risk was minimized. Interest rates were high, and the stock markets seemed to be in upward mode. Even Japan must have bottomed out by now, they told themselves.

This is not to suggest that international financiers lived in a state of delusion. But they certainly seemed inclined to look on the bright side, not realizing that behind the slick façades of the new Asia, an old one lurked menacingly.

Kovan Khrishnaswamy, a tourist visiting Laos in 1991, was delighted to find that he could get clean bottled water, a modern, air-conditioned room, and even french fries. But he was much more surprised when he hopped on to a local bus — in diametric opposition to the strict instructions of his government-sponsored tourist guide — and headed out of town into the Laotian countryside.

'As we left Vientiane, slowly the houses fell away, until we were just driving alongside the occasional shack,' he said. 'Then the shacks fell away, and we were on a road with nothing on either side. Then the road fell away. Then we were just driving along in the dirt in a jungle with no signs of civilization at all.'

Hey, Where Did it All Go?

The Asia-Pacific crash was like no other in history. For a start, it wasn't a crash. It was a series of discrete and individual financial battles, strung out over a wide swathe of the planet. Second, it happened in slow motion, with a year between the first cracks in the concrete and the thud of the later pillars collapsing. Third, it was focused on currencies and bad loans instead of stock markets, the general large-scale financial battleground of choice. And fourth, there appeared to be a human malevolence about it, although to a lesser extent than some commentators — notably Malaysian Prime Minister Mahathir Mohamad — would like to think.

Nineteen ninety-seven started normally enough, with many Asian countries filing their usual healthy figures as far as the leading indicators were concerned. The Japanese economy appeared to be in recovery mode after its recession, but the advances seemed depressingly small. Thailand, South Korea, Singapore, Taiwan, and Malaysia had all seen economic growth slow in 1996, but they were all still getting richer.

There appeared to be nothing major to worry about. In Indonesia, for example, figures released in early 1997 showed that the country had received US$22 billion in approved foreign investment in the first eight months of 1996. Investments meant growth, right? Economists predicted that average growth in the years to the millennium would be at least 7.1 percent a year.

But not long after the New Year drinks were cleaned up, things started to go wrong. The first problems appeared in Thailand in January, when the country's currency was shaken by a wave of speculative attacks. This didn't appear to be a deliberate attempt to ruin a country's economy, but rather a case of the financial markets spotting a weakness and going on the offensive to turn a profit — which is, after all, what markets are designed to do. The financial community was turning negative about Thailand for several reasons. There was a fat current account deficit, and export growth had slowed. The two were bad signs which were particularly negative when seen together. When analysts noticed the alarming size to which Thailand's private foreign debt had grown, a monstrous 250 billion baht in the property sector alone, the 'tiger' label lost its magic. Shaky debts are shaky debts, whether they are owed by an individual, a business, or a whole nation. Worries crept from the property sector to the finance sector: if there was all that unsafe debt in property, were the banks truly safe? Or was there something seriously wrong here?

The Thai government dipped into its coffers to fend off the attacks, but with little success. By mid-February, the stock market was suffering, down 14 percent from its mid-January heights. By March, large corporate victims of the financial problems had started to show up. A large and stately Thai company, Somprasong Land, surprised the business community by defaulting on a $3.1 million Euro convertible bond. Observers waited for more skeletons to turn up.

By early summer, economists inside and outside the country were doing the math and didn't like what they saw. There was a huge amount of private foreign debt — some US$81.6 billion — and about half of it was in the form of short-term loans locked into the property business. The trouble was, the property business wasn't performing, so how could they be paid back?

The growing fears were increasingly justified by events. A major finance company, Finance One, collapsed in April. A wave of financial panic then set in, and efforts to calm the markets down got nowhere. A string of government financiers left their posts or were sacked. In the end, the government abandoned all pretences of democratic process and resorted to enacting executive decrees to push through urgent policies in the finance sector.

Another 16 finance companies were suspended on June 27, and Thai government officials met in secret to decide on what dramatic steps they could take to restore stability to the teetering economy.

After a middle-of-the-night meeting on July 2, a big step was taken: the baht, standing at 25 to US$1, was decoupled from the U.S. dollar. It immediately fell to 28 to US$1. It then was revealed that US$23 billion had been spent defending the baht, and some US$14.8 billion of that was lost.

Thailand turned to Japan for help, but that country had its own problems and its officials couldn't countenance taking on such a large entity as a whole collapsing country. Officials in Tokyo suggested the Thais go, cap in hand, to the International Monetary Fund, and that's what they did. On August 5, tentative austerity measures were introduced and a further 48 finance companies were suspended. On August 11, the IMF unveiled a rescue package for

Thailand in Tokyo totaling US$16 billion from the IMF and other Asian nations.

* * * * *

Indonesia's troubles had mainly been political. President Suharto's family had become spectacularly wealthy at the country's expense. There was some uncomfortable news in the financial sector, too. The current account deficit had more than doubled, from US$3.5 billion in 1994 to US$8.8 billion in March 1997. Private debt, the problem which had worried analysts in Thailand, was clearly a huge problem in Indonesia, too. It had reportedly doubled in three years, from US$28 billion to US$56 billion by March 1996. But ministers tried to keep the people calm. As long as the country's energetic economic growth continued and the currency remained stable (which had not been a problem up till now), financing the deficit with capital inflows would be straightforward enough.

But when it became apparent that Indonesia's debts were bigger than Thailand's, and the real figure was a massive US$65 billion, confidence started to evaporate. Capital started to flow out. Currency speculators, seeing opportunity, rushed in, and the rupiah was badly savaged, dropping to a fraction of its mid-summer value. The problems escalated. By the year's end, the Indonesian government's total foreign debt was revealed to be a staggering US$117 billion.

Indonesia's currency meltdown was a long, slow nightmare that stretched from August well into the following year. Suharto was compelled to agree to the liquidation of 16 banks, including three partly owned by members of his family. He, too, had to go cap in hand to the IMF, which promised him a US$33 billion rescue package.

* * * * *

It quickly became obvious that Malaysia, neighbor to Indonesia and Thailand, shared many of the same problems. It, too, had a large current account deficit, looming asset bubbles in its property and stock markets, and a highly leveraged economy. That eroded confidence, with disastrous consequences for both the ringgit and the Kuala Lumpur Stock Exchange. By October, the situation was reaching crisis proportions.

Prime Minister Mahathir Mohamad blamed the troubles on American financier George Soros and other currency traders. He threatened to ban currency trading in Malaysia — a threat that wasn't carried out. Mahathir was certainly correct in that there is an undeniable human element in attacks by currency speculators. But their motivation — profiting by spotting or manipulating movements in markets — isn't much different to the motivations of any other financial market, be it equities, or gold, or soybean futures. Perhaps it's the way they attack, rather like a pack of hounds looking for a wounded deer, that makes them raise the ire of non-financial people.

Malaysians learned in October that certain mega-construction projects were to be cut, but the Kuala Lumpur markets failed to rally. The government ignored the negative response and instead continued to pour out blame in the direction of the West. Mahathir hinted darkly about Jewish conspiracies against his largely Muslim country.

* * * * *

In the north, South Korea had been having a really bad year all by itself, without taking much notice of the crisis taking place to the south. A series of major business collapses had kept the government in hot water all year. It started on January 23, when Hanbo Iron and Steel collapsed under a debt load of 5 trillion won. The loans amounted to some 16 times its own capital.

The discovery that the chairman of the company, Chung Tai Soo, had paid bribes to politicians turned the collapse into a government scandal — which escalated when it became known that the son of President Kim Young Sam had been involved in the deal.

On March 20, another steel-maker, Sammi, went bankrupt when it failed to make payment on its 1.9 trillion won debt. Further collapses followed, most notably that of the Kia Group, a car-maker.

With the country demoralized and debilitated by the corporate disasters, it seemed inevitable that it should catch a bad dose of the 'Asian flu' that was doing the rounds of the countries to the south.

By August a full-scale financial disaster was in progress in South Korea, with the currency sliding and share prices plunging. The country was on the verge of bankruptcy. By late November, officials gave up the fight and the IMF was contacted to bail it out.

* * * * *

Although corruption, nepotism, cronyism, and similar sins which run through the Asian financial systems received much of the blame for these crises, in hindsight the problems appear to be much more to do with the international markets simply losing confidence in Asian countries, one after another.

The other negative factors just seemed to act as proof of poor management — and proof that the officials concerned were not going to be able to pull their countries out of the mess in which they found themselves. When confidence evaporates in a country, it has a host of predictable, and instant, repercussions: capital stops flowing into the country, loans from foreign banks are called in, the currency comes under attack, companies go bankrupt, the stock market is driven down, and prospects for economic growth dwindle or disappear.

It seemed to be almost by chance that Thailand was the first victim. Once the international business community had withdrawn from that ravaged country and was mopping its brow, it decided to take a look-see at Malaysia, Indonesia, and other countries — and found exactly the same problems in each of them. Confidence fled from each in turn.

Hong Kong at first seemed immune to the problems of the other economies. However, in October 1997, speculators hit the currency hard and the overnight interest rates banks charge each other shot up to 300 percent. The currency survived, but the stock market didn't. On Thursday, October 23, the Hang Seng Index plunged 10.4 percent, and on the 28th, it fell 13 percent.

To the south, the Singapore dollar had fallen 9 percent against the U.S. dollar by October, and the markets followed the same route down. Although the government insisted it was confident the city-state could weather the storm, it was obvious that Singapore, being so small, would be affected by the problems of its neighbors.

The Seeds of Destruction

The Asian crisis of 1997 hit hundreds of millions of people at all levels. Thousands quickly lost their jobs, in Indonesia, South Korea, Thailand, Malaysia, and elsewhere, and tens of thousands of further job losses were expected over the following few years. Unemployment, previously not a problem in Asia, suddenly became top of the agenda. The people who retained their jobs were also hit. Their income and savings, in international terms, suddenly fell by 30 percent or more, wiping out all the interest payments and wage inflation of the past three to five years.

The losses of the wealthy, including many of Faber's friends and clients, were counted in hundreds of millions of U.S. dollars. Faber estimated that, in 1997 alone, Asia's 500 richest families outside Hong Kong and Taiwan lost, on average, between 50 and 70 percent of their net worth. Most were hit by falling equity prices and currency depreciation, and their losses were multiplied by their cross-shareholdings. These families' wealth tends to be principally tied up in their own companies' publicly traded shares, of which they were frequently majority shareholders and against which they often borrowed in order to finance private deals.

Furthermore, it had become quite common for many Asian families and their companies to borrow funds offshore, where interest rates were lower than in their local capital markets. 'A large number of these families' private investments, including factories, hotels, commercial and residential properties, boutiques for the mistresses, golf clubs, casinos, etc, will lose money for a long time and may even become white elephants,' Faber said.

Asian governments were also feeling the pinch, since most countries had large foreign borrowings. Following the Asian currencies collapse, interest charges and repayments became heavier. Banks started to experience the problems of soaring numbers of bad commercial and consumer loans.

Financing new projects immediately became more expensive, as Asian companies saw their credit ratings downgraded. Raising funds through equity issues also became tough as the appetite of foreign investors for Asian equities diminished — or disappeared entirely.

Faber had repeatedly written in his reports about the booms and busts which are endemic to rapidly growing emerging economies, with particular reference to Asia. In 1993 and 1994, he had expressed serious concern about the grossly inflated stock markets of Asia. 'These reports were largely ignored by investors, whose optimism about Asian stock markets was fueled by buzzwords about Asian values, the rise of the East, the tiger economies, and so on,' he said. He was particularly suspicious of the phrase 'paradigm shift,' which sounded dangerously akin to 'new era' when used in a financial context.

The rather unwieldy title of his newsletter of April 12, 1994, had been: 'No Joy for Foreign Investors in Asia (and Elsewhere Too) ... and Even Less to Come!' He gave clear warnings about the blind spending in Asia.

> No matter how badly a company is run, how poor its future prospects may be, or how obsolete its assets and technology are, it can sell its shares to the public at a substantial premium to its private market value. This is especially true for a company blessed with a location in a politically unstable country such as China, India, Thailand, or Indonesia, where neither asset values nor earning power can be precisely appraised.

Which of the world's many investments was most to be avoided? 'Since the gold boom of the late 1970s, I cannot recall any investment theme that has caught investors' fancy on a global scale as much as the Asian emerging stock markets.'

Despite the fact that the crash vindicated him to some degree, Faber had to admit that the scale of the disaster stunned him. 'The

Asian crisis has left me shellshocked,' he wrote to his clients in February 1998. 'I have never read of, or seen, such a total economic breakdown and massive destruction of wealth as has occurred, against all expectations, in Asia in the last six months.'

Faber traces the problem back to 1990, when he believes the seeds of destruction were planted. During the 1985–1990 boom period, Asian exports were growing at about 25 percent a year, far above the long-term growth trend. This was laudatory, certainly. But it wasn't sustainable, and couldn't be. Export growth had to slow down. This was inevitable, for at least five reasons.

First, overseas customers weren't spending. The 1990–1991 recession in Europe and the U.S. caused the Western consumer to cut back his spending: consumption growth came to a standstill. In the recovery phase which followed, the spending increase reached only moderate rates of growth. The consumer was burdened with 'negative equity' on real estate he had purchased in the boom-times of the late 1980s. Also, after 1990, Japan went into depression and cut back on its spending on Asian raw materials, such as plywood, lumber, and base metals.

Second, the Asian nations simply didn't notice the growth of competition. A number of other developing nations went through structural, economic, and political reforms which had a direct effect on Asian business. These nations opened up and began to compete with Asia in exporting to the large Western consumer markets. The competition of new entrants such as China in export markets had an impact. In the 1990s, the former main exporting countries in Asia had become too expensive. Suddenly, it was almost impossible to afford an office and staff in South Korea, Taiwan, Hong Kong, or Thailand. They had lost their competitiveness.

Third, the natural cycles called for a slowdown. Even without the competition from the *nouveau arrivistes* in export markets, Asian export growth was on a downtrend. Asia's export volume had grown from US$400 billion in 1985 to US$1.4 trillion in 1996. Think about it. When your exports make up less than 15 percent of total global export trade, you can grow pretty fast, at speeds of up to 30 percent a year. But when you find yourself with close to 30 percent of the market in a world competing vigorously for market share, you aren't going to be able to keep up that rate of expansion.

Fourth, the Asian nations didn't have the right balance of imports and exports. Just as their exports began to slow down, imports started to increase at an accelerating pace. With rising prosperity, Asia's new rich developed an almost insatiable appetite for foreign brands. The successful Asian business person wanted to wear Ferragamo shoes, Pierre Cardin suits, Gucci belts, Hermés ties or scarves, and Ralph Lauren shirts. 'Asia's *jeunesse dorée* also wanted to own Mercedes, BMWs, and Harley bikes, and to furnish their flats with Italian furniture and Japanese consumer electronics,' says Faber. 'They drank lots of Hennessy XO and later switched to expensive French wines, smoked Cuban cigars, and traveled and shopped more and more overseas.' Thus, as Asian consumption rose, imports of consumer goods soared.

Fifth, many Asian businesses made the classic mistake of increasing capacity just when they should have been reducing it. By the early 1990s, companies had become accustomed to the 25–30 percent export growth rates of the late 1980s and perceived this export boom to be a permanent feature and not just an aberration of the long-term trend, argues Faber. As a result, manufacturing capacity was added everywhere in order to meet the Western consumer demand that was expected to rise forever — in Faber's book, a typical case of the 'error of optimism.'

The foreign investor — surprise, surprise — also made silly mistakes. Outsiders increased their direct investments in Asia in order to capitalize on the promising domestic markets of Asian countries. But while foreign direct investments had a favorable multiplier effect on economic growth in Asia, they also meant the trade accounts suffered from further deterioration. Practically all capital goods had to be imported. 'They were usually imported at inflated prices — in order to get even with the local partner, or for tax purposes,' says Faber. Once the factories were operational, higher-value assembly parts such as car engines had to be purchased from foreign suppliers in Japan or elsewhere.

So, at the end of the 1980s, import growth rates began to exceed export growth rates, which led to a gradual but nevertheless visible deterioration in Asia's trade surpluses.

A large sector of business in Asia which suffered from poor calculation was tourism. During the global prosperity of the late 1980s, inbound tourism in East Asia increased at about 20 percent a year and provided Asian hotel owners with very high rates of return. The Bela Vista in Macau was charging US$20 a night in 1987, and, in renovated form, around US$380 a night just ten years later.

Many of Faber's rich Asian clients liked to own a hotel, or even better, a golf course. In the case of Thailand, hotels were useful as a way to launder money. In the 1980s, there seemed to be no reason why they shouldn't expect tourism to continue to grow at 20 percent a year, so a range of hostelries, from business inns to resorts, were built in every country in Asia. World tourism slumped with the Iraq war of 1990. From then onward, it recovered very slowly, because Asia's favorite tourists — the Japanese — stayed at home, worried about their moribund stock market and wounded property market.

Worse still, new tourist destinations such as Eastern Europe, China, Vietnam, and Latin America started to offer good-value holidays in the 1990s. As a result, many Asian cities — with Bangkok being one of the worst cases — became glutted with hotel rooms. 'They are now largely vacant,' Faber says.

There was worse to come. Just as inbound travel was slowing down, Asians began increasingly to travel to Europe, Australia, and the U.S. It was no coincidence that East Asia's travel trade surplus started to dwindle. This, together with worsening trade balances, led to a general deterioration in the current account balances.

But perhaps the worst-managed sector in Asia was property, Faber believes. During the late 1980s, excess liquidity badly inflated Asian property prices. The problem was further exacerbated by the tendency of Asians, at this time, to flee their rural farms and seek their fortunes in the bright city lights. Businesses built export-oriented manufacturing plants on the outskirts of cities, to take advantage of these cheap workers. The rapid industrialization led to wage increases. In the meantime, foreign companies opened offices and built factories in and around Asian urban centers, and staffed them with well-paid expatriates, which increased the demand for real estate even more. Thus, in the busiest urban parts of Asia, residential and commercial real estate prices rose several-fold.

Again, real estate prices rising relentlessly on the back of strong domestic and foreign demand was regarded as a permanent feature of the Asian region. People saw no reason for such increases to stop — forgetting that prices don't need reasons to stop rising. They pause and go into retreat from time to time because of their in-built cycles.

Property buyers simply forgot that in the 1970s and early 1980s, Asian real estate prices had been steady or even falling. The result of all this mass amnesia was an unprecedented construction boom which swept across Asia in the 1990s, leading to the present situation — literally millions of apartments standing empty over the region.

Another imbalance was the mismatching of asset inflation and real wage gains. In most Asian countries, the inflation of real and financial assets over the past ten years or so has far exceeded median real wage gains. Income disparity has widened. Families who owned properties became immensely rich, on paper anyway, while workers and pensioners who rented their homes were impoverished. This latter group either had to pay higher and higher rents, or were forced to borrow heavily to buy homes at inflated prices. Naturally, this wealth discrepancy, which has lately been further aggravated by the currency devaluations, leads to a slowdown in consumption. (For a look at how the under-consumption business cycle works, see Chapter 4.)

In purely theoretical terms, Faber was pleased to have been proved right about the weaknesses in the financial infrastructure of most Asian countries. But he was distressed at having been so far out on timing — after all, in the investment business, timing is everything.

Why had he been so mistaken? Faber later identified five factors that staved off the economic collapse, which, he believes, should have happened in Asia several years previously.

First, consider Asia's relative imperviousness to the Black Monday stock crash on Wall Street that shook the world. A number of Asian stock markets were hardly touched. The South Korean stock market actually rose on the day following the Wall Street crash of October 19, 1987. By 1988, most Asian stock markets had already exceeded their 1987 highs. At their 1989/90 peak, the Taiwanese and South Korean stock markets had both risen dramatically from their pre-1987 crash level, by another 300 percent and 250 percent, respectively. Indonesia, whose stock market had remained totally inactive and depressed until 1987, rose almost sixfold between 1987 and 1990. In Japan the Nikkei Index soared from a pre-1987 crash high of 26,646 to 38,915 in late 1989.

This sensational recovery in Asian stock prices boosted investors' confidence in the merits of Asian equities. 'It reinforced their belief that Asia was really something special and that any setback in share prices was actually a lifetime buying opportunity,' says Faber.

There was a second boost to investors' confidence shortly afterward. In 1990, there was a recession in the U.S. and Europe. East Asia hardly felt the effects, because strong domestic consumption growth offset the temporarily weaker exports. The exports subsequently bounced back in 1991. The theory in the investment community was, then, that Asia's economic cycle had 'decoupled' from the Western world and no longer depended on exports for growth.

Third, concerns about the slowdown in outbound exports were set aside. After all, Asia-philes said, interregional trade was expanding so rapidly that it would eventually replace exports to the industrialized countries. Who needs the West? People in the Asian investment community really felt that the world's business cycles no longer applied to them, says Faber. Conveniently, strategists and economists took Japan (which by then had gone into recession) out of the Asian region and began to talk about 'Asia ex-Japan.'

Fourth, the curious currency situation also misled investors in Asia. Since many Asian currencies were closely linked to the U.S. dollar, exchange rate risks were perceived to be minimal. This led investors around the world to invest more and more of their savings into higher-yielding Asian currency deposits.

Then came the Mexican crisis in early 1995 which had the curious effect of raising confidence in the infallibility of the Asian economies even further. Asia's incorrigibly optimistic pundits argued: 'See, Mexico and Latin America have a financial crisis because they depended largely on portfolio flows. We in Asia, however, are recipients of far larger foreign direct investment than portfolio flows. And since foreign direct investment flows are far more stable than portfolio flows, which can leave a country overnight, we'll never experience similar problems.' Needless to say, Asian strategists failed to notice that after the Mexican peso collapsed in 1995, and as a result of the North American Free Trade Agreement (NAFTA), Mexican exports became extremely competitive and displaced some of Asia's exports, such as textiles.

Why did no one ring the alarm bell over the growing trade deficits? They were dismissed as irrelevant because they were due to imports of capital goods which were designed to produce consumer products for export, the fantasists said. In reality, they were used to produce consumer goods for the domestic market, Faber believes.

Faber's scoresheet would have looked much better if the Asian turmoil had occurred when the emerging stock markets fell sharply in 1994. It was, however, postponed for various reasons, some of which were delineated above. Having survived 1994, they were buoyed up by the powerful bull market in U.S. stocks which ran from 1995 onward, during which money continued to pour into the emerging economies until 1997. These money flows, although smaller than they had been in 1993, kept Asian stock markets fired up, and allowed Asian companies to issue shares and foreign currency-denominated fixed income and convertible securities in the international capital markets.

'After the global bond market rout in 1994, bond prices around the world rallied strongly, with spreads between lower-quality bonds and U.S. treasuries falling continuously after the 1995 Mexican crisis,' Faber wrote to his clients. 'Therefore, performance-oriented and yield-hungry investors, disregarding any risk, were only too eager to invest in domestic- and foreign currency-denominated fixed-interest securities of emerging economies, as they could profit from falling interest rates and narrowing yield spreads.'

Faber points to the naivety of many people in the Asian financial scene as another cause of the crash. By the early 1990s, the financial districts of Asian cities had become crowded with local and foreign brokers, investment bankers, portfolio managers, and battalions of private bankers. 'I've lived in Asia since 1973, and I have yet to meet a Thai, Filipino, Malay, or Indonesian stockbroker who wasn't consistently bullish about his respective stock market,' says Faber. 'These brokers traveled around the world with the sole purpose of having foreign investors purchase securities in their own capital market.' Excessive confidence, rising nationalism, and increasing self-awareness in Asia also had an impact. For a Thai broker to have been negative about Thailand would have been a national disgrace.

And the so-called sophisticated economies were just as bad as their less-mature neighbors. In Hong Kong, the head of the monetary authority vowed not to place any funds with foreign fund managers who were believed to have sold the Hong Kong dollar short. And in Singapore, any foreign-based analyst who made unflattering remarks about the Singapore economy risked losing his employer valuable government-related investment business, or even his own job, said Faber. 'Obviously, this doesn't shed a particularly favorable light on the quality of Asian leaders and government officials.'

Many of the Asian portfolio managers Faber met were about 27 years old and had maybe two years' investment experience. 'Most of them wouldn't even know what a map of Latin America or Eastern Europe looked like; nor would they have the slightest knowledge of capital markets outside Asia.' Their knowledge of economics isn't much better, either. When China began to open up in earnest in the 1990s and expanded its exports at a torrid pace, Faber appeared to be alone in identifying an obvious danger: that China's exports would gradually displace some of the other Asian countries' exports, or lead to a shift of foreign direct investment flows away from Thailand, Malaysia, and Indonesia.

Since the portfolio managers' livelihoods depended solely on raising as much money as possible for their Asian funds, they expended a great deal of energy discrediting skeptics of Asia's economic miracle. Experts who were critical of Asia, including Faber, were pooh-poohed at all levels. When no less an economist than Paul Krugman, a distinguished professor at the Massachusetts Institute of Technology (MIT), published a critical article about Asian growth prospects, numerous articles by Asian fund managers and strategists appeared saying that Krugman didn't know what he was talking about.

Faber sniggered at one such article by a noted Asian economist, published in the *Asian Wall Street Journal* on November 6, 1996, which concluded: 'For the time being, the tigers' structure looks firm. They will sooner or later ride out their present cyclical problems.'

The Swiss investment economist says a small number of serious analysts in Asia did identify problems. He picks out Paul Schulte (ING Barings), David Shairp (Caspian Securities), Jim Walker (Credit Lyonnais), and David Scott (W. I. Carr) as economists who questioned the sustainability of Asia's economic miracle well before the 1997 crash. He noted that 'their concerns were carefully worded as they faced being criticized by the management and sales staff of their own firms.'

Faber believes that international investment banks and private banks played a major role in the disinformation of foreign investors. Having just undertaken costly expansions in the region, their principal concern was to place stocks and bonds of Asian issuers in international capital markets. They didn't want their analysts to be negative about a company or a country, because that would jeopardize that bank's chances of getting a corporate finance mandate, or of participating in an underwriting syndicate. Similarly, many largely inexperienced private bankers told their private clients that relatively risk-free returns could be obtained by borrowing foreign currencies and investing in Thai baht or Indonesian rupiah deposits using high leverage.

Boomtime literature was much in evidence. Between 1993 and 1996, numerous books were published with titles like *Asia Rising*, reminding Faber of the bullish 'Japan Inc.' books which appeared in the late 1980s. 'Still, I don't wish to be too harsh on anyone for having been too optimistic about the Asian region, since I have been totally wrong about so many other issues since I started in this business 27 years ago,' he said.

'But I believe that in Asia, businessmen, brokers, government officials, investment managers, and economists, more often than not, put their self-interest ahead of objectively reporting the facts. Even to a layman, it should have been quite obvious that the fundamental positions of many Asian economies were showing signs of stress — and not just recently, but for the last few years. Everybody is putting the blame on someone else, and Asian economists who until six months ago lauded Asian leaders and central bankers for their economic management now blame them for their ill-conceived economic policies.'

In Faber's opinion, the accusations of blame that were made were pointless and irrelevant. 'If we accept the principles of free markets and a capitalistic system; and if accept that we have created, over the last ten years or so, a practically unregulated global capital market in which funds can flow from one corner of the world to another, then we must accept booms as well as busts. After all, capitalism without bankruptcies would be like Christianity without Hell.'

Medicine for Tigers

The bulls argue that following the currency devaluations, Asian countries' exports will be cheap again and start to expand, while the impoverished citizens will buy less, causing imports to decline, and bringing about an improvement in trade and current account balances. But by how much will Asia's trade and current account balances improve? And will they really lead to renewed vigorous economic growth?

Faber admits that devaluation can help in the long run. Following the 1995 Mexican peso devaluation, many Asian countries' export growth suffered. After China's 55 percent yuan devaluation in 1994, it gained a significantly larger share of total Asian exports. U.S. imports from China as a proportion of U.S. imports from Asia rose from 4 percent in 1983 to 26 percent in 1997. Thus, to some extent, recent devaluations in Asia should improve some countries' competitive position.

However, the beneficial effect of the recent Asian currency devaluations shouldn't be overestimated, he warns. Mexican and Chinese labor costs are still lower than their equivalents in Thailand, Malaysia, Indonesia, and the Philippines. Mexico continues to enjoy the advantage of lower U.S. import tariffs, being a member of NAFTA. Also, it is right next to the United States — which cuts shipping time to practically nothing.

To some extent, the pain will be shared around the world. Faber picks out Thailand as an example. Domestic consumption indicators are all in negative territory, so imports are likely to continue to decline. Foreign direct investments are also likely to fall — possibly sharply. After all, who would want to build another factory when consumption is collapsing and over-capacity is part of the problem? Also, infrastructure projects which have a high content of imported materials will either be abandoned or postponed. So, if imports of consumer and capital goods decline, it will curtail exports from the industrialized countries, especially Japan. And if Thailand is representative of the whole Asian region, then the industrialized world (and especially Japan) is due to suffer further.

How will the Japanese economy recover if its exports to Asia diminish? Asia now consumes 40 percent of Japan's total exports. Asia takes more from Japan than the United States and Europe put together.

The U.S. and Europe will suffer, too. In 1995, the ten leading Asian developing countries imported US$748.4 billion worth of goods from around the world. Given the size of that figure, the prospect of Asian imports stagnating or declining quite sharply should be disconcerting to the pundit who argues that 'the Asian tigers' structure looks firm.'

The ten leading Asian economies outside Japan have long been big spenders (see Table 8.1). These will all shrink.

To put the size of Asia's imports in perspective, Faber reminds his audiences that in 1995, small, now-virtually bankrupt South Korea's imports were 40 percent the size of those of mighty, richest-country-in-the-world Japan. If Asian imports decline, the industrialized nations' economies will surely be affected. The recovery of many

Table 8.1 Leading Asian Importers, 1995

	US$bn
South Korea	135.1
China	132.0
Taiwan	103.8
Malaysia	77.7
Singapore	76.0
Thailand	69.1
Hong Kong	53.7
Indonesia	42.2
India	31.7
The Philippines	27.1

industrialized countries in the 1990s was fueled by strong export growth to the developing countries. So Asia will buy less from the industrialized countries and they, in turn, will have less money to spend on items from Asia or on direct investments in the region. 'In short, this is a vicious circle similar to that in the 1930s,' Faber warns.

He also points out that Asia today is the world's largest user of commodities. The demand is likely to suffer, reinforcing the global deflationary trend he believes is now a major threat.

There are further threats to Asia's economic rehabilitation, he believes. Electronic products are now dominant exports in a number of Asian countries. It is easy to see how over-capacity could develop in this sector. For one thing, China is likely to wreak havoc for the other Asian manufacturers once its production facilities come on-line, which they will do by 1999 at the latest. Or the market for PCs and related products could slow down in the industrialized countries. 'Then even the prospect of this rapidly expanding export industry could be dimmed — another shoe to drop for Malaysia.'

Of course, economists naturally focus on macroeconomic factors, but problems like this are really human ones. The reduction of income for workers will have social ramifications, and political unrest has already been seen. Riots of the poor and dispossessed have been seen in Indonesia and China since 1996. These are likely to depress further the confidence of foreign investors.

But from a purely economic point of view, Faber picks out three immediate lessons to be learned from the fall-out of the Asian stock markets:

1. The business cycle is alive and well and hasn't been tamed.
2. Equities and economies which outperform for a while eventually regress to the mean.
3. Investors should always be wary of countries that depend on large foreign capital flows in order to sustain their excessive spending, 'a condition which will certainly one day also haunt the United States.'

1 *Asia 1997 Yearbook* (Far Eastern Economic Review, Hong Kong, 1998).
2 John Naisbitt, *Megatrends Asia* (London, 1995).
3 ibid.
4 *Asia 1997 Yearbook*, op. cit.

ADVENTURES IN *21*ST CENTURY
FINANCE: *A* PROPHECY

S cience fiction and financial analysis rarely overlap. But they do for Faber's followers. He has a penchant for projecting himself 20 or 30 years into the future and giving illustrative lectures or writing predictive papers which 'recap' on things that are yet to happen. Having studied these, the present writer offers the following fictional treatise, based on specific writings of Faber, and largely using his own words.

* * * * *

There's a slight sizzling noise as the electronic chopsticks in Faber's hand send a sanitizing current through the plump, pink *har gow* he has just picked up. The smell of burnt soy-plum sauce is curiously intoxicating.

But he pauses, the shrimp dumpling halfway to his mouth, and turns his head. 'What *is* that strange sound?' It isn't the hiss of the chopsticks, but the undulating rhythmic whirr from the window, that has caught his attention.

'Bicycles,' explains Geri Mulan Xi, a blue-eyed Chinese graduate student who had been assigned to be his personal assistant. 'There was a long power cut last night, and most of the electric cars have got no power today. People are using their old bikes instead.'

'Good,' mumbles Faber, referring both to the welcome absence of car horns and to the dumpling he is now carefully chewing with his remaining teeth.

The year is 2017, and Professor Marc Faber, now aged 70, is in the staff room of an imposing stone educational edifice on Nanjing Road, the main thoroughfare through Shanghai. Although technically in his fifth year of retirement, he has found himself unable to stop work. Today, a bright, temperate morning in September, he is about to give a press conference at the MBA school attached to the new Shanghai Museum of Financial History.

The Swiss economist lowers his chopsticks and flicks his wrist to trigger his watch. 'Ten fifty-nine local time,' says a synthesized version of his grand-daughter's voice. He stands up creakily, his old ski injury affecting his posture, and glances in the mirror. His ponytail and most of the rest of his hair have disappeared, but the mischievous eyes are as sharp and interrogatory as ever. He checks the top button of his shirt, takes a deep breath, and enters the lecture hall.

'I am in awe,' he begins, after he is effusively introduced in English and Mandarin by the museum's Director Lu. 'Shanghai is now Asia's most important commercial, industrial, and financial center. New York, London, and Moscow pale beside its wealth, opulence, and glamor.'

He looks at the rows of impeccably dressed, highly educated faces before him, and nods at a vaguely familiar young woman with a miniature television camera styled into her beehive hairdo. 'Even the fashion industry here has displaced Milan as a world trendsetter. Today, no other city in the world is as cosmopolitan as Shanghai in attracting artists, celebrities, business people, bankers, showbiz types — and ladies of the night — from all over the world.'

There is a chuckle from the audience at the last item listed. Faber smiles. 'Director Lu has given you all the information you need about the new museum, including a copy of my keynote speech from the ceremony last night. Are there any questions, comments, or items you wish to discuss?'

Ten hands rise, but the woman with the camera in her hair is already speaking. 'Is it true you are predicting doom for the Chinese economy?'

Faber leans forward, his palms flat on the table, and grins. 'Doom? No. A little trouble in the near future for local equities? Yes. Do you mind if I sit down?'

He lowers himself slowly into the seat and makes himself comfortable. 'Let me put this in context,' he says into the microphone that hovers in front of his lips. 'China has done extremely well. Shanghai especially. Real estate prices here exceed those of Tokyo, New York, Paris, and London, and are five times higher than those of Hong Kong. We are also in the midst of the greatest stock-market boom that China has ever experienced. Since the financial reform of 2001, the Shanghai Stock Exchange Index has risen by more than 30 times. Following its 85 percent gain so far this year, China's total stock-market capitalization now exceeds the combined value of all Japanese and U.S. equities.'

Next to him, Director Lu beams and bows her head slightly, as if she has achieved all this by herself. The old-fashioned reporters are scribbling with lightpens into their net-linked electronic notebooks, while others mumble into microphones slung across their mandibles, or use tiny remote controls to adjust the focus on webcams built into their spectacles.

Faber's face grows serious. 'But clearly, the present parabolic uptrend in equity prices, which is largely a function of huge inflows into the domestic mutual fund industry, isn't sustainable. A crash is likely to occur sooner or later.

'Whenever euphoria and excessive optimism lead to investment mania, caution and a reality check are warranted, even at a time when the economy has never been healthier. Moreover, the outlook for future growth appears to be exceedingly promising and has led our leadership to talk about "the dawn of a new era" for the people of China. Director Lu, I noticed, used precisely that phrase this morning. That means trouble.'

Director Lu's smile freezes on her face.

Another hand shoots up. 'What has been your worst mistake as a forecaster?'

Typical, thinks Faber. No coherence, no flow of ideas. Each reporter is focused entirely on the question that he or she wants answered. The Swiss investment advisor sucks in his breath through closed teeth. 'That's a difficult one. I have made so many. Some lost money for me, and with some I lost face, which was worse. I think that missing the U.S. bull market of the mid-to-late 1990s was one of the more painful financial mistakes I have made. That period seemed to last forever. I simply predicted the end too early.'

He lowers his chin on to his fingertips. 'My critics always say that it is easy to be a prophet of doom, since if one keeps predicting crashes, one will eventually occur. Yet the 1990s, when the U.S. stock market defied all calculation and logic for several years, shows that nothing in the prediction business is inevitable. The crash was a long time coming. But it came. Praise be to Kondratieff.'

'Why were fund managers so vilified in the early years of this century?' asks the woman with the camera in her hair.

'We all need someone to blame when we do something stupid. Individual investors have shown an uncanny ability to buy the wrong types of funds at the wrong time, and this was particularly true in the last decade of the previous century. They bought biotechnology funds in 1991/92, emerging market funds in 1993/94, and aggressive growth stock funds in the late 1990s.'

Faber explains how, in the mid-to-late 1990s, investors were buying huge amounts of index funds — funds which are tied to equity indexes, but which weren't managed or diversified, and held no safe cash portion. Because index funds had been outperforming active fund managers, fund managers were increasingly forced to buy stocks which had a heavy weighting in the S&P 500 in order to keep up with these indexes. 'The professional investment community was thus following the lead of the unsophisticated retail investor, who, not knowing the difference between McDonald's and Microsoft, had piled into index funds.'

This meant there had been a hidden role reversal in the late 1990s, he says. For decades, retail investors had worshiped active fund managers and followed their investment ideas. But fund managers had begun imitating the behavior of retail investors. 'We one-eyed portfolio managers were no longer leading the blind. The blind were leading us.'

A young man with Mongolian features interestingly offset by green hair raises his hand. 'Can you tell us about the great Wall Street crash?'

'Which one?' Faber asks. 'No, never mind. Let me talk about both of them. There were a remarkable number of similarities between the end of the 1990s and the end of the 1920s. At least, let me see, ten. Perhaps more. Yet so few economists noticed.'

He leans forward. 'Let me give you a little history lesson. From its low in 1920 to its peak in 1929, the U.S. stock market had gone though a spectacular bull run, having risen by more than 700 percent. In the latter bull run, the market had risen 1150 percent from a low in 1982 to May 1998, when I began to realize that a crash was really becoming extremely likely at last.'

Both were boom periods in the United States, Faber says. Investors in the last decade of the 20th century decided that there was no danger of a crash because they had already had one. There had been a reasonably sizable crash in October 1987, they recalled.

'That was a fatal error. They didn't realize that that was exactly what people were saying in 1928 and 1929. Most investors didn't know that there were several crashes before the great crash of 1929, with particularly severe "corrections" in 1926 and 1928. By 1929, people were saying that these should have been seen as buying opportunities, which is just what was said in the late 1990s about the 1987 crash — "I wish I'd got in then, when prices were on the floor."'

Just like in the late 1990s, people were saying in 1929 that the business world was entering a new era of prosperity — and just like people are saying today in China, says Faber. 'A respected commentator named Bernard Baruch said, in *The American Magazine* in June 1929: "The economic condition of the world seems on the verge of a great forward movement." Sounds like Director Lu this morning, right?

'In the late 1920s, many economists, including university professor Irving Fisher, became well-known figures running investment trusts. The *Wall Street Journal* reported in September 1929 — I don't remember the date now, it will be in one of my books — that this new system "concentrates large sums in the hands of experts ..." The most popular trusts, it said, were "managed by interests who have built up widespread reputations for financial acumen ..."

'Fast forward 70 years. A typical late-1990s' headline was one I clipped from the *International Herald Trubune* in the spring of 1998: "Economists Becoming Academia's Superstars." Investment banks were advertising themselves by pushing the personalities of individual star fund managers. You don't need me to tell you that similar things are happening today in this country.'

'Did you predict the 1929 crash, too?' asked a young woman who looked like she was about 12 years old.

'Come on! Please, I'm not *that* old,' says Faber with a theatrical frown. 'But I took an interest in my counterparts in that period. In the final years before the 1929 crash, a few bears had courted unpopularity by repeatedly advising people to get out of the market. William Peter Hamilton of the *Wall Street Journal* published four warnings between 1927 and 1929. The last of these was on October 21, 1929, eight days before the great crash occurred. Paul Warburg, head of Kuhn Loeb, had warned in March of that year that the amount of stock speculation threatened to lead to a market crash which would "bring about a general depression involving the entire country." Warburg was criticized for failing to grasp that the country had moved into a new era. Eventually, the nervousness had spread from bearish advisors to government officials. On February 7, 1929, the Federal Reserve Board of the United States warned about "the excessive amount of the country's credit absorbed in speculative loans."'

'Were you the only person to predict the millennium crash?' the same young woman asked.

Faber sighed. What a lot these young people had to learn. 'There are always bears and there are always bulls. Many economists, far more learned and far more significant than I, were forecasting trouble ahead in the 1990s. It wasn't just investment advisors who became nervous. Students of economic history may recall the words of Federal Reserve chairman Alan Greenspan in 1996 about the "irrational exuberance" of the market. One of the more vocal long-term bears, Robert Prechter, who had published an excellent historical study, *At the Crest of the Tidal Wave*, in 1996, predicted the demise of the equity cult. Before the millennium crash, he was also discredited.'

'Is it easier to be a bear or a bull?'

Faber pauses. 'Good question. The right answer should be that the hardest thing is to be a bear at the right time and a bull at the right time. But if you have to choose one, I would say that being a bull is an easier life. Less strain. Fewer complaints by financial people who feel you are scaring off their investors.

'In contrast, bears have always had a hard time. The 1929 crash, just like the millennium crash, started slowly. There was a series of small slips from September 3, 1929, when the Dow had peaked at 381 points. By October 1, a commentator in the *Wall Street Journal* peevishly wrote, concerning stock-market newsletters, "I find that 75 percent of them are bearish. They cannot see anything but bad news ... Now, why is it that everyone seems to get bearish when stocks have had a bad break? ... Don't forget to buy a few stocks when 75 percent of the trading element is bearish."

'After a brief rally upwards from — if I remember rightly — 329 points on October 4, the real fall began on Tuesday, October 24, when the Dow fell to 305 points. A commentator in the *Wall Street Journal* said: "The air has been saturated with pessimism for the last two weeks, but things will change. They always do." Famous last words. On October 29, the market imploded dramatically, wiping out the life savings of hundreds of thousands of investors. The more recent crash, as you know, affected hundreds of millions of investors around the world and the negative effects were felt in the United States' economy until very recently. We bears often have to wait a long time until we are vindicated.'

A hand was raised at the back of the auditorium. 'Professor Faber, the Chinese economy is doing fine. Why do you expect trouble? Surely there is only trouble when things are looking bad?'

Faber shook his head. 'On the contrary, things usually go wrong when everything is looking just fine. In the U.S. in the 1920s and the 1990s, the U.S. economy was in fine shape, everyone agreed. Straight after the crash of 1929, the richest man in the world, John D. Rockefeller Snr of Standard Oil, spoke publicly for the first time in decades. He said: "Believing that the fundamental conditions of the country are sound, my son and I have been purchasing sound common stocks for some days." The comedian Eddie Cantor responded: "Sure, who else has any money left?" After the millennium crash, Bill Gates of Microsoft made similar statements, as did Warren Buffett. Director Lu, your Prime Minister, and your other senior officials are saying the same thing about equities in China today.'

Faber goes on to explain how in both of the big U.S. crashes of the past 90 years, business leaders and government officials repeatedly made the point that any setback could only be temporary, since the American economy was in good condition and had no serious problems. President J. Edgar Hoover had said in 1929: 'The fundamental basis of the country ... is on a sound and prosperous basis.' President Gore had said at the turn of this century: 'This financial upset will not derail us for more than a brief moment in the overall big picture of the ongoing triumphant rise of these, the United States of America.'

'In both instances, many people blamed the fickleness of foreign investors for the problems, saying that many overseas investors had pulled out their money in ways that had triggered a panic,' continues Faber. 'Others said the problem was that so many people were borrowing money to speculate with. Then there was the media, which was publishing literally dozens of magazines and books every week trumpeting how easy it was to make money by investing in equities.'

It was unthinkable in the early 1930s and in the first few years of this millennium that the good times wouldn't return. 'The Harvard Economic Society made positive forecasts throughout 1930 and 1931, and did so until it was disbanded,' says Faber. Everyone was so confident. Yet the Great Depression followed. With few exceptions, each month saw the index lower than the previous month, and this situation continued until June 1932. By then, most indices had fallen by a further 80 percent from their lows of November 13, 1929. 'Most investment trusts either went bankrupt or their shares collapsed by 99 percent,' says Faber. 'Seventy years later, in the late 1990s, Wall Street strategists made positive recommendations for the next four or five years, until most of them were sacked. Many funds were wound up. Literally dozens of financial publications collapsed in the first five years of the 21st century. More than 85 percent of investors lost money in mutual funds by the year 2004.'

'How did you know the more recent crash would be so bad?' asks a tall youth of uncertain sex or provenance from the corner of the room.

'It was clear by 1997 that a period of global deflation was inevitable. At turning points from inflation to deflation, profits tend to collapse because prices fall and demand shrinks. This, I knew, could occur even if the corporate sector wasn't leveraged. Excessive government and consumer debts were sufficient to increase the debt burden by pushing real interest rates up, forcing aggregate demand down. Whereas the stock market in the United States in the crash of 1929 took three years to decline by 90 percent, in the more recent Asia crash, most markets declined by 90 percent in dollar terms in the nine months from the summer of 1997. For me, this was a clear indication that the financial markets had become a monster, unreasonably large in comparison with the size of the real economies they purported to serve. With the increase in financial instruments such as securitization, and with the growth of instant communication, I became convinced that the public would panic and dump stocks at a torrid pace.'

The young man looks unhappy. 'Could you explain that a bit more simply? What were the signs you spotted?'

Faber rubs his chin. 'Let me try. To young people like you, the 1990s — which is when most of you were born, I suspect — are part of ancient history, just like 1929. But people in the 1990s, including your parents, felt they were on the cusp of a new era of prosperity. In the 1920s and the 1990s, some stocks and groups of stocks were selling at huge multiples because mergers were expected to boost earnings and productivity.

'Then there was the technological revolution that was perceived to be taking place. A report published in 1929 by the Commission of Patents stated that more patents had been granted during the past ten years than during the 100 years from President Washington's inauguration — that is, from 1789 to 1899. One of the most far-reaching developments was the discovery that electricity could be distributed for huge distances through wires. Until 1912, electric generators provided power by moving transmission belts, as one used to see in car engines. Other dramatic developments included the growing popularity of radio and the fast growth of the American movie industry.

'In the 1990s, we had the same thing, but with a different set of mergers. There was Citicorp and Travellers'. There was AT&T and TCI. And the same thing was happening with new innovations. There was the whole digital revolution, the internet, personal computers, satellite links, high-speed cables, and so on.

'On a financial front, there was the huge appetite for pooled shares. In the 1920s, they called them investment trusts. In the 1980s and 1990s, they were mutual funds or unit trusts. Today, we in China call them People's Joint Money Pools. In all cases, the public were told that they took the risk out of speculation. First, they were managed by experts; and second, they were diversified across a range of stocks. Get a high rate of return with a greatly minimized downside. You'll read the same things in the Chinese financial press today about your People's Joint Money Pools.'

The young man with the green hair still looks perplexed. 'You said there were at least ten signs that tipped you off about the millennium Dow crash. I only wrote down seven. Could you go through them again for me?'

'Sure,' the economist replies, uncertainly. 'If I can remember them. I'm not a young man anymore.' Faber rubs his left temple to trigger the oxygen-pumping electrode tucked under his skin. The television lights are giving him a headache. 'Right. Ten similarities. 1: There was the merger fever. 2: The widespread amount of investing on margin and leverage. 3: The heavy presence of foreign investors in the U.S. market. 4: The widely confident outlook on business — in both cases, they were enjoying the advantages of automation, downsizing, improved labor conditions, and stable prices. 5: The presence of investment trusts, mutual funds, or whatever you want to call them. 6: The potential seen in new-technology industries. 7: The record number of patent applications. 8: The presence of 'boomtime literature' with a torrent of books and magazines highlighting the delights of investing in stocks. 9: The prevalence of optimistic forecasters touting the "new era" of prosperity. And 10: The way economists and leading Wall Street figures had become celebrities. There. You got all those?'

'Yeah. Thanks.'

'I've thought of a couple more. In Asia, there were further worrying echoes of the great crash. You had the presence of government and business leaders who continuously made optimistic statements which flew in the face of the facts; and you had the widespread belief, from the first months of the Asian crisis of 1997, that the worst had passed.'

A dark-skinned man who seems about seven feet tall raises his hand, his fingertips almost touching the light fitting. 'Did you realize the financial turmoil which started in Asia in 1997 would spread around the world and last so long?'

'Sure. My observations showed me that following a colossal collapse in a financial market — the United States in 1929, Japan after 1989, Latin America in the 1980s, Asia in 1997 — repeated extremely sharp rallies take place, but they usually give most of their gains back sooner or later. Thus, these rallies were false rallies, because they didn't lead to new highs for the indices in U.S. dollar terms. They were merely a common and necessary feature of a longer-term base-building period, a healing period for the economy. These do lead, eventually — normally, many years later — to sustained bull markets. In the case of Latin America, the base-building period lasted six to eight years, while Japan has been taking much longer. In the case of Asia, the false rallies of 1999 and 2000 were followed by the lows being retested, largely as a result of a bear market in U.S. and continental Europe stocks.'

A tremor runs through the audience, as a newsflash causes all the digital receivers in the room, wheresoever attached to the body, to vibrate. The Swiss investment advisor glances over at the news watch on Director Lu's wrist to read that the Finance Minister of Japan has just resigned.

A dozen hands shoot up. 'Please to comment on the resignation of the Finance Minister of Japan, Faber-san,' asks a Japanese reporter. 'Why Japanese financial system have so much trouble?'

'They come, they go. What can you say?' says Faber. 'You are used to hearing bad news about the economy of Japan, but if you stepped into a time machine and went back 30 years you would be amazed at what was being said. In January 1990, *Institutional Investor* published an article headlined "Will the Japanese Soon Own the World?" After the crash of the Nikkei Index later that year, people kept expecting a recovery. It eventually did start, but there were many years of base-building first. In financial terms, Japan's best days are still ahead.'

A middle-aged man who Faber vaguely recognizes as the anchor on an internet television financial news show raises a hand. 'Professor Faber, can you talk a little about the rise of China? In the 1980s and early 1990s, there was much talk about "the Pacific Century." This line of argument disappeared in 1998, when there was a lot of trouble in the economic miracle countries of East Asia. Then we heard people talk about "the second American century." The Europeans claimed that the future was theirs, after the Euro single currency was launched. But today, China is the most economically dynamic country. Can you comment, please?'

'Certainly, Stan,' says Faber, delighted that the man's lengthy question had given him time to recall his name.

'I was born in Europe, studied in London, and worked in New York, before I came to Asia in the early 1970s. Looking back, it amazes me how almost everyone got geo-economics so wrong.'

He pauses and takes a sip of water. 'Time for another history lesson. In hindsight, it can be seen that for much of recent history, Asia as a region was largely cut off from the world economy. China was on another planet — hard for outsiders to get into — and impossible for insiders to leave. All of the Central Asian republics, plus Vietnam, Myanmar, and other countries, were under communist rule. India, Pakistan, and other countries had strong socialist tendencies and a damaging belief in self-reliance. As a result, more than three-quarters of Asia's population was completely inactive in economic terms. The one Asian country which was properly linked into the world financial system was Japan — but that was small. Japan's entire stock-market capitalization in 1970 was smaller than that of America's IBM alone.

'Why did the countries of this region go through dramatic changes in the 1980s? The key wasn't any action on their part, but activity in the United States. In 1982, U.S. President Ronald Reagan implemented fiscal reforms which led to a surge in U.S. consumption and to rapidly rising budget and trade deficits in the U.S. during the 1980s. Japan and the so-called Asian tigers — countries like Thailand, Singapore, South Korea, Taiwan, and so on — took advantage of the strong growth in U.S. consumer demand. They supplied the American people with consumer goods such as televisions, video recorders, Nike shoes, garments and, later, personal computers and semiconductors.

'The East Asians had a great time. But they didn't look over their shoulders. All this was going on in the absence of any competition from China, the Soviet bloc, India, or Latin America, all regions which were at the time still under communist or socialist rule, or mired in recessions. Further, inflation, which had been rampant through the world in the 1970s, began to cool down. This led to a secular decline in interest rates from about 1982 onwards.

'As a result of all these factors, the late 1980s and very early 1990s became a golden era for South-east Asia. The small Asian tiger countries were flushed with liquidity, thanks to their growing trade and current account surpluses.

'Not surprisingly, Asian stock markets went through the roof. South Korea, the Philippines, and Thailand all had markets which rose about tenfold, while the Taiwan stock market rose more than 20-fold between 1985 and 1990. In fact, today, given the poor state of the economy in China's Taiwan province, it is difficult to believe that, at the end of the last century, this island was one of the world's fastest-growing and richest countries. At its height, Taiwan's foreign exchange reserves were far larger than those of China, and at its peak in 1990, its stock-market volume frequently exceeded that of the New York Stock Exchange. Can you believe that?

'Equally hard to believe, given the current depressed state of Japanese equities and their low price/earnings ratios of about ten, is that Japanese stocks sold for about 60 times earnings at their peak in late 1989. Let me also remind you that at that time, the Nikkei Index peaked at about 39,000. However, since then it has failed to reach a new high, and it is now the year 2017 — 27 years have passed.'

Faber is almost in a trance by now. He has stopped focusing on the faces in front of him. His eyes are glazed, as he immerses himself in the world of economic history in which he feels so much at home.

'In the 1990s there was a growing belief among old leaders that capitalism and totally free markets would lead to the best of all possible worlds. Globalization, privatization, downsizing, and emerging markets became buzzwords. Communist countries, including China, began to open up, trade barriers fell, foreign exchange controls were lifted, and modern banking techniques permitted capital to flow from one corner of the world to another. The opening up of the world in the late 1980s and early 1990s, combined with huge strides in new technology, led investors to believe in the dawn of a new era which would bring prosperity to everyone on earth. Note that dangerous phrase, "new era."'

Director Lu gives him a hostile glance.

Faber fails to notice. 'Also, because of the strong growth rates that the Asian economies enjoyed at the time, Western investors fell in love with Asia and poured money into the region in the form of direct and portfolio investments. Nineteen ninety-three, in particular, saw huge inflows of foreign portfolio investment which led to the early 1994 peak in the Malaysian, Thai, and Singaporean stock markets. The Hong Kong, Indonesian, and Philippine stock markets reached subsequently marginal new highs in 1997.'

The economist's brow suddenly darkens and he wags an admonishing finger. 'However, it was in this period of great euphoria, the 1990s, that investors made crucial mistakes. Several important economic events were either ignored or totally overlooked.

'With the demise of communism and socialism, as well as the disappearance of policies of self-reliance, we essentially saw an opening up of much of the world. More than 3.5 billion poorly paid people joined the world's free economy. This had profound implications. Wages for unskilled workers in the industrialized countries began to decline in real terms, leading to slower consumption growth. In turn, this slowdown in consumer spending growth in the industrialized countries — which was reinforced through unfavorable demographic trends and heavy personal debt burdens — led to a significant slowdown in Asian exports. By 1996, Asian export growth rates had fallen to about 5 percent per annum, down from about 25 percent per annum in the late 1980s. Meanwhile, the Asian tigers had become quite fat and had developed a ferocious appetite for imported goods, which led to larger and larger trade and current account deficits.

'The slowdown in export growth had another important implication. Local business people and foreign investors had become accustomed to rapid export growth rates and, therefore, had expanded their manufacturing capacity to meet future demand which they expected to grow at a fast pace. Alas, when these expectations led to disappointment, many industries suffered from tremendous over-capacity which brought about a downturn in foreign direct investment, starting in about 1997.'

He focuses again on the audience of reporters and realizes that he has lost them. Some are chewing their lightpens, while others are reading reports on pocket news-receivers. He is being too technical, using too many economics terms. Must try to simplify.

A woman in a hover-wheelchair raised her hand. 'Professor Faber, what were the greatest investment follies you saw in your lifetime?'

'There are many. They seemed to spring up every few years to keep me entertained. First, the rush for oil, gold, and silver in 1980. Oil rose to about $50 on the spot market. By the late 1990s, it was about $12. Silver's high was $50, and it fell to below $4 in 1992. Gold hit $850 in 1980, and languished at $270 in 1998.

'Later, we had the Japanese stock-market mania of 1989. Then we had the Hong Kong property and red-chip stocks crazes of 1997. What next? One of the great investment follies of 1998 was the fact that stocks in the United States and continental Europe continued to rise, perceived as safe havens. But people should have assumed, as I did, that if the emerging economies which were home to some 80 percent of the world's population were in trouble, the industrialized nations would soon follow down that path. Then, I would include Japanese bonds in 1998, when their yields had fallen to less than 1.3 percent. They are now yielding more than 8 percent.

'More recently, I would say Shanghai property prices in 2010. As you know, real estate in Shanghai collapsed in 1999–2000 because of the huge over-supply. But then it rose 15-fold over the next ten years, starting in about 2002. There are many others. There was the vanilla boom of Madagascar in the early years of this century. There was the North Korean land boom of the year 2005. And some of you in this room probably suffered from the bubble in collectors' cards of Chinese football stars which burst in 2015.'

There were a few guilty laughs at this. The same woman spoke again. 'Can I have a follow-up question? Those were like the stupidest things that people bought. What were the best things that people bought?'

Faber nodded slowly. 'Yes. You are asking about what I like to call lifetime buying opportunities — unobvious investments that turn out to bring huge capital gains. Well, there have also been many of these. First, U.S. Treasury bonds in 1982, before most of you were born. When the dollar was depressed and when the yield on long-term government bonds rose to 15 percent. I might add that zero coupon bonds outperformed U.S. equities, even during the share-market boom of 1982 to 1998.

'Second, I would put the Asian emerging markets in the years 1985 and 1986, and Latin American markets in the years 1989 and 1990 as key opportunities. They multiplied the investments of the few people who put money into them by ten-, 20-, or 30-fold.

'Then came gold, silver, oil, and agricultural commodities in the years 1999 and 2000, as the Kondratieff wave bottomed out. This great buying opportunity in commodity markets went largely unnoticed as investors focused their attention entirely on equities and on the recovery potential of equities following their 1998–1999 crash. People overlooked the fact that commodity prices had been in a 20-year bear market and were ready to embark upon a secular bull trend. As you know, gold has risen by ten times from its levels of the late 1990s.

'What other once-in-a-lifetime buying opportunities have there been? Let me see. The Asian markets again became opportunities in 1999, after they hit the floor. Indonesia and Russia were the big winners there in terms of bargains. The stock markets of Iran, Azerbaijan, and Kazakhstan at the turn of the millennium were under-appreciated treasures. The development of the Caspian Sea oil reserves combined with rising oil prices after 2000 brought unprecedented prosperity to the central Asian region. Real estate in Angola and Mozambique was good, providing you bought it before the year 2001. Shanghai property in the year 2002, after the big shake-out, well rewarded long-term buyers.'

An older man raises a bionic arm, using its telescopic function to reach higher than the people around him. 'Professor Faber, are you a rich man?' he asks in a Serbian accent.

The old Swiss economist grins. 'Well, as a financial advisor I committed a number of errors, like being short on U.S. stocks in the 1990s. But I fully recovered my losses during the subsequent crash. One of my more fortunate investments was the purchase of gold in the late 1990s.'

'What made you buy gold?'

'In the 1990s, I became very apprehensive about the speculative nature of financial markets — the increase in the global debts of governments, corporations, and the private sector. I realized that it would lead to defaults and eventually rising inflation as governments were likely to panic and start printing money. There was one specific incident in 1998 that stuck in my mind. In 1980, when gold was at its most expensive, most Swiss bankers had some 20 percent of their money in gold. In 1998, I tried to interest a Swiss banker in buying gold. "No," he replied. "There is absolutely zero interest in gold these days." That was the reason he wouldn't buy any. And that was the reason I went straight out and started stocking up on the stuff.'

'Was the fall of Hong Kong a surprise to you, Professor Faber?'

Faber blinks and sees a reporter from his former home town in the far left of the room. 'Not at all. Hong Kong's economic decline was the most inevitable of all. All the East Asian tigers have been languishing to some degree through the first couple of decades of this century. But for Hong Kong, it has been a long, slow, painful, downward drift. I knew it would happen. That's why I left Hong Kong in 2001 and moved my office here. I had been saying throughout the 1990s that Hong Kong's property prices would crash disastrously. When it happened in 1998, I was amazed that anyone was surprised, since —'

Director Lu interrupts. 'Professor Faber, you have not spoken enough about the triumphant and glorious rise of the People's Republic of China. Could you please do so?'

Faber has been in China long enough to know an order when he hears one. 'Certainly, Director Lu. The biggest mistake economists, investors, and financial commentators made in the late 1990s was their total misjudgment of the significance of China's opening up and how it was to permanently change the economic landscape of the world.

'From history books, we know that Shanghai and the Manchurian region were the dominant industrial and commercial centers before the communist takeover of China. In 1930, these two areas attracted more than 80 percent of foreign direct investment. Even the British, who ruled Hong Kong, had more than 76 percent of their investment in Shanghai, compared to only 9 percent in Hong Kong. The closure of China to the outside world in 1949 — a historical accident, I might add — led to a temporary change in the economic geography of the world, particularly Asia. .

'China wasn't in the game from 1949 to about 1997. The door opened in 1978, but it took some time for business to get going. This period was long enough for people to convince themselves that it was permanent and irreversible. What was overlooked, however, was that countries like Taiwan, South Korea, and the British colony of Hong Kong owed their successful rises solely to the fact that China wasn't an economic factor after 1949. Until the late 1980s, its absence as a competitor for foreign direct investment flows and the world's export markets had enabled the non-Chinese Asian region to prosper. This wouldn't have been the case if China had remained a market-based economy and was open to the outside world after the Second World War.'

The middle-aged television anchor raises his hand. 'Let me get this straight, Dr, er, Professor Faber. Are you really saying that in the post-Second World War period, the boom in the economies of the Asian tigers was simply a direct result of China's economic absence from the world's market?'

'Yes,' says Faber with a curt nod. 'That was a major reason. Another factor delaying China's rise was the Western nations' perceived threat from communism. How so? The U.S. was afraid that the communist movement would spread, so they engaged in a policy to strengthen the economy of China's then renegade province, Taiwan, together with South Korea, in order to serve as a bulwark against communist China.

'The threat that China would become a mighty world competitor and economic powerhouse was never seriously considered until after the 1997 financial crisis. This was because the opening of China was initially — from 1978 to the early 1990s — beneficial to the other Asian economies. China's industries needed to import capital goods and foreign parts for assembly.

'By about 1997, investors woke up to what was happening in China. In that year, it was noted that Chinese exports accounted for

Adventures in 21st Century Finance: A Prophecy

close to 30 percent of total exports from Asian countries other than Japan. In the mid-1980s, the figure had been just 6 percent. Furthermore, by 1997, China was attracting more foreign direct investments than all the other Asian countries combined, which meant that more and more capital was directed from other Asian countries into China.'

A white-haired woman with a camera strapped to one eye waved a long-range pen-microphone in her hand. 'Why did you move to Shanghai instead of Guangzhou or Beijing?'

'The centers of prosperity were shifting not only outside China, but within it. In the 1980s, China's manufacturing centers had been in the south of the country. But in the 1990s they moved into the Shanghai area, particularly the Shanghai-Tianjin corridor. This echoed the way that U.S. manufacturing had shifted from the east coast at the beginning of the 1800s to the Great Lakes region by the 1850s, as a result of the widespread railroad infrastructure built across America. Later, in the early years of the 21st century, a further shift occurred toward Chongqing. That, as you know, has now become the Chicago of China. Most of these changes were gradual and went unnoticed by the bulk of investors.

'By the late 1990s, many multinational companies moved their headquarters in China from Hong Kong to Shanghai. Within a few short years, Shanghai was totally transformed. Bridges, ring roads, tunnels, modern sewage systems, had all been put into place almost overnight, while residential and commercial structures suddenly mushroomed. Pudong, on the east side of Shanghai's stretch of the Huangpu river, initially suffered from over-construction. But it started to thrive after the new Shanghai airport was opened in 1999. By the year 2005, and to the surprise of the pundits, traffic at the new Pudong airport exceeded the traffic at Hong Kong's new Chek Lap Kok airport. Shanghai airport became the main air hub for China. Practically all flights between Asia, the Americas, and Europe started using the polar route.'

Director Lu is beaming again, and Faber realizes that he has redeemed himself.

The man from Hong Kong has his hand up again. 'But Hong

231

Kong was part of China by then. Why didn't it benefit from the boom in the rest of the mainland?'

'Hong Kong has always lived in its own little dream world,' says Faber. 'And it has always been contemptuous of its rivals, inside and outside China. You see, the people in Hong Kong didn't realize that by 1997, trading volume on the Shanghai Stock Exchange was already frequently exceeding that of the former British colony. By 2000, following the Hong Kong stock-market crash of late 1997, the total stock-market capitalization of Shanghai grew to twice that of Hong Kong. In fact, if ever investor perception was far from economic reality, it was the outlook for Hong Kong's economy in the late 1990s. It was ironic that in the summer of 1997, an academic produced a book entitled *The Hong Kong Advantage*, just ahead of one of Hong Kong's greatest stock and property crashes.

'In what I consider to have been one of economic history's greatest follies, Hong Kong property prices soared to record levels in the first half of 1997, because it was believed that the integration of Hong Kong into the rapidly modernizing Chinese economy would benefit the city — a view I never shared. However, given the shift in China's economic development away from the south to the Shanghai–Tianjin corridor, Hong Kong's high property prices, which were ten times higher than in Shanghai, were clearly not sustainable.'

'Was the withdrawal of the British in 1997 a factor?'

'It contributed in at least one way. What investors in Hong Kong totally failed to notice was that while Chinese cities like Guangzhou, Shanghai, Dalian, Tianjin, Beijing, and many others were becoming more cosmopolitan and hospitable to foreigners, Hong Kong was increasingly becoming a Chinese city both culturally and economically. It was one of several problems. By 1998, Hong Kong's economy began to suffer as property and stock prices collapsed. In addition, Hong Kong was no longer price-competitive — particularly after the 1997 Asian currency devaluations — so re-exports and tourism declined. In addition, after the handover, Hong Kong was poorly run by grossly overpaid government officials who were more eager after their own self-interest than the well-being of the Hong Kong people.'

Jim, a BBC man, is waving his hand. 'You still haven't really said how China became more economically dynamic than practically everywhere else in the world.'

'I apologise. Let me put it this way. Around the turn of the millennium, we saw a major shift in the economic geography of China. The greater Shanghai region became the nucleus of economic activity, whereas the Asian tigers, which had thrived as long as China had been hibernating under communist rule, lost out. The fact that such a change occurred is very obvious from the divergent performances of the Shanghai Stock Exchange Index and other Asian stock indices. While the Shanghai stock market has risen by 30 times since the financial reforms of Zhu Rongji in 2001 — a reform which paved the way for China's stunning economic development in this century — the indices of the Thai, Taiwanese, Malaysian, Tokyo, and Hong Kong stock exchanges are still, in U.S. dollar terms, well below their highs reached between 1989 and 1997.

'There was also the long-lasting secular New York stock-market decline which began in the second half of 1998, and which brought about a devastating wealth effect on American consumers. Falling consumption led to the deflationary global recession. That hit the U.S. and Europe very badly.'

'Professor Faber, can you — '

'I haven't finished my answer to the gentleman from the BBC. I'll get back to you, sir,' says Faber. 'Or miss,' he adds, blinking at the nondescript shock-haired figure in the front row.

'China's path out of hibernation wasn't smooth. In the late 1990s, China had excess capacity in all sectors of its economy, while the country had become significantly overbuilt. In 1998, export growth began to slow and even declined briefly in 1999. However, by then, the structure of the Chinese economy had begun to change. As prices for manufacturing goods declined because of existing industrial over-capacity and the global deflationary recession, they became more affordable, stimulating domestic demand. In the process, the domestic economy began gradually to replace exports as the engine of growth and development.

'While some of China's Asian neighbors suffered from political and social instability — Indonesia being a prime example — China was calm, and therefore continued to attract large foreign direct investment flows, albeit nothing compared with their peak levels in 1996. Thus, while the global deflationary recession in the early years of this century also produced economic hardship in China, the damage was relatively small when compared to other nations. And when the global economy finally recovered after 2003, China surged forward at a breakneck speed, leaving behind all the other Asian nations — to the great surprise of many pundits.'

'Can other nations learn from the methods China used?'

'China's problems were pretty unique, and needed unique answers. In my opinion, three factors contributed to the economic takeoff. The financial reform of 2001 led to a resolution of the triangular debt problem. All debt of the state-owned companies was exchanged for equity. As a result, state-owned enterprises became publicly owned companies overnight, as banks sold off debt in the form of shares to the public. Thus, an unprecedented streamlining and rationalization of China's state-owned enterprise system was under way.

'And while this process of revitalizing the state-enterprise sector was at first painful, as more than 20 million workers lost their jobs, its beneficial effects didn't fail to materialize shortly thereafter. Formerly unproductive workers who had been paid off were forced to seek employment at much lower wages than they had been paid by the state-owned enterprises. But since the overall cost of living in China was declining, real wages hadn't actually suffered by much. In any event, as a result of the financial reform of 2001, approximately 50 million workers were shifted from unproductive to productive jobs — a structural shift in China's economy which created miracles.

'The second factor which contributed to China's rapid economic development was a combination of its entry into the World Trade Organization, liberalization of its financial system, and implementation of the yuan's convertibility as part of the financial reform of 2001. As a result, many foreign banks shifted their Asian headquarters away from Singapore and Hong Kong to Shanghai, as it became obvious that the huge pool of idle domestic savings in China dwarfed that of every other nation in Asia except Japan. This shift in Asian banking to Shanghai was naturally facilitated by the important legal reform of 2003 which established the rule of law in China. The period of robber baron capitalism which was characteristic of China in its early years of modernization — when a well-defined legal structure was clearly missing — came to an end, and was replaced by a strictly enforced and binding legal system.

'Lastly, another factor contributed to the rapid expansion of the Chinese economy after 2002. While I don't have many kind words about the communist period and the Cultural Revolution, in a strange way, the hardship the Chinese people endured during that period bound them together and cemented their society. Furthermore, communism had failed to produce significant economic gains. But through oppression of individuals and private initiative, it created a very large pool of ambitious and driven people.

'Once they were economically liberated, they rebounded as powerfully as a coil that is suddenly released. According to the historian Arnold Toynbee, adversity, pressure, and hardship can have a very stimulative impact on a society. This was the case with China's society after the demise of the communist system. While the Asian tiger societies had grown spoiled and complacent during the boom years of the late 1980s and the 1990s, and then struggled during the recession at the end of the 20th century, China's society was still largely unspoiled, as it was in the very early stages of economic and social development. This, in my opinion, may have been the greatest contributor to the quick resumption of the Chinese economy's growth in the early part of this century.'

Director Lu is smiling from ear to ear.

'That's the good news. Now the bad news,' says Faber.

Director Lu turns her head slowly to glare at him, her smile changing angle.

'Today, 15 years after China's secular bull market began, albeit interrupted by several serious bear market periods, I feel that a serious setback is only a matter of time. China's stock market has risen by more than 30 times since 2002. Foreign brokers, investment bankers, and fund managers from all over the world are crowding the hotels in order to participate in the boom. Taxi drivers in New York, Tokyo, and London are buying Chinese shares on the internet. My grand-daughter told me that they had formed an investment club specializing in Shanghai shares at her school.'

At this point, Faber notices Doctor Lu's hostile stare and decides to introduce a more positive note. 'While business cycles, financial booms and busts, excessive optimism and pessimism, and changing centers of prosperity will continue to be recurrent features of our global economic landscape, I have no doubt that China will continue to prosper in the long run.'

'I think that would be a good place to end the press conference,' says Director Lu.

Faber flicks his wrist. 'Eleven-thirteen, local time,' says his grand-daughter's voice. 'I think maybe I'll take one or two more questions,' says the aging economist. 'I'm enjoying this. It's like old times. Besides, I promised to answer the question of the young — er — person in the front row.'

'What has been your biggest financial surprise?' it asks.

'There have been many,' says Faber, looking into the middle distance. 'So many. I was pleased when Latin America took off in the early 1990s, after I tipped it as a place to be in 1988 and 1989. There was Russia, Sri Lanka, the London Docklands ... so many.' Faber shifts in his chair and puts his chin in his hands.

'I'll tell you. There was one thing that caught many people on the hop. At the turn of the millennium, there was one place that was never mentioned by financiers. It was just off the map as far as the investment banking community was concerned. Which was amazing if you think about it, because it was and is one of the biggest and richest land masses on earth. Do you know what I am talking about?'

A pale-faced young woman raises her hand. 'Africa,' she says.

'Correct,' says Faber. 'For decades, Africa was considered by many people to be a continent in despair. Since becoming independent nations, most African countries had been plagued by poor leadership, widespread corruption, economic mismanagement based on Marxist ideology, and ethnic and civil wars, as well as plagues and droughts. The 1980s were particularly difficult, when, in addition to these factors, falling commodity prices led to a real GDP per capita fall in black Africa of 1.2 percent per annum.

'It was in early 1997 that I began to believe that the African continent had bottomed out. Over the next few years, it provided direct as well as portfolio investors with rewarding investment opportunities.

'What changed? First, attitudes. I attended the London School of Economics in the late 1960s and I remember well the heated debates I had daily with African students about socialism, imperialism, and the exploitation of the Third World by Western powers. Then the view was that only state ownership, the nationalization of foreign-owned companies, and policies of self-reliance would lead to improved economic conditions.

'But by the late 1990s, a fresh wind was blowing. Hostility toward foreign investors had given way to recognition that the transfer of capital, technology, and know-how was indispensable for economic development, and that private companies tend to be more efficient than the state sector. By the millennium, the spirit of capitalism had been gaining acceptance and had already led to renewed economic growth.

'There were other factors. With the influence of socialism diminishing, most African countries embarked on structural adjustment programs in the late 1990s. In the first few years of the new millennium, free-market economic policies were being implemented. The focus was on export promotion, to attract foreign investors and to lessen the involvement of the state in the economy through wide-ranging privatizations. African central banks were better run, became increasingly independent, and started to act based on a goal of maintaining price stability and controlling inflation through sound monetary policies. This enabled them to lift foreign exchange controls.

'Social changes were very important. The tribalism which led to civil strife and political instability in many African countries diminished. Broader-minded politicians and far better-educated technocrats brought about — albeit slowly — an era of reconciliation. Some were educated at American business schools. They recognized that the issue was not "class struggle" but rather economic development, which lifts all classes of society. And while corruption was still a problem, the Bokassa and Mobutu type of kleptocracy came to an end.

'The civil wars came to an end because the opposing factions simply grew tired of the costs and atrocities of the armed conflict. War and hatred such as prevailed in countries like Angola, Liberia, and Mozambique then gave way to peace and national unity, which are the most important preconditions for economic development.'

'What do you think about the loss of foreign aid to Africa 15 years ago?'

'Surprisingly to some, the loss of foreign aid was a big plus. In the early years of the new millennium, African leaders understood that foreign investments, unlike foreign aid, create jobs and stimulate education standards by transferring technology and know-how. Instead of moaning for additional funds from donor countries, many African leaders started to create an economic and legal environment which was attractive to foreign investors.'

'You said Africa was rich. But it is still a poor continent compared to the others.'

'It is rich in resources, and rich in people. This, rightly handled, should make it rich in commercial terms eventually. I did a survey of Africa, what? 15 or 20 years ago, after visiting Abidjan in the Cote D'Ivoire. The 50-plus countries which made up the African continent, when combined, were the world's largest exporters of gold, platinum, diamonds, vanadium, bauxite, manganese, chromium, cobalt, phosphates, cocoa, tea, and tobacco, and the world's second-largest exporters of copper, coffee, crude oil, and cotton. Africa was endowed with such natural resource wealth that it became prosperous through the production and processing of food, minerals, and oil. But I knew this potential would only be fulfilled after it embraced peace, political stability, and economic reforms.'

'The relationship with Asia also helped in the first decade of the 21st century. Most of Asia's raw material needs were met by Africa.

Asia supplied Africa with capital and consumer goods, while Africa supplied Asia with resources. Cote d'Ivoire was the first place to blossom, but others followed, including Angola, Mozambique, Uganda, Liberia, and Zaire.'

Another tremor runs around the room. This time the reporters are visibly affected by the news flash, and several let out whoops of excitement.

'What's the story?' Faber asks.

'Just the World Cup football results,' says Stan, looking at his wrist.

'I had a little wager. If China has won the World Cup, I shall be a rich man,' says the Swiss economist.

'In that case, you're a rich man, Professor Faber,' says the BBC man. 'The score's China 2, England nil.'

Faber looks around at the happy faces in the room. 'Looks like pretty much everyone in this room was betting on China to win the match. And what sensible person would bet any other way?' he says.

But Director Lu is unexpectedly scowling.

EPILOGUE

—·—·—·—·—·—·—·—·—·—·—·—·—·—·—

The person who knows that he doesn't know much, knows much. So anyone who claims to understand something about the workings of the world in the present, and especially he who dares to predict its future, needs to do so with humility.

'With respect to our history, geography, and evolution, we may know where we are relative to data available to us. However, we know little about where our planet is located vis-à-vis the rest of the universe, or whether our civilization is the only one that has ever existed,' Faber wrote to his clients in April 1996.

'The same applies to economics. We may know our "economic position" relative to the depression years of the 1930s, the bear market low of 1974, and the peak in commodity prices in 1980. However, we have little knowledge about where we stand with respect to the history of capitalism. Are we in the early stages of capitalistic development, or are we close to the end of the "capitalistic age," as Ravi Batra has suggested?'

There are no hard-and-fast answers to questions like these. The forecaster, although his job is to give flesh to intangible hunches, tends to be a person who knows how few hard-and-fast rules there are in life.

Faber shies away even from the assertion that he makes money for his clients. He gives them the ideas, he says. They make the money for themselves.

Every investor is an amateur forecaster, and few realize how tough a game they are playing. Investment, if you like, is a math exam where the powers that be work out the answers based on new formulae they develop after your papers have been handed in.

Epilogue

And even if you get all the answers correct, the complexity and interconnectedness of an endless number of factors mean that there is no guarantee that the final outcome will be what you expect. This can be illustrated by another parable, this one based on a 1933 analogy by Irving Fisher:

Once upon a time, there was a land called Alphabetia, where 26 people lived.

Mr A owed a million dollars to Mr B. But he wasn't worried. Mr A reassured Mr B: 'Fear not about your money. Mr Z owes me a million dollars, and as soon as he pays me, I'll pay you.'

'That's good news,' said Mr B. 'Because I owe Mr C a million dollars, and he wants me to pay him back soon.'

'Quite right,' said Mr C. 'I need the money back because I owe Mr D a million dollars.'

Mr D owed a million dollars to Mr E, who owed a million dollars to Mr F, and so on.

The last man in Alphabetia, Mr Z, was an economist. He worked out that the net debt of the land of Alphabetia was zero. All the money and all the debts canceled each other out.

'None of us need worry in the long run,' he announced.

But then Mr Z, busy with his sums, forgot to organize any sort of payment to Mr A by the deadline. He was declared bankrupt. And so, one after another, were all the other 26 residents of Alphabetia.

'What on earth went wrong?' said a puzzled Mr A. 'One day we were all rich. And the next day we are all poor.'

A little knowledge can help the investor avoid outcomes such as that. And a little philosophizing can be a great comfort in the investment business. 'No one ever makes a loss by taking a profit,' Faber tells clients who worry that they have sold their shares too soon. 'Better to miss a little than to lose a lot.'

But Dr Doom's favorite financial quotation is as comforting to those who actually lose money as it is to those who make it. After all, money is just one factor among many which shape our lives. Napoleon Bonaparte once said: 'Riches do not consist in the possession of treasures but in the use made of them.'